Mindfulness-Informed Relational Psychotherapy and Psychoanalysis

Mindfulness-Informed Relational Psychotherapy and Psychoanalysis: Inquiring Deeply provides a refreshing new look at the emerging field of Buddhist-informed psychotherapy. Marjorie Schuman presents a cogent framework which engages the patient at the levels of narrative, affective regulation, and psychodynamic understanding. Blending knowledge of contemporary psychoanalysis with the wisdom of Buddhist view, she examines how mindfulness can be integrated into psychodynamic treatment as an aspect of self-reflection rather than as a cognitive behavioral technique or intervention.

This book explores how mindfulness as a "self-reflective awareness practice" can be used to amplify and unpack psychological experience in psychodynamic treatment. Schuman presents a penetrating analysis of conceptual issues, richly illustrated throughout with clinical material. In so doing, she both clarifies important dimensions of psychotherapy and illuminates the role of "storyteller mind" in the psychological world of lived experience. The set of reflections comprises an unfolding deep inquiry in its own right, delving into the similarities and differences between mindfulness-informed psychotherapy, on the one hand, and mindfulness as a meditation practice, on the other.

Filling in an outline familiar from psychoanalytic theory, the book explores basic concepts of Self, Other, and "object relations" from an integrative perspective which includes both Buddhist and psychoanalytic ideas. Particular emphasis is placed on how relationship is held in mind, including the dynamics of relating to one's own mind. The psychotherapeutic approach described also delineates a method for *practicing with problems* in the Buddhist sense of the word *practice*. It investigates how problems are constructed and elucidates a strategy for finding the wisdom and opportunities for growth which are contained within them.

Mindfulness-Informed Relational Psychotherapy and Psychoanalysis demonstrates in clear language how the experience of Self and Other is involved in emotional pain and relational suffering. In the relational milieu of psychotherapy, "Inquiring Deeply" fosters emotional insight and catalyzes psychological growth and healing. This book will be of great interest to psychoanalytically-oriented clinicians as well as Buddhist scholars and psychologically-minded Buddhist practitioners interested in the clinical application of mindfulness.

Marjorie Schuman is a licensed clinical psychologist and certified psychoanalyst specializing in mindful psychodynamic therapy. Currently in private practice in Santa Barbara, California, Schuman is also a member of the faculty of the Los Angeles Institute and Society for Psychoanalytic Studies. She co-founded the Center for Mindfulness and Psychotherapy in Santa Monica.

Mindfulness-Informed Relational Psychotherapy and Psychoanalysis

Inquiring Deeply

Marjorie Schuman

Routledge
Taylor & Francis Group

LONDON AND NEW YORK

First published 2017
by Routledge
2 Park Square, Milton Park, Abingdon, Oxon OX14 4RN

and by Routledge
711 Third Avenue, New York, NY 10017

Routledge is an imprint of the Taylor & Francis Group, an informa business

British Library Cataloguing in Publication Data
A catalogue record for this book is available from the British Library

Library of Congress Cataloging in Publication Data
Names: Schuman, Marjorie, author.
Title: Mindfulness-informed relational psychotherapy and psychoanalysis:
inquiring deeply / Marjorie Schuman.
Description: Abingdon, Oxon; New York, NY: Routledge, 2017. |
Includes bibliographical references and index.
Identifiers: LCCN 2016033812 | ISBN 9781138699342 (hardback: alk. paper) |
ISBN 9781138699359 (pbk.: alk. paper) | ISBN 9781315517056 (e-book)
Subjects: | MESH: Psychotherapy—methods | Psychoanalytic Therapy—
methods | Buddhism—psychology | Mind-Body Relations, Metaphysical
Classification: LCC RC480.5 | NLM WM 420 | DDC 616.89/14—dc23
LC record available at https://lccn.loc.gov/2016033812

ISBN: 978-1-138-69934-2 (hbk)
ISBN: 978-1-138-69935-9 (pbk)
ISBN: 978-1-315-51705-6 (ebk)

Typeset in Times New Roman
by Deanta Global Publishing Services, Chennai, India
Printed and bound by CPI Group (UK) Ltd, Croydon, CR0 4YY

Contents

Acknowledgments

Writing this book has been a major chapter in the story of my life. For five years, it has been the centerpiece of what I now recognize to have been a dedicated practice of Self-Inquiry. In this process, again and again things have unfolded synchronously in a way which instantiated what I was writing about and made it very real for me. At many points I felt like I was receiving a kind of wisdom teaching. Be that as it may, the book wanted to be written.

One of the themes in the book is the co-creative process by which new aspects of ourselves come into being in relationship with others. In this regard, I want to acknowledge, especially, my husband and deepest conversational partner Robert Shafer, who, more than anyone, has encouraged my creativity and brought my clinical self into being. I also want to express my appreciation to my close friend and dharma brother Fernando Mata whose intelligence and erudition have been a consistent source of inspiration to me over decades of shared philosophical discourse. Other special friends have also been my companions on this path, especially Jean Holroyd, Trudy Goodman, Concetta Alfano, Karen Redding, and Radhule Weininger.

Special thanks go to two analytic patients who, mostly unbeknownst to them, have been co-creative partners in the development of my thinking. I will let them remain anonymous here, although they will recognize themselves in what I have written about them. I thank them also for generously giving permission to me to publish very intimate, albeit disguised, details of their lives.

I also want to recognize and express my gratitude to various editorial partners, whose constructive criticisms were instrumental in helping me define my written voice. My friend, dharma colleague, and editor-in-chief Dave Leggatt labored long hours with me as I crafted the structure of the book. His conceptual acuity contributed enormously to my ability to write clearly about the dharma. Noelle Oxenhandler was a superb editorial consultant whose comments affirmed and validated the value of this work. Janet Surrey, Joseph Bobrow, Fernando Mata, Sylvia Bercovici, and Phillip Moffitt read drafts of the entire manuscript as it progressed. Their comments helped me sculpt the narrative into a form that readers could assimilate. Last but not least, Elizabeth Berlese gave painstaking attention to the construction of every sentence.

Many teachers, too numerous to mention by name, have guided me in my dharma practice through dharma talks, interviews, and the written word. Here I give special mention to my mentor, Phillip Moffitt, and to Jason Siff, both of whom have had major formative influences on my thinking. I also want to acknowledge Gregory Kramer for important insights he provided to my understanding of relational suffering. Nonetheless, the understanding of the dharma conveyed in this book is my own, and I gladly take responsibility for any and all errors contained herein.

The writing of this book has been an exercise in self-discipline, a word which (as I am fond of saying) comes from the same etymological root as the word *disciple* and means to follow oneself with love. Be that as it may, I have lived with the questions I address in the book on as deep a level as I have known how to do. I feel very fortunate to have had the opportunity to undertake this kind of awareness practice, and I am happy to be able to authentically say that the path continues to deepen.

Marjorie Schuman
Santa Barbara, CA
March, 2016

Prologue

> *Hokusai says Look carefully.*
> *He says pay attention, notice.*
> *He says to keep looking, stay curious.*
> *He says there is no end to seeing.*[1]

Introduction

Inquiring Deeply grew out of my compelling personal desire to understand how to blend Buddhist mindfulness and relational psychotherapy into an integrative approach to working with psychological problems. I knew intuitively that there was wisdom in problems and opportunities for growth contained within them. I loved the Buddhist metaphor of the lotus flower with its roots in the mud growing toward the sunlight, and I could see for myself that problems always seemed to point exactly where I needed to look and reveal what I most needed to see. Early on in my meditation practice, I recognized the profound truth that *this very moment is the perfect teacher*, as Buddhist teacher Pema Chodron famously said (Chodron, 1997).

I also knew from my work as a relational psychoanalyst that problems have many layers, and that the meaning we assign to them is a very powerful catalyst in how they resolve (or don't). At the core of problems, there is often some rejecting attitude toward the problem itself and/or toward some aspect of one's experience. Indeed, the essential meaning of "problem" is that there is a circumstance or situation which one regards as unwelcome and needing to be dealt with or overcome. Sometimes we hold the view that problems are a punishment for something we have done, or failed to do; something in ourselves we deem blameworthy or shameworthy. Beyond the particular circumstances, there often seems to be an embedded view that having problems is itself a problem; as if life could be without problems, or that having problems were an indication of deficiency or failure.

I could see that finding an effective frame in which to hold problems, a "right view" in Buddhist terms, plays an important role in someone's ability to find a path through their suffering. (And, it was clear that most often there is no way out of the swamp except through the alligators!)

So, my first set of questions became: *What is a wise relationship to problems? What is a skillful way to "be with" problems?* And/or: *How can someone best "practice with" problems, in the dharmic sense of practice?*[2]

It was apparent to me that this skillful means could not be *looking for* something; it needed to be *looking deeply into* something. Whatever answers I arrived at would have to honor both of the interpenetrating strands of my own life experience: psychoanalysis and Buddhism.

****

I searched for answers to these questions in many ways and in many different places, including of course the burgeoning literature on Buddhism and psychotherapy. Many of the available approaches were, by and large, not a good fit. For starters, most of the popular clinical applications of mindfulness—mindfulness-based cognitive therapies (MBCT), dialectical behavioral therapy (DBT), and acceptance and commitment therapy (ACT), for example—were cognitive-behavioral and problem-centered, whereas my own clinical work was psychodynamic/relational and depth-oriented. I was not drawn to mindfulness as a clinical *technique* but rather as an aspect of self-reflection. I sought to understand how to incorporate mindfulness into psychotherapy as an aspect of intimate relationship, not as a technique for modifying behavior. I also found that my own mindful awareness seemed to invite a resonating depth and immediacy in patients, enhancing the depth of our connection. My primary interest was relational psychotherapy, not applied mindfulness.[3]

In my own work, the focus tends to be on communication, both conscious and unconscious. Mindfulness is only one facet of a multifaceted effort to uncover previously unseen surfaces of experience. As the reader will see in the many clinical illustrations I have included in this book, I do sometimes incorporate mindfulness practice into the clinical protocol where appropriate, but the primary emphasis is not mindfulness practice.

I gradually crafted a "signature" clinical style which I call "inquiring deeply." This approach interweaves psychodynamic principles and Buddhist thinking; it is both Buddhist-informed and what one of my patients calls "Buddhist-affirmative," in that it blends Buddhist view into its interpretive framework. The best way to convey inquiring deeply is through clinical example; many of the clinical illustrations in this book come from my work with patients who are Buddhist practitioners, which may provide an added dimension of interest to readers.[4]

One preliminary caveat is that "Buddhist view" is not homogeneous, but rather varies across different schools of Buddhism. (A similar point can be made in regard to the various schools of psychoanalytic thought.) The principle Buddhist ideas in inquiring deeply are insights available in the practice of mindfulness meditation; that said, however, it should be noted that mindfulness is only one of many different Buddhist practices, one which is not included in every form of Buddhism. The primary focus of *Inquiring Deeply* is how Buddhist view is relevant to the practice of relational psychoanalysis and psychotherapy. While the basic ideas on which *Inquiring Deeply* is based are outlined later in this chapter and the next, the intended emphasis is how Buddhist view and psychoanalytic treatment can be blended into an integrative whole.

Inquiry

As I pursued these questions over a period of many years, it gradually dawned on me that the process I was engaged in is the one called "inquiry"—"living in the question of something." This recognition further stimulated my curiosity about the process of inquiry itself. I looked into dharma teachings on this topic and I reflected on it a great deal. Some of what was generated by that process is written in this book.

Inquiry feels to me like an extended conversation that takes place within me and in the "external world" simultaneously. The typical sequence is generally something like this: first, a question arises in my mind. Sometimes this begins with a word or a phrase that starts to echo in my thoughts. Then, generally within a day or two, I find that something—just the "right" something—emerges: an insight; a comment someone makes as we are speaking together; or something that comes up in a therapy session with a patient. In the mystery of unconscious process, it feels as though life itself is alive and responsive to my inquiry; that answers are generated from (called forth by?) my intention to "answer" a particular question.

I have found inquiry to be a wonderful frame for relating to emotional problems. Exploring its value has remained the center of my interest and my attentional focus as I have practiced Vipassana meditation[5] and worked with patients in psychotherapy over a period of many years. Over this time, my questions have broadened in scope and taken on different forms, but these have been the main ones:

- What are the essential similarities and differences between Buddhism and psychotherapy?
- Is Buddhist practice itself a form of psychotherapy? Or conversely, is psychotherapy a subcategory of dharma practice?
- Can mindfulness practice help bring psychodynamic efforts to fruition? And, if so, how?
- Can dharma practice be broadened to include the "relational field": i.e. the implicit representation of our relationship to others that exists both in our minds and in the interplay between self and other?

And pragmatically:

- What is a skillful way to explore problems; to look deeply into them in a way that breathes space into them, decodes their hidden meanings, and allows them to resolve?
- Could awareness practice in everyday life be used as an effective adjunct to working with psychological problems in psychotherapy? Could this be done

in the spirit of self-reflection rather than using mindfulness meditation as a cognitive behavioral technique?

This book, *Inquiring Deeply* (designated in italics to distinguish it from the framework/method I call "inquiring deeply"), describes some of what I have learned from my own process of inquiry about these questions.

****

I have spent more than three decades concurrently involved in the practices of Buddhist mindfulness meditation and psychoanalysis.[6] At some earlier points in my life journey, these practices not only felt *disparate*, they lived in my experience as disjunctive aspects of my *identity*: For many years I felt that I had to keep my involvement in Buddhism "in the closet" in order to be accepted as a psychoanalyst. The reflections on theory and clinical practice that comprise this book have developed in the context of my efforts to integrate these two different narrative strands in my own life experience. So the inquiry that gave rise to this book was not only a matter of intellectual or theoretical interest. As is obvious in hindsight, it was also a way of working through a personal issue.

My identity issues also lived in me at deeper levels which at times took the form of problematic situations in my personal life. Beyond professional identity, I could see that I was at core seeking to *become* somebody (and to discover who I am). Over time, the drive toward self-expression and self-actualization began to predominate over my concerns with validation. I began to feel that *Inquiring Deeply* was the outer form of a new level of integration within myself. And so, the writing of this book is for me the completion of something: the "working through" of a multilayered psychological issue. It is also a living example of how sustained inquiry can lead to and unfold into the solution for personal problems.

In any event, the two narrative strands—Buddhist and relational/psychodynamic approaches to working with emotional problems—have over time become woven together in my mind into a fabric of understanding that feels both seamless and rich. Inquiry is a process I often liken to clarification of butter; the essence gets increasingly more refined (and defined) as the questions "cook." The framework of my inquiry became gradually clarified, fleshed out, and filled in as inquiry progressed. What I have learned is expressed in this book.

Inspirations

There are many insights from psychoanalysis embedded in the discussions in *Inquiring Deeply*. I resonate especially strongly with D. W. Winnicott's idea that psychological reality involves both creation and discovery; we *participate* in the construction of our psychological world (Winnicott, 1971).

In mindfulness meditation practice, the boundary between creation and discovery is explored by bringing mindful awareness to the emergent moment of Here and Now. In psychoanalysis, it is explored through examination of the intersection of two or more subjectivities as we relate to one another. I discovered in the consulting room that powerful things often happened when attention was brought to bear on the relational/intersubjective field. Many examples of how this looks and feels in clinical practice are given throughout this book.

My clinical approach is also predicated on several other basic principles that are pillars of any psychodynamic approach: First, the ability to put experience into words is extremely important. Second, being deeply understood by others is vital. And third, the stories we tell are essential to how the human world is constituted.

As readers can easily confirm for themselves, relational narratives often occupy center stage in the mind. That fact, in my view, is a strong argument in favor of including this aspect of mind in dharma practice. The mind is organized in and for relationship.

In my view, the most elegant concepts which describe the relational structure of the mind are those found in contemporary psychoanalytic theory. At the same time, I cannot overstate how important Buddhism has been in both my personal life as well as in my professional work. At meditation retreats, and whenever I listen to a good dharma talk or read a good dharma book, I invariably experience a "felt sense" of deep truth which lives within me as the comforting presence of something. I think that this is a relational function of dharma practice which is insufficiently acknowledged.

****

Inquiring Deeply: A Contemplative Relational Psychotherapy

This book is intended to provide a coherent rationale for Buddhist-informed relational therapy: what can perhaps be described as "contemplative relational psychotherapy."[7] It is written primarily for two groups of readers: (1) psychotherapists who want to explore how to blend Western psychological understanding with Buddhist psychology; and (2) dedicated Buddhist practitioners who are psychologically minded. (I imagine that many readers will fall into both of those categories!) In addition, the reflections in the book will likely be of interest to "seekers" of many different stripes and to any serious student of the mind.

The book explores what I consider the three-legged stool of psychotherapeutic change processes: mindful awareness, self-reflection, and deep connection. It describes a listening stance in psychotherapy that is infused by clinical training as well as by depth of experience with mindfulness meditation practice. It elucidates a paradigm of understanding which can inform the practice of relational psychotherapy and/or be used as a framework for "working on oneself."

All of the reflections revolve around the importance of relationship and how relationship is held in mind. Special emphasis is placed on the importance of psychological narrative—"storyteller mind"—which tends to be viewed very differently in Buddhism and in psychotherapy. *Inquiring Deeply* argues that "wise understanding" of the stories we tell about our experience is essential in cultivating insight.

In sum, inquiring deeply can be described as mindfulness-informed psychotherapy which has a psychodynamic and relational orientation. It can be equally well described, in some instances, as psychologically-minded dharma practice: "mindfulness of mind" with special emphasis on the way relationships are held in mind.

Overview of the Book

Each chapter of *Inquiring Deeply* consists of a series of reflections about a particular dimension or theoretical aspect of Buddhist-informed psychodynamic/relational psychotherapy. Filling in an outline familiar from psychoanalytic theory, the various chapters explore basic concepts of Self, Other, and the "object relations" between self and other from an integrative perspective which includes both Buddhist and psychoanalytic ideas.

- **Chapter 1 (Prologue)** introduces the psychotherapeutic approach called "inquiring deeply," a blended clinical strategy which integrates the knowledge of psychoanalysis with the wisdom of Buddhism in a single coherent frame. In addition to describing the questions which the book will address, it describes the personal and philosophical context in which *Inquiring Deeply* came about.
- **Chapter 2** consists of a series of preliminary reflections on the process of inquiring deeply as a psychodynamic/relational psychotherapeutic approach informed by Buddhist view. It defines inquiring deeply, presents its fundamental premises and assumptions, and discusses the role which mindful awareness plays in psychological healing. Mindfulness in psychotherapy and mindfulness in Buddhist practice are compared.
- **Chapter 3** explores basic ideas of mindful self-reflection as it is understood in inquiring deeply. Introspective awareness practices of mindful noticing, investigation, and inquiry are introduced. These practices are used in inquiring deeply as adjunctive methods which can amplify and "unpack" psychological experience. The clinical process of inquiring deeply is illustrated with case examples.
- **Chapter 4** presents a framework of questions that can be used for clinical inquiry in psychodynamic/relational psychotherapy and/or as a structured process for psychological self-reflection. The process of deep inquiry helps to define and clarify the crux of psychological problems and issues, highlighting problematic aspects of self-experience, relational needs, and existential attitudes. It opens new options and choices for relating to problems and finding the innate wisdom within them.
- **Chapter 5** describes the role of connection in relational psychotherapy and how the quality of Presence which is cultivated in mindfulness practice is relevant in deepening therapeutic intimacy. It describes the receptive, meditative frame of inquiring deeply, and introduces the concepts of "relational field" and "transcendent relational field."

- **Chapter 6**, the heart of *Inquiring Deeply*, is a series of reflections on different aspects of connection. Because the mind is inherently relational—organized by and for relationship—interpersonal problems are the primary sphere of emotional difficulties. This chapter gives a conceptual framework for understanding conflicts and fear of intimacy with others; explores the importance of how relationship is held in mind; and explains the importance of intimacy with self.

- **Chapter 7** consists of a series of reflections on the nature of thinking. How the mind creates experience presents an important set of questions which are at the heart of both psychotherapy and Buddhism. A clear understanding of the function of thought is essential in developing a wise relationship to the thinking mind.

- **Chapter 8** gives a clear and coherent account of the psychological self and its organization, highlighting the development of self-awareness and the role of self-reflection. The interpersonal origins of self-identity are explained, with special emphasis on the narrative construction of the self. Finally, the "problem of self" as it is understood in Buddhism is elucidated and the role of mindfulness in the development of subjectivity is explored.

- **Chapter 9** takes up the different meanings of the concept of "object" in Buddhism, Western philosophy, and psychoanalysis. Emphasis is placed on the psychoanalytic concept of "the mind-object" which has important bearing on how we relate to our minds and so is very pertinent to understanding both mindfulness practice and psychotherapy. The mind-object in clinical work is illuminated with clinical examples.

- **Chapter 10** presents a summary and synthesis of the various topics in *Inquiring Deeply* as they pertain to understanding the processes of psychological change and growth. It describes *how we change* in terms of ten component factors. It presents conclusions about a *wise relationship to problems*. Core questions about whether mindfulness and psychotherapy are essentially the same or different are revisited. Finally, the nature of psychological healing is considered and contrasted with the Buddhist goal of liberation.

To summarize, *Inquiring Deeply* describes a framework for psychotherapy which is intended to integrate the knowledge of psychoanalysis and the wisdom of Buddhism into a single coherent frame. It thoughtfully compares Buddhist and psychoanalytic ideas about working with emotional pain and shows in an experience-near way how to go about combining the two into a blended clinical approach. While *Inquiring Deeply* is based in contemporary psychoanalytic thought, it is best described as a book about how to "practice with problems" in the Buddhist sense of the word *practice*: how Buddhist methods of practice (mindfulness, investigation, and inquiry) can be used to amplify and "unpack" psychological experience. This strategy can be used in psychodynamic psychotherapy (or psychoanalysis), and it is also applicable to working with the problems of everyday life outside of the consulting room.

There is already a large professional literature that presents a scholarly comparison of Buddhism and psychoanalysis with respect to their essential areas of similarity and difference.[8] *Inquiring Deeply* is not this kind of comprehensive analysis; it is, rather, a series of reflections which is intended to guide readers in making their own discerning comparisons. Its purpose is to give an overview which will help provide a conceptual bridge between Buddhist and Western psychology for those who would like to integrate them in their own practice, personally and/or professionally.

Inquiring Deeply endeavors to present a theoretical overview of basic ideas from contemporary psychoanalysis and to explain how these concepts help us understand experience. The language or "idiom" used in this book is psychoanalytic because this is the theoretical foundation of my clinical work. While basic ideas are presented in a condensed and simplified form so that they will be accessible even to readers who are not trained in psychotherapy,[9] I hope that the level of discourse will be both interesting and informative even to those with a lot of clinical experience. Clinical illustrations are provided to add depth and texture to the discussion and to show what Buddhist-informed relational/psychodynamic work looks like in my consulting room.

****

A Thousand Words Are Worth a Picture ...

As further context for *Inquiring Deeply*, I want to elaborate a bit about my personal experience. I hope to be able to convey "who I am" as well as give the reader an up-close and personal view of where "inquiring deeply" fits into the picture of my life. I hope that this will not only explain but also *show* and *evoke* where inquiring deeply comes from in me.

Big picture view: Philosophical and intellectual by nature, I have had a lifelong fascination with fundamental questions about mind, brain, and self. Always in search of deeper understanding and answers, even in the early years of my childhood, I came of age in the psychedelic era, which opened my mind to the mysteries of consciousness. I then pursued answers over several decades of academic and experiential study encompassing psychoanalysis, neuroscience, and Buddhism as well as participation in many different "transformational workshops."

Not wanting to digress into a lengthy autobiographical narrative here, as I write these words I sit, close my eyes, and turn my attention inward, awaiting some inspiration about what to say. A question crystallizes in my mind: how *did* "inquiring deeply" become my "life project"?

Several early memories arise:

- I am about two years old and I am standing in the sunshine, aware for the first time I can remember that *I am aware*. I think of this moment as my birth into self-reflective awareness. (A photograph taken of me in that moment has always been in my possession, so perhaps that *image* is what framed the significance of this particular moment.)

- I am sitting on the sandy bottom of a beautiful brook in Connecticut, with my head beneath the surface of the water. I am three years old. I have a stone in each hand and I am clinking them together, deeply fascinated by the way the sound reverberates in my ears. I am in a state of consciousness in which there seems to be little need to breathe.
- I am sitting on the bed in the bedroom of my childhood, looking out the window. There is a diamond-shaped metal grating/guardrail on the window and as I gaze out with soft focus, the diamond pattern telescopes out and expands into a deep three-dimensional space. The experience is compelling. I repeat it often.
- Not yet five years old, I wonder often where I was before I was born.

When I told these experiences to a meditation teacher many years later, his response was: "you were a Zen child!" Be that as it may, these memories are emblematic of many similar experiences which have informed my life and which ultimately evolved into the writing of *Inquiring Deeply*.

Self-reflective and compassionate by nature, I was drawn to a career in clinical psychology. As I traversed the ordinary ups and downs of life and encountered thematic iterations of what I would term my core psychological issues, it began to feel important to me to articulate my understanding of how to find a path through problems. This became a "life project."

Many layers of "answers" emerged in different reflections and at different moments—many of which are narrated throughout this book—but several major insights stand out:

1   As life unfolds there is always opportunity to make conscious choices about the meaning we assign to our significant events—even if it doesn't always seem that way in the moment. This insight has been the bedrock of my personal life and my professional work.
2   Who we *are* is ultimately the most important contribution we make to others.
3   When we peel away the layers of problems, eventually we get to a common core which is communicated very well by the cartoon in Figure 1.1.

What we are holding onto imprisons us, and what we are blind to in ourselves is the limiting boundary of our freedom. We need to see our predicament clearly in order to "free the spirit from its cell" (Brandschaft, 2010).

I have explored many interesting ideas in this long process of inquiry. The process of study and reflection has been deeply satisfying at a personal level, and my hope is that what I have written here will add insight, depth, and texture to readers' understanding.

Because it has come into being as part of my own psychological, meditative, and existential reflections, *Inquiring Deeply* bears the stamp of my humanistic and philosophical nature. It has taken its shape from the process of inquiry which has informed it. Again and again, I have circled back to the observation made by Hokusai in the lines of poetry that open this book: there is no end to seeing.

****

Figure 1.1

In his book *Relational Freedom*, Donnel Stern (2015) makes a comment that is apropos and which I strongly resonate with: all theories of technique and therapeutic action are basically statements of values. I have an inquiring mind, and— (as my early memories attest)—I have "inquired deeply" as the natural expression of my being throughout my lifetime; expanding awareness has been one of the major organizing principles in my life. Self-reflective, contemplative inquiry seems built into the very structure of my character. "Inquiring deeply" seems a very apt name for this kind of "awareness practice."

Inquiring Deeply is a book about how the process of deep inquiry and self-reflection can be incorporated into the framework of psychodynamic/relational psychotherapy. It is a guide to how to practice with psychological problems in the Buddhist sense of the word *practice*: how to apply Buddhist methods of practice (mindfulness, investigation, and inquiry) to deepen psychological experience. It is pragmatic rather than academic and expresses what I have learned from and with my patients as we have inquired deeply together in a psychodynamic and relational frame.

What I mean by "inquiring deeply" will be defined and elucidated in the next chapter, and its theoretical foundations will be described. The remainder of the book consists of a series of reflections which summarize some of what I have learned during more than three decades of daily practice of Vipassana meditation, many years of advanced training in psychoanalysis, and thousands of hours doing psychotherapy.

Inquiring Deeply is intended to illuminate the intersection at which Buddhism and psychotherapy meet. It is written for psychotherapists, Buddhist practitioners, or for anyone who is interested in understanding the similarities and dissimilarities between psychodynamic and Buddhist approaches to working with emotional pain. My hope is that it will further the reader's own personal integration of the two paradigms of experience and allow the two practices to be blended into one cohesive whole.

Notes

1   Poem by Roger Keyes. Unpublished work used with written permission of author. (No copyright.)
2   Buddhist concepts and view are frequently referred to in this book as "dharma" or "Buddhadharma," meaning in a general sense the teachings of Buddhism. In similar manner, the practice of Buddhism is called "dharma practice."
3   There were some very notable exceptions of course—important writings by others who creatively integrated psychotherapy and Buddhism and whose ideas helped shape the contours of my own journey. The references at the end of this chapter include a selected list of authors and sources that have informed my thinking. I want to especially recognize the work of the group at Institute for Meditation and Psychotherapy in Boston, which is the foundation on which this book rests.
4   I refer to the people I work with as "patients" rather than "clients" throughout, in accordance with the psychoanalytic clinical model.

5   "Vipassana" is Buddhist insight meditation, mindfulness practice in the Theravadan tradition of Buddhism. My dharma study has been primarily in this school of American Buddhist thought.
6   As already indicated, my dharma study has been primarily in the American Buddhist/ Theravadan-Vipassana tradition. My clinical work has been most influenced by the traditions of psychoanalytic Self Psychology, Intersubjectivity theory, Relational Psychoanalysis, and British Middle School Object Relations.
7   "Contemplative relational psychotherapy" was a term co-created by myself and my colleague Concetta Alfano when we taught together at the Center for Mindfulness and Psychotherapy in Santa Monica, Calif., in 2006–2007.
8   See for example: Aronson (2004); Bobrow (2007, 2010); Epstein (1995); Magid (2002); Jennings and Safran (2012); Rubin (1996) and Safran (2003).
9   A glossary of terms is also included for easy reference.

References

Aronson, H. (2004). *Buddhist practice on western ground.* Boston, MA: Shambhala Press.
Bobrow, J. (2010). *Zen and psychotherapy: Partners in liberation.* New York, NY: Norton Professional Books.
Brandschaft, B. (2010). *To free the spirit from its cell.* In Brandschaft, B., Doctors, S. and Sorter, D. (Eds), *Toward an emancipatory psychoanalysis: Brandschaft's intersubjective vision* (pp. 125–145). New York, NY: Routledge Press.
Chodron, P. (1997). *When things fall apart: Heart advice for difficult times.* Boston, MA: Shambhala Publications.
Epstein, M. (1995). *Thoughts without a thinker: Psychotherapy from a Buddhist perspective.* New York, NY: Basic Books.
Jennings, P. and Safran, J. D. (2010). *Mixing minds: The power of relationship in psychoanalysis and Buddhism.* Somerville, MA: Wisdom Publications.
Magid, B. (2002). *Ordinary mind: Exploring the common ground of Zen and psychotherapy.* Boston, MA: Wisdom Publications.
Rubin, J. (1996). *Psychotherapy and Buddhism: Towards an integration.* New York, NY: Plenum Press.
Safran, J. D. (Ed.). (2003). *Psychoanalysis and Buddhism.* Somerville, MA: Wisdom Press.
Stern, D. (2015). *Relational freedom: Emergent properties of the interpersonal field.* New York, NY: Routledge Press.
Winnicott, D. W. (1971). *Playing and reality.* London, England and New York, NY: Routledge Press.

Chapter 2

Preliminary Reflections

Definition and Fundamental Premises of "Inquiring Deeply"

This chapter provides a conceptual introduction to "inquiring deeply." In general terms, inquiring deeply can be defined as psychodynamic/relational psychotherapy informed by Buddhist view. It is relational psychotherapy which integrates mindfulness into therapeutic exploration to engage the patient at the levels of narrative, *affect regulation*, and psychodynamic understanding.

"Inquiring Deeply" Defined

The phrase "inquiring deeply" is used in this book in several different ways, as follows:

- *"Inquiring deeply" refers to mindful, psychodynamic, relational psychotherapy.* It is a psychotherapeutic approach for working with emotional problems which blends the wisdom of Buddhist psychology with the knowledge of contemporary psychoanalysis. It is a psychotherapeutic framework informed by relational psychoanalysis, Buddhist view, and the practice of mindfulness meditation.
- *"Inquiring deeply" refers to an attentional or listening stance in psychotherapy; a therapeutic frame.* Inquiring deeply can be defined as mindful self-reflection held in a context of psychotherapeutic investigation. It engages an attitude of receptive, mindful, and compassionate attention toward experience.
- *"Inquiring deeply" refers to a psychotherapeutic strategy which incorporates "self-reflective practices" adapted from Buddhism (mindfulness, investigation, and inquiry) to amplify and "unpack" psychological experience.* All of these are mindful methods for deepening self-awareness and gaining a grasp of the mind's potential.
- *"Inquiring deeply" refers to the self-reflective methodology used in this psychotherapeutic approach.* Self-reflection is used strategically to investigate subjective experience from a point of view that is informed by Buddhist, psychodynamic, and relational ideas. This methodology can be incorporated into psychotherapy as an aspect of the therapeutic dialogue and/or it can be

prescribed as an intervention to further the work. It can also be done as a self-guided process.

• *"Inquiring deeply" refers to a method for "practicing with problems" in the Buddhist sense of the word practice.* It investigates how problems are held in mind: how we can best understand them and how we can create a wise context for relating to them.

To reiterate, "inquiring deeply" in lowercase letters refers to a framework for psychotherapeutic exploration which is informed by Buddhist view and which engages the strategic use of self-reflective practices to deepen awareness of emotional experience. It can also refer to self-guided inquiry that proceeds along similar lines. Further delineation of the self-reflective practices themselves will be reserved for Chapter 3, and a set of questions for clinical inquiry will follow in Chapter 4.

In italics, *Inquiring Deeply* refers to this book as a whole. It comprises an unfolding deep inquiry in and of itself, delving into the similarities and differences between mindfulness-based psychodynamic treatment, on the one hand, and mindfulness-based Buddhist meditation practice, on the other.

****

The major purpose of this chapter is to clearly describe the key premises and assumptions of inquiring deeply as a psychotherapeutic approach in order to show where it fits within the broad framework of psychodynamic, relational, and psychoanalytic treatments. Because it is grounded in my dharma practice and was developed in my clinical work, this "signature therapeutic approach" is in some sense particular to me. My hope, however, is that sharing the way I think about clinical work will be in some way illuminating and will pave the way for readers to forge their own integrative paths.

I want to emphasize at the outset that inquiring deeply is not a new "brand" of psychotherapy. It is better described as a new *slant* on psychodynamic/relational psychotherapy, an integrative clinical framework which is informed by Buddhist view and mindfulness practice. As a synonym, I sometimes refer to this therapeutic approach as "contemplative relational psychotherapy."

Inquiring deeply is not something the therapist *does* as a clinical intervention, not something the therapist *teaches* the patient, nor even something *done by* the patient under the direction of the therapist. It is not something which requires any particular state of consciousness. It is, rather, a paradigm for psychodynamic understanding which is conceptually informed by Buddhist psychology and experientially informed by mindfulness practice.

The organization of the discussion in this chapter is as follows: first, the conceptual and philosophical underpinnings of inquiring deeply as a psychotherapeutic framework will be articulated. Next, the basic aspects of mindfulness (mindful awareness) will be described. Together, these summaries will begin to construct a conceptual bridge between Buddhist practice and psychodynamic work. The strategic application of mindfulness in amplifying psychotherapeutic exploration can then be explained. Finally, by contrasting the two sets of ideas, the discussion will highlight some basic differences between mindful psychotherapy and mindfulness meditation.

Presumably some readers will already be quite familiar with one or the other of these two basic content areas (or both) so that this preliminary discussion may be a review. Be that as it may, my intention has been to present all of the important ideas in a way that is lucid and clear; simple yet not superficial. My summary will hopefully provide conceptual common ground for readers to stand on as the discussion progresses to greater levels of complexity.[1]

Readers should be aware that this book is not intended as a scholarly exposition of either Buddhism or psychotherapy, nor does it try to make a comprehensive comparison of the two. Rather, *Inquiring Deeply* explores the "psychological world of lived experience" from a pragmatic point of view which needs to be grounded in one's own introspective practice. Its overarching purpose is to provide a guide to understanding how mindfulness informs the practice of psychotherapy, and vice versa.

View of Psychological Healing in Inquiring Deeply

As has been said above, inquiring deeply is a blended psychotherapeutic approach which integrates mindfulness with therapeutic techniques that engage the patient at the levels of narrative, *affect regulation*, and psychodynamic understanding. Some basic definitions were unpacked in the opening paragraph of this chapter. Before exploring further the elements which mindfulness contributes to psychodynamic/relational treatment, it will be useful to first spell out the foundational psychodynamic principles on which this therapeutic approach is grounded.

1 We all fall under the influence of unconscious dynamics which negatively affect and suffocate our ability to feel, think, work, and love. These are psychodynamic "knots" which are associated with psychological wounds of varying severity.
2 These psychodynamic knots show up in the psychological world of our lived experience as areas of unprocessed or unmetabolized experience—termed in this book *non-experienced experience*. Non-experienced experience corresponds to areas of trauma.
3 Tangles in the mind symptomatically present as recurrent upsets, problems, and long-standing, repeated, painful patterns of reactivity. They show up in interpersonal entanglements, personal dramas with others which are painful and construed as problems. These reaction patterns reveal underlying areas of wounding: "unfinished psychological business" from our relational history with others. They reveal aspects of experience which are dissociated, things in ourselves which we are denying or are otherwise frightened to see.[2]
4 Because problems call attention to areas of unprocessed experience, they can be a useful guide to healing. A foundational assumption in inquiring deeply

is that problems have innate intelligence in them by virtue of calling attention to what most needs to be seen. Analogous to pain in the physical body, they call our attention to underlying wounds. Psychological healing can then occur as a function of bringing awareness to what is unconscious.

5   Humans are relational beings and a great deal of our psychological wounding occurs in our relationships with others. Relational wounds are best addressed in the context of a psychotherapeutic relationship that both explores problems and provides a corrective intimacy between self and other.

6   Relational healing occurs when the deep pain of one person is met with empathy, compassion, and understanding from another. This relationship—all relationship—is a two-way street: inherently bidirectional, always co-created, and mutually transformative. Healing in psychotherapy is a function of the relational intimacy of the therapeutic connection and the new experiences that occur.

7   Psychological healing is a function of the ***relational field***: the fabric of interconnectedness which is continually and dynamically created and re-created between the participants. The relational field is both interpersonal and intersubjective. Therapeutic intimacy in the relational field is the heart and soul of psychotherapeutic change.[3]

In addition, we can also delineate the following ways in which mindfulness can enhance psychodynamic/relational work:

8   Psychological healing requires more than mere recognition of something at the level of conscious thoughts, attitudes and views, and ideas. The optimal way to relate to experience is *deep emotional understanding*: intuitive understanding grounded in embodied experience, the felt sense of things. Mindful awareness cultivates and deepens this dimension of experience.

9   Healing is also a function of the quality and depth of our relationship with our own experience—the ability to *be with* (i.e. *be present with*) experience. This ability to *be with* is a function of both mindfulness and self-compassion. It can be developed in the psychotherapeutic milieu, aided and abetted by the therapist's own mindful awareness and compassion.

10 Psychological healing involves re-organization of the experience of self and other, facilitated by the *cultivation of self-reflective awareness* both inside and outside of the consulting room. Mindfulness develops the capacity for self-reflection.

11 Relational healing is a function of our understanding of the dynamics of interpersonal relationships and requires self-awareness as we relate to others. In inquiring deeply, these goals are facilitated by conscious exploration of *how relationship is held in mind*—both through *psychotherapeutic inquiry* and through *mindfulness of connection*.

12 Mindfulness enhances the capacity to witness experience without identifying with it. It is a meta-level awareness of *how we relate to our own minds* (i.e. our relationship with ourselves).

13 The view in inquiring deeply is that psychological healing is a function of relating to the **background field**[4] which both holds and frames our awareness. This concept may be conveyed by analogy with the process of looking into a mirror: we can invite awareness of the surface of the mirror as well as of the images reflected there. Explicit recognition of the background field contributes to the ability to witness and observe, thus enhancing self-reflective function.

14 Inquiring deeply includes focus on aspects of the mind that are addressed in Buddhist psychology, for example the tendency of the mind to grasp onto and push away experience. It *brings Buddhist view into the psychological narrative*.

15 Healing is supported by an *attitude of acceptance, receptivity, and faith in the wisdom of whatever emerges*. When we can relax into what is happening, rather than struggling against it, we are more likely to see clearly and make good choices. These therapeutic attitudes are supported by the practice of mindfulness.

16 As the focus of attention shifts to the background field, it also becomes possible to access healing experiences in which we intuitively glimpse a way of being which transcends suffering. In this book, I term such experiences **transcendent subjectivity**. *into formless?*

17 Even brief experiences of transcendent subjectivity may transform the way that we relate to problems. Transcendent subjectivity entails the insight that deepening the experience of problems is a necessary part of how they are resolved. *Problem and solution are two sides of a single coin. This insight is both transformative and healing.*

Mindful of What?

The core meaning of "mindfulness" is the ability to *be with* what is; to be intimate with the present moment of experience. Mindfulness is a function of how we pay attention. Unfortunately, the word has become so diluted in common usage that for many people it serves as a simple synonym for awareness of something. In the course of writing this chapter, for example, I heard the word used conversationally in phrases such as "mindful of the time," and "mindful of the presence of others." It is important to recognize that in Buddhism, "mindfulness" has a much more specific meaning: it is a particular *quality* of awareness that is honed by the practice of systematic and careful noticing of experience.

The Buddhist concept of mindfulness is often defined as systematically paying attention to what is experienced Here, Now: intentionally cultivated, receptive, non-judgmental awareness of the present moment.[5] A nuanced discussion of mindfulness as it is understood in Buddhism goes beyond the intended scope of this book. For present purposes, it should be emphasized that "mindfulness" does not reference any one particular experience or state of mind. Rather, it references a

mind is sense door

span or continuum of states of awareness which may differ greatly both in regard to the *content* of awareness and to the *subjective texture* or *quality of awareness* that is present. Mindful awareness deepens as meditation practice cultivates an increasingly stable, clear, and penetrating quality of attention.

The two basic parameters of experience are its *content* and its *context,* understood as the figure and ground of experience, respectively.[6] In general, Buddhist meditation privileges what is called *direct experience*: simple, unelaborated awareness of the content of experience at the six sense doors (sight, sound, touch, smell, taste, and mind). Direct experience can be conveyed by calling to mind the difference between standing outside in the rain vs. watching the storm through a window. It varies in vividness and intensity as a function of mental state, and deepens with meditation practice. The practice of insight meditation repeatedly calls attention to simple ("bare") awareness of each of these six kinds of experience.

The experience of the background field of awareness in which experience arises is also an important part of Buddhist meditation practice. We may refer to the experience of this background field as *awareness of awareness.*

As most readers probably know, there are *four foundations of mindfulness* addressed in Buddhist mindfulness practice:[7] (1) how experience feels in the body; (2) its pleasantness or unpleasantness; (3) states of mind; and (4) mental "objects"—i.e. the various mental phenomena which Buddhism recognizes as basic truths about human mind and life ("**dharmas**").

"Right mindfulness" of each of the four foundations means to repeatedly and closely observe whatever experience is occurring. Across all of the four foundations, it involves noticing certain central features of experience, especially the fact that it is recurrently unsatisfactory, impermanent, and devoid of any independently-existing self. In following the Buddhist path, one can come to know each of these truths (the "three marks of existence") for oneself moment by moment in the flow of experience.

The first foundation of mindfulness is experience of body: bodily sensations, posture, activities, and functions. Often the first foundation is taught through mindfulness of breathing—for example, registering the sensations of the breath coming in, going out; the belly or chest rising and falling. As we follow the breath with focused attention, we can become aware of increasingly subtle experiences of breathing.

Over time, we recognize that even our relationship to the very act of breathing varies impressively: at times the breath may feel labored; at other times it is so effortless that the body seems to be breathing *us* rather than the other way around. With repeated practice, mindfulness of breathing cultivates relaxation, stillness, and attentional focus, which collectively constitute *presence with* the basic experience of being alive. It becomes increasingly clear that our breath mirrors the state of mind and state of being moment by moment.

The second foundation of mindfulness is the *feeling tone* of experience: its felt sense of being *pleasant, unpleasant,* or *neutral.* Feeling tone is the core sense of pleasure and pain; what we like and what we don't. Mindfulness of the second foundation reveals how rapidly feeling tone becomes elaborated into emotions, reactions, and action tendencies: for example, the effort to hold onto experience or to push it away. This mindful awareness makes it possible to see emotions and judgments as they first emerge. Mindful awareness of the second foundation illuminates the challenge of staying present with experiences of pleasantness and unpleasantness just as they are.

The third foundation of mindfulness is termed *mindfulness of mind*. To be "mindful of mind" means to be aware of our states of mind: to know both the subjective qualities of moment-to-moment experience and how the mind is relating to that experience. In Buddhist meditation practice, the third foundation refers especially to experiences of lust or greed, anger and aversion, ignorance and delusion which may cloud the mind. By being mindful of the mind, we learn to discern when such experiences are present and when they are not; to notice different qualities and textures of mind states—concentrated or distracted; expansive or contracted; confused or clear; calm or agitated.

Mindfulness of mind is inclusive of everything we may become conscious of: moods, thoughts, feelings, and subjective states. It registers the subjective qualities of mind states, our reactions to our states of mind, and even our awareness of being aware of them. Contemplation of the third foundation highlights how the mind enters into and becomes entangled with the world which it creates, grasping after what is pleasant and attempting to avoid what is unpleasant.

The fourth foundation of mindfulness includes the constituents of our experience moment by moment. It includes the "five aggregates" of form, feeling, perception, thought, and consciousness; mind observed in the acts of sensing, feeling, observing, and knowing. It includes awareness of what arises at the six sense doors of sight, hearing, taste, smell, touch, and the mind. The fourth foundation of mindfulness also includes all of the "dharmas" described in Buddhist teachings: the entire landscape of phenomena which arise and then vanish from experience. Among the dharmas which can be observed are the hindrances to concentration; the "factors of enlightenment"; and the four noble truths. Mindfulness of the fourth foundation yields penetrating insight into suffering and its causes.

Taken together, contemplation of the four foundations of mindfulness schools the mind in awareness of *what* occurs *as* it occurs. Its basic goals include:

• enhanced awareness of the bodily dimension of experience;
• clear seeing and knowing what is happening in the mind as it is happening;
• relaxed, stable, and continuous attention; and
• non-reactivity (equanimity).

By shifting attention from complex objects of awareness to elementary information at the sense doors, mindfulness meditation reveals to us that mental states, even painful ones, are a kaleidoscopic play of experience at the six sense doors and that "this too shall pass." This practice helps us to "decenter" from the content of experience and counteracts the automatic tendency to get caught up in the thinking mind and its abstract or symbolic knowing, which the philosopher/ Zen enthusiast Alan Watts famously described as confusing the menu for the meal. This fundamental human confusion, Buddhism teaches, goes to the heart of suffering.

Moreover, mindfulness of mind (including elements of both the third and fourth foundations of mindfulness) develops awareness of increasingly more refined and subtle objects of mind, and in so doing sharpens the distinction between what we are aware *of* and awareness itself. This was likened above to the difference between noticing images in the mirror and paying attention to the surface of the mirror itself. This emerging clarity about the distinction between figure and ground—the *content* vs. the *context* of experience—cultivates our capacity to dis-identify with particular experiences that may be occurring. Mindfulness practice develops the ability to discern and sustain awareness of the background field—the field of sentience from which experience continually arises and disappears. As bumper sticker wisdom proclaims, *mindfulness is the state of mind in which we realize that we are not our state of mind.*

It is important to recognize that "mindfulness" is not a single state of mind. Rather, every state of mind has its own distinct mood, felt sense, and organ-ization of self-experience, including the degree to which mindful awareness is present. Inquiring deeply as a psychotherapeutic approach focuses on the importance of mindfulness as self-reflective awareness. I liken it to a "clutch" function which allows the mind to shift gears so that new points of view can emerge.

With depth of practice, mindfulness can ripen into many states of mind which are unusual in the ordinary consciousness of everyday life. Such states of *"trans-cendent subjectivity"* as they are termed in this book, yield an altered perspective on self and world which can be instrumental in resolving problems. Sometimes the very sense of self and the experience of *agency* can shift, allowing a direct experience of reality without the usual boundaries. In such moments, seer and seen can merge transcendently into the experience of existence unfolding itself seamlessly moment by moment.[8]

Inquiring Deeply: Mindful, Psychodynamic, Relational Psychotherapy

The fundamental elements of inquiring deeply are mindfulness, self-reflection, and deep connection. Its most essential premise is that emotional well-being is a function of the quality of our connections with others. It explores inner experience from this perspective, looking into how experience with others comes about and the developmental factors that contribute to making it that way. Like all psycho-dynamic work, its aim is the transformation and reorganization of the patient's self-experience.[9]

It is widely understood in the mental health professions, but not always in Buddhist circles, that the mind is inherently relational. This fact explains why the issues which are most often problematic for people are emotional/interpersonal in nature: they are embedded in unseen relational patterns. Inquiring deeply explores experience through this relational lens, using self-reflective awareness practices adapted from Buddhist mindfulness practice.

Like Buddhism, inquiring deeply is based on a quest for insight into the nature of suffering. But whereas Buddhist practice systematically focuses attention on the four foundations of mindfulness, the primary focus in inquiring deeply is on the *psychological world of lived experience*: the subjective, "experience-near" world as it lives in peoples' minds. For most people most of the time, problems comprise a significant part of that subjective world, and so what we can also say is that inquiring deeply focuses on deepening awareness of problems. One of its fundamental premises is that there is intelligence in problems. Analogous to pain in the body, problems call our attention to what we need to see.

Problems have many layers. The starting point of exploration is generally some narrative of complaint about what is wrong or some aspect of experience which feels problematic (an emotional reaction, event, psychological upset, or symptom).[10] As we "inquire deeply" about a problem, several things need to happen (albeit not in linear sequence):

- We invite "fully receiving" experience in the Buddhist sense—i.e. relaxing into it and being mindfully present with what is going on.
- We focus attention on the problem in a way which invites deeper emotional understanding of what is involved. This includes exploring the narrative themes in which the experience is embedded in order to illuminate their psychological context, the feelings that are involved, and the meanings that we have assigned to the experience.
- We invite deliberate investigation of problematic aspects of experience, including representations of self and other. As needed, self-reflective awareness practices are created and "prescribed" for use as adjunctive therapeutic strategies to help amplify those aspects of experience that need to be seen more clearly.
- We help the patient tune into the unseen aspects of how they are relating to this experience in a way which enacts resistance rather than acceptance.
- We use the therapeutic relationship to help the patient relax into the background field in order to create space for the problem to unfold. This, in turn, facilitates the creation of new templates of experience.

Inquiring deeply focuses on the content of psychological narrative. The stories that we tell—about ourselves, about others, and about what we consider to be real—comprise the system of meaning in which we live. The therapeutic approach described in this book is based on the view that not only are these stories not "beside the point," as Buddhist teachings often suggest, they are vital to self-understanding. As writer David Loy puts it, our world is made of stories (Loy, 2010).

To summarize what has been said so far, inquiring deeply is mindful, psychodynamic, relational psychotherapy. The following basic premises can be articulated:

- Inquiring deeply is a psychodynamic approach. By investigating problems and tracking experience as it unfolds over time, many psychodynamic processes can emerge clearly into view in a way that deepens self-understanding. Because the story lines of the person's narrative can and will be understood differently by every listener, the therapist's attuned understanding is an essential ingredient of good psychotherapy. Perceptive mirroring on the part of the therapist is essential. (If we could see our own blind spots, they wouldn't be blind!)
- Inquiring deeply is a *relational* psychotherapeutic framework. It explores the relational dimension of how the mind is organized. Relational patterns in the patient's life are explored, especially those which are problematic in nature. By focusing closely on what is enacted in the patient's life and the stories that are being told about those events, it becomes evident that the psychological world of lived experience is constructed around a complex "***relational matrix***" which encodes our history with others.
- Inquiring deeply is a psychoanalytic approach. Since the Here and Now of psychotherapy is a microcosm of the patient's way of being in the world, the therapeutic relationship itself is often a fruitful area of inquiry. By bringing the process of the shared therapeutic experience into the foreground, insight emerges. To do this well, therapists need to participate in the emotional experience—in the *being*—of the other. Being "up close and personal" in this way is the best way to develop understanding of a patient's problems.
- Inquiring deeply is a mindfulness-informed approach. The depth of mindful awareness of the therapist is a basic therapeutic factor which bears upon achieving a mutual and clear comprehension of the patient's emotional experience.
- Inquiring deeply is a strategic approach. As dynamic exploration reveals important aspects of experience that the patient may not have been aware of, this suggests what the person might benefit from seeing more clearly and becomes the basis for devising strategies of awareness practice which can help in making things more clear.

Moreover, the therapist's empathic inquiry into the patient's experience models the possibility of compassionately accepting one's experience. The therapeutic relationship, which includes the therapist's mindful and compassionate awareness, is gradually assimilated by the patient into a new framework for relating to his or her own experience.

Mindfulness-Informed Psychotherapy and Buddhist Practice Compared

Inquiring deeply is a mindfulness-informed psychotherapeutic process which focuses on events in the mind which are anchored in individual history and experience. In contrast, dharma practice generally focuses on becoming aware in one's experience of what the Buddha taught about the origins of suffering and the path to its cessation. Although Buddhist practice explores these factors as they surface in our own experience, they are not fundamentally personal. Despite this basic difference between psychotherapy and dharma practice, mindfulness, self-reflection, and psychotherapeutic exploration are confluent in their effect on deepening awareness.

The prescribed objects of attention in Buddhist mindfulness practice derive from the fundamental tenets of what the Buddha taught and bear the conceptual imprint of that foundation. The specific mental skill cultivated in mindfulness meditation is the ability to sustain relaxed, wakeful attention in the here and now, and the correlated ability to avoid getting lost in thoughts. So-called "disidentification from experience" invites attention to shift to the background field.

From this perspective, in Buddhist practice it is often thought to be unwise to focus on the psychological story-line of experience. The "manifest content" in the mind (to borrow Freud's phrase for describing the story line of night dreams) can easily hijack attention, and it tends in any case to devolve into more layers of thinking we can get lost in. Meditators are therefore encouraged not to focus on what thinking is *about*. In my view, this throws out an important baby with the bathwater.[11]

In contrast, exploration of experience in inquiring deeply begins with the painful psychological dramas and stories in the psychological world of lived experience. For some people, such dramas tend to occupy center stage in the mind. Be that as it may, there is wisdom inherent in whatever is arising, dual and non-dual experience alike, and that we can open to that wisdom through investigation and inquiry. We can use mindful awareness of problems to discover opportunities for growth.

****

Mindfulness and Psychotherapy: Are They Distinct?

Mindfulness is the meditative heart of Buddhism, and it seems to have found a secular home in Western psychotherapy. This makes sense because Buddhist practice, like psychotherapy, is fundamentally a method for addressing psychological pain. Westerners have been turning to mindfulness in increasing numbers as a means for coping with emotional distress; paraphrasing the titles of some best-selling books, they are seeking ways to free themselves from old habits and fears; find out what to do when things fall apart; and find clarity in the midst of emotional chaos (to mention just a few).

Certainly dharma practice has a psychotherapeutic dimension. Its very purpose is to help people get beyond suffering, and psychological pain is fundamentally what attracts people to it. An implicitly psychotherapeutic view of Buddhist practice is also invited by the work of contemporary dharma teachers who have been educated in Western psychotherapy and who have been the authors of our current

Buddhist psychological narratives. For example, when we look at inspirational stories of transformation which occur during mindfulness meditation practice (such as those recounted in Jack Kornfield's (1993; 2008) books) we see that they can be aptly described either as dharma practice or as Buddhist psychotherapy. Both narrative frameworks feel valid.

Following this train of thought, we might say that meditation practice itself, and/or the deep intimacy and presence of *being with* the teacher, provides a powerful "psychological container" in the analytic sense. One can easily imagine the transferential needs and wishes the practitioner brings to the situation, including deep longing for transformative connection with other. The compassion of the teacher and the experience of being deeply seen, understood, and accepted are deeply healing in a psychotherapeutic sense.

However, there are also confusions created when psychotherapeutic and Buddhist narratives are conflated. What gets lost is that healing in the psychotherapeutic sense is not the intended goal of Buddhist practice. Buddhist practice is defined in its own terms; it aims toward a radical re-contextualization of identity in which suffering ceases to have its usual personal meaning and significance. This goal, "*liberation*," is distinct from psychological healing.

Using the metaphor that was introduced above, psychotherapy is intended to relieve pain by untangling the relational knots which engender psychological suffering. In contrast, dharma practice is a method for radically transforming our relationship to the entire field of our experience—our fundamental way of perceiving and being—in a way which obviates the necessity for untangling. Liberation is not the same as psychological healing, although the two are closely intertwined. In any event, mindfulness cannot be adequately understood apart from the Buddhist philosophy from which it derives.

The "psychologizing" of mindfulness has one additional unfortunate implication, which is the notion that gets conveyed that even a brief exposure to mindfulness equips a clinician to understand what mindfulness is and teach others how to "do it." While the rudiments of mindfulness meditation may perhaps be learned in a weekend or an afternoon, and while mindfulness can certainly be used as a psychotherapeutic intervention, tool, or technique, this misses the depth of mindful awareness that is available in sustained practice, as well as the mature wisdom and compassion which are the goal of dharma practice.

The following quote bears upon the distinction between the psychotherapeutic and the Buddhist paradigms. (In reading the quote, think of "myth" = subjective understanding of the world.)

> We are all living within a myth, the myth or myths that provide us with our fundamental world view. Psychotherapists (often read) the Buddhist myth in terms of their psychotherapeutic myth. But to understand Buddhism, one must enter the Buddhist myth, and once we are within that myth, then we will naturally read psychotherapy in terms of Buddhism.
>
> (Kearney, 1999, p. 11)

Although inquiring deeply is informed by the Buddhist "myth" or world view, through the long series of reflections that are described in this book I have concluded that the distinction between the psychotherapeutic and Buddhist narratives is neither clearly delineated nor fixed. Inquiring deeply is *both* Buddhist-informed psychotherapy *and* psychologically-minded dharma practice. On the one hand, I recognize a distinction between psychological healing and liberation, as presented above; on the other hand, I also experience the boundary between the two as complex and fluid. For this reason, I have settled on defining inquiring deeply as a blended set of reflective practices, one which includes psychodynamic exploration of experience.

Perhaps, when all is said and done, Buddhist and psychotherapeutic narratives are simply that, narratives, and whatever practice we do is only liberating to the extent that it is. This is implicit in Hokusai's message: experience is endlessly unfolding exactly as it does, and there is no end to seeing.

Notes

1   As Shunryo Suzuki (1970) famously said, "in the beginner's mind, there are many possibilities, in the expert's mind there are few." I hope that readers will approach *Inquiring Deeply* with beginner's mind!

2   Readers who are familiar with the concepts of dissociation and enactment in relational psychoanalytic theory will recognize this basic idea in the statement of this premise.

3   The relational field established by the psychotherapist is the essential mechanism of therapeutic action, created through meeting the basic needs of the human being to be recognized, validated, and accepted—a quality of 'being to being' which will be further described in Chapter 5. A good introduction to the basic premises of relational psychotherapy may be found in the work of Mitchell and Aron (1999); Stern (2003); Stern (2010); and Stern (2015).

4   Although the term "background field" is not a Buddhist idea, it is congruent with the core of Buddhist teachings. It may be thought of as the field of sentience or interconnected Being in which experience arises.

   The background field exists *prior to* experience in some sense. It "contains" all that has not yet come into being; it is the potentiality from which all experience emerges. This view entails complex philosophical questions which are not the intended subject of the present discussion. The term "background field" is not intended to imply that the field is some *thing* we can become aware of. Awareness of the background field, or of anything else, is a particular constellation of experience which arises and passes away just as everything does.

5   This definition of mindfulness is the one most frequently cited in the popular and professional literature. A full and more nuanced discussion of the nature of mindful awareness cultivated in Buddhist practice is beyond the scope of this book. For an in-depth introduction, I recommend Gunaratana (2002) and Analayo (2003).

6   These two basic parameters may sometimes be conflated in discussions of mindfulness.

7   A full description of these and other basic Buddhist concepts is beyond the scope of *Inquiring Deeply*. The interested reader might be well-served by a more scholarly and detailed guide such as Nyanaponika's (1965) book *Mindfulness: The Heart of Buddhist Meditation*.

8   ***Transcendent subjectivity*** is defined vis-à-vis inquiring deeply in Chapter 8. The meaning in a spiritual context is roughly equivalent to "non-dual awareness" or

"unconditioned awareness" (see for example Fenner, 2007)—subjective states in which the commonplace reality of separation between the subject and object of experience are transcended.

9 Inquiring deeply is informed by many different schools of thought in contemporary psychoanalysis (self psychology, intersubjectivity, and relational psychoanalysis as well as object relations theory). Though predicated on these psychoanalytic views of the mind, inquiring deeply does not, however, necessarily focus clinically on what gets enacted between patient and therapist (as would generally be done in relational psychoanalysis). There may or may not be explicit emphasis on the transference and counter-transference in any particular case. Be that as it may, the relational dimension of the work is key.

10 Selecting what to attend to is the creative aspect of this psychotherapeutic approach. This will be elaborated and discussed in detail in Chapters 3 and 4.

11 This is not to say that Buddhist psychology does not investigate the process of thinking. Buddhism has its own way of working with the content of experience and of the unconscious mind.

References

Analayo (2003). *Satipatthana: The direct path to realization*. Birmingham, UK: Windhorse Publications.

Fenner, P. (2007). *Radiant mind: Awakening unconditioned awareness*. Boulder, CO: Sounds True.

Gunaratana, B. H. (2012). *The four foundations of mindfulness in plain English*. Boston, MA: Wisdom Publications.

Kearney, P. (1999). *Still crazy after all these years: Why meditation isn't psychotherapy*. Online blog published by Dharma Salon. www.buddhanet.net/psyche.htm.

Kornfield, J. (1993). *The path with heart*. New York, NY: Bantam Books.

Kornfield, J. (2008). *The wise heart*. New York, NY: Bantam Books.

Loy, D. (2010). *The world is made of stories*. Somerville, MA: Wisdom Publications.

Mitchell, S. A. and Aron, L. (1999). *Relational psychoanalysis: The emergence*. Hillsdale, NJ: Analytic Press.

Nyanaponika, T. (1965). *Mindfulness: The heart of Buddhist meditation*. York Beach, ME: Samuel Weiser Press.

Stern, D. (2003). *Unformulated experience: From dissociation to imagination in psychoanalysis*. Hillsdale, NJ: Analytic Press.

Stern, D. (2010). *Partners in thought: Working with unformulated experience, dissociation, and enactment*. New York, NY: Routledge Press.

Stern, D. (2015). *Relational freedom: Emergent properties of the interpersonal field*. New York, NY: Routledge Press.

Suzuki, S. (1970). *Zen mind, beginner's mind*. New York, NY: Weatherhill Books.

Chapter 3

Inquiring Deeply
Mindful Self-Reflection in Psychotherapy

Psychotherapy, like mindfulness meditation, has the purpose of helping us get to know our minds. Inquiring deeply is a psychotherapeutic framework in which this happens in two interwoven ways: through mindful self-reflection, and in dialogue with a mindful therapist. This amounts to a creative synthesis of mindfulness meditation and psychodynamic/relational psychotherapy in which we discover our own deepest, subjective truths.

To reiterate some of the primary conclusions in the preceding chapter, inquiring deeply in psychotherapy is *not* a particular method nor a particular state of consciousness. It is *not* something the therapist does as a clinical intervention, *not* something the therapist explicitly teaches the patient, nor even something *done* by the patient under the direction of the therapist. Rather, it is a stance of mindful reflection that arises as a function of shared psychotherapeutic intention in the therapy relationship.

While we can "inquire deeply" by ourselves, either in formal periods of meditation practice or in the process of daily life, there are ways in which collaborative inquiry is optimal. Just as a fish is unlikely to be aware of the water in which it swims, there are some aspects of ourselves that are essentially invisible except in the mirror of another. For this reason, this kind of psychological exploration is well-suited to the psychotherapeutic process.

Because each therapeutic situation is unique, the therapeutic strategy can vary a great deal. The most essential element is the stance of mindful presence that is brought to clinical listening.

The clinical signature of inquiring deeply as a psychotherapeutic approach includes the fact that (1) it is Buddhist-informed and incorporates dharma practice methodology and Buddhadharma into the process of exploring psychological suffering; and (2) it is psychoanalytically informed and highlights the relational dimensions of suffering. It creatively interweaves psychotherapeutic dialogue, mindful awareness, and intentional self-reflection into new narratives of understanding. This allows us (both therapists and patients) to become aware of things that might otherwise escape our notice.

Inquiring Deeply into Psychological Problems

Psychotherapy invariably begins with an inquiry into why a patient has come. Most often I begin with some question like "what brings you?," but there are many different ways to open the therapeutic dialogue.

Most often the patient gives a narrative about a problem they are having, frequently one which has been stubbornly recurrent and troublesome. One slogan which summarizes what I have learned in the process of doing this work is that "insight often begins with bad news." I may or may not make this comment out loud, but it is an implicit part of my clinical paradigm.

Patterns of emotional reactivity, upsets, or "meltdowns"—places where there has been a breakdown in the capacity to metabolize emotional experience—are useful points of departure for inquiring into the psychological structures that organize experience. As we inquire about a problem, we first endeavor to trace emotional reactions to their roots in unmet psychological needs. Most often we discover that problems are rooted in our views of self and other.

The overall goal of dynamic psychotherapy lies in establishing a therapeutic conversation (and therapeutic relationship) which supports a deeper emotional understanding of the nature of the patient's difficulties. At various points in the therapeutic dialogue, opportunities for reflective practice may unfold, as will be illustrated in the clinical vignettes which follow.

I will begin my description of this therapeutic approach with an entry from the journal of a patient, "Alice," who used her meditation practice to investigate an experience of anxiety.

Clinical Illustration 3.1: Alice

*I noticed that I was anxious. I tried to see where it was coming from [**investigation**] but it was opaque to me, so I decided to sit in order to explore what the anxiety was about. A lot of thoughts came up about a conversation I had yesterday with my sister regarding a fight she had with her husband [**reflection**]. Suddenly it became clear to me that I am upset about my relationship with John [Alice's significant other]. I am worried that he may be attracted to Betty [a woman John works with].*

*I spent the rest of my meditation trying to locate the roots of my jealous feelings. I also thought about the nature of jealousy, and what you said to me once about my tendency to confuse jealousy and love. I could see clearly that my jealous feelings are based on feelings of insecurity [**self-reflection**].*

As she meditated, Alice had a spontaneous insight about the link between thoughts she had about her sister's marriage and jealous feelings she has regarding her own partner. Had Alice and I been talking together, I would likely have had the same thought and said so. Clarifying and making interpretive links of this sort are among the basic skills of effective clinical listening in any psychotherapy.

Note that in the example given, inquiry began with the associative framework of psychological meanings, as in the example given. For most people, this is a very "natural" place to begin as we look within ourselves, because the raw material in the mind tends to consist of these kinds of associations. (In dharma practice, all of this would fall into the category of "personality view"—a very basic aspect of our conditioning.)

In my own consulting room, the process of inquiry unfolds in ordinary psychotherapeutic conversation. It develops both out of observations contributed by the patient and/or from creative or intuitive clinical ideas of my own. I may "invite" a patient to further investigate some particular aspect of their experience. I may suggest an "empirical experiment" to notice what feelings arise under certain circumstances, or I may just ask a pointed question that invites reflection. I may comment on something that seems to me to be happening in the Here and Now of the session and ask the patient to take a moment to see how he or she is actually feeling in that moment. I may introduce a clinical "pause" by inviting the patient to spend a few minutes getting a "felt sense"[1] of what they are talking about. I may make an interpretation of some sort and ask the patient to notice whether or not it seems true to them, or I may invite them to investigate what evolves as life unfolds. When I work with meditators, I may sometimes "prescribe" a question for meditative investigation or inquiry: for example, "what is at stake here?" or "what aspect of yourself are you attached to here?" There are sometimes interesting comparisons to be made between daily life and meditation practice, and there may also be important points that bear upon the perspective of the dharma (whether or not Buddhist ideas are made an explicit focus).

Reflective Practices in Inquiring Deeply

Inquiring deeply includes a number of different "reflective practices." I delineate various kinds of introspective awareness under this umbrella, including noticing, investigation, inquiry, and self-reflection. All of these involve mindful awareness, but it is sometimes helpful to distinguish among them, so I will define each before I proceed with further illustration and discussion.

"*Noticing*": Awareness of psychological events and experiences as these arise during daily life or during meditation. Noticing is one of the basic experiential modes of the conscious, cognizing mind. However, it is important to recognize that the experiential quality of noticing varies a great deal from moment to moment. Here, I am referring to "mindful noticing" as distinct from ordinary noticing.

"*Investigation*": Focused mindful exploration of some specific aspect of experience, including the thoughts, images, body sensations, emotions, mood, and mental state that are present.

"*Inquiry*": Looking into the nature of something in a deliberately open and receptive state of mind in order to discover something about it. As I use the term, inquiry is a deliberate, strategic, and sustained process, "living in the question" of something, whereas investigation is the probing of experience as it arises. Finding the right questions is the art of inquiry, and is itself a process; questions become progressively more refined and clear as we *be with* them over time. Once a question has been posed, the major task is simply to keep questioning and looking, sustaining an attitude of curiosity and receptiveness.

(When inquiry is done as a formal meditation process, it can also be called "contemplative inquiry.")

The optimal state of mind in inquiry is aptly described as "opening the hand of thought" (as Uchiyama called Zen practice in his 2004 book). This is a state of mind which is open and receptive, one which neither holds onto nor pushes away thoughts. It rests on a platform of mindful attention. This quality of mind invites an experience of not knowing, which can be both creative and generative.[2]

"Self-reflection": A process of introspective inquiry into the connections between the present moment of experience and the broad network of associations in the mind. We ponder and/or contemplate what something means to us or we try to understand what is happening within us in the light of what we know about ourselves. Thoughts and feelings are examined to see how things are connected, what memories are called up, and what context of *personal meaning* is present. Self-reflection helps us to see more clearly and understand more deeply how we are relating to our experience. A process of deliberate self-reflection can be engaged in order to invite insight or to create wise intentions for future experience.

Self-reflection is not necessarily "meditation," nor vice versa. For example, self-reflection occurs frequently in ordinary conversation as we respond to something someone has said with our own associations. Self-reflection occurs when we start thinking about something and follow thoughts as they deepen along their own path;[3] ("having a good think," as the British psychoanalysts are wont to say). Self-reflection can be regarded as a continuum of states: at one end of the continuum, it is a casual mental process, barely noticed; at the other end, it can be a formal, self-guided inquiry practice (holding some question of interest in mind throughout a period of sitting meditation[4]). Ordinary psychotherapeutic conversation falls somewhere in the middle of this self-reflective spectrum.

Collectively, I refer to these various methods of exploring experience—mindful awareness, noticing, investigation, and inquiry—as "self-reflective practices." They are used as adjunctive interventions in inquiring deeply to discover or encounter what is subjectively true—i.e. to become directly aware of how we experience something. This is somewhat distinct from the same methods as forms of dharma practice in that psychotherapy focuses selectively on what feels psychologically important, generally aspects of experience that have to do with personality, with self. We look into psychological experience with the intention to discover the *subjective* truth of something; to the best of our ability, to strip away the biasing influences of fantasy, belief, and desire, and to invite discovery of what is so that has not yet been seen.

Inquiring deeply is a psychotherapeutic approach which is based both on self-reflection integral within psychotherapeutic exploration and self-reflection which is engaged as a deliberate awareness practice. Although inquiring deeply uses mindful investigation, inquiry, and self-reflection as adjunctive strategies in psychotherapy, it should be emphasized that inquiring deeply cannot be equated with meditation as a process nor with any particular state of awareness.

What we choose as the object of self-reflective practice may be focused and specific (for example, "what about being with that person makes me so anxious?") or it may be general and abstract ("what am I not seeing?" or "what experience am I pushing away?"). A framework of questions for clinical exploration informed by contemporary psychoanalytic concepts will be provided in the next chapter.

As we have said at other points in this discussion, inquiry and other reflective practices engage both intuitive awareness and analytic thought, so they should not be considered to be only cognitive processes. Optimally, they are grounded in the immediacy of deep experience, including feelings.

With this nomenclature in mind, the first clinical illustration ("Alice 3.1") that was given above will now be re-examined as an illustration of these various reflective practices, as follows:

Clinical Illustration 3.2: Alice

I noticed that I was anxious. I tried to see where it was coming from [investigation] *but it was opaque to me, so I decided to sit in order to explore what the anxiety was about* [inquiry]. *A lot of thoughts came up about a conversation I had yesterday with my sister regarding a fight she had with her husband* [reflection]. *Suddenly it became clear to me that I am upset about my relationship with John [Alice's significant other]. I am worried that he may be attracted to Betty [a woman John works with].*

I spent the rest of my meditation trying to locate the roots of my jealous feeling. I also thought about the nature of jealousy and what you said to me once about my tendency to confuse jealousy and love. I could see clearly that my jealous feelings are based on feelings of insecurity [self-reflection].

R.A.I.N.: Mindfulness Meditation vs. Mindful Psychotherapy

By way of contrasting psychotherapy and mindfulness meditation in working with emotional problems, I will first briefly describe a paradigm designated by the acronym R.A.I.N. which is taught at many Vipassana mindfulness retreats (Kornfield, 2008).[5] The method delineates four essential principles in Buddhist practice which together can transform difficulties: *Recognition*, *Acceptance*, *Investigation*, and *Non-identification*.

Although not a linear sequence of steps, in the R.A.I.N. strategy the meditator first learns to *Recognize*—notice—the moments when the mind becomes "hooked" or caught in moments of reactivity. The second aspect of this mindful awareness is to relax or soften into—i.e. *Accept*—the experience. Then, to the extent appropriate, the person *Investigates* the experience so that it can be fully received mentally, somatically, and emotionally. With mindful noticing each experience of reactivity is recognized and accepted. Feelings are named and investigated with respect to whether the mind state that accompanies them is pleasant or painful, contracted or relaxed. One notices what emotions are present and where they are felt in the body; thoughts and images, memories and fantasies, judgments and beliefs associated with the difficulty are acknowledged. But also, the practitioner is cautioned against identifying with experience (*Non-identification*): refraining from analyzing what is happening or buying into the stories the mind tells about it. Consider for example the following anecdote related by meditation teacher Sylvia Boorstein (2012):

> *It recently happened to me that a grumpy mood filled my mind and for some while I thought about it: "Why this? Why now? What happened? What does this mean?" Quite soon I realized that rather than being mindful of the mood, seeing it as a passing phenomenon, I'd engaged in a struggle with it. I laughed. I knew it for the grumpy mood it was. And it disappeared.*

The message here is a familiar one to Buddhist practitioners: don't get caught up in experience, or struggle with it, since it soon changes and it has no fundamental or substantive reality. Buddhist thinking points toward the truth that we create a world of illusion with our thoughts and with our personality, that these are merely fleeting experiences in the mind which have no real core to them; as one teacher puts it, they are foam on the sea of experience and have no real substance (Sumedho, 2007). In other words, to use more technical Buddhist language, experience is "empty"; moments are constantly arising and passing. One need only be mindful of them.

The Buddhist psychological approach of R.A.I.N. holds the promise that mindful attention to experience will, over time, result in a lessening of emotional reactivity, and indeed it may often do so. Mindfulness practice cultivates equanimity and the capacity to be with experience. However, as every psychotherapist knows, each of us has areas of emotional reactivity within ourselves which can be quite intractable. Patterns repeat themselves despite one's best and most mindful intentions to the contrary; in psychoanalytic language, a "repetition compulsion" holds sway.

From a psychoanalytic perspective, intractable and dysfunctional patterns of experience are held in place by areas of unconsciousness. Reflective practices in psychotherapy have the aim of illuminating problems so that they can be seen more clearly and in order to help experience unfold in ways which are positive (i.e. making the unconscious conscious and promoting growth and healing).

Inquiring deeply borrows from contemporary psychoanalysis the understanding that for experience to be transformed it must be relationally as well as mindfully received. The "knot" of experience around which problems have formed must be empathically understood and articulated; the experience must find a "relational home" (Stolorow, 2007). This entails a shift in emphasis from mere recognition to deep emotional understanding of experience. Deep understanding is an intersubjective process in which patient and therapist arrive at emotional comprehension in collaboration with one another. This is the essence of relational psychotherapy.

To reiterate the major points of difference between mindfulness meditation practice and mindful psychotherapy, dharma practice privileges embodied awareness deconstructed into moment-by-moment experience at the six sense doors. It counsels letting go of personal perceptions and stories because identifying with them only creates more layers of illusion. We notice experience and, in doing so, we let it go. (This is what Sylvia Boorstein was pointing to in her example, cited above, of noticing a grumpy mood.) When we investigate experience in mindfulness practice, we seek to discern the impersonal causes and conditions at work in our minds. To the best of our ability, we let go of ordinary and everyday (personality-based) narratives.

In contrast, in a psychotherapeutic frame we "start where we are," first mindfully noticing problematic experience but then trying to illuminate that experience in the light of a deeper psychological and emotional understanding. For example, in Alice's journal entry quoted above, she reflected on her feelings about herself, her sister, and her husband, as well as on the nature of jealousy. This psychotherapeutic investigation creates a different kind of "wise discernment" than in dharma practice; it heightens our understanding of our attachment to particular views of ourselves.[6] We can think of this as awareness practice with a focus on ourselves as personalities and as psychological beings. This may naturally deepen into dharmic understanding as we discover deeper and deeper levels of the truth within ourselves.

When we engage in reflective practices, a salient component of what comes up in the mind are the aspects of self and other which comprise the psychological world of lived experience. Exploring these experiences in psychotherapy does not substitute psychological awareness for mindfulness of the present moment. As in the practice of R.A.I.N., the aim is to clearly see what is so (recognition) and to find a foundation of compassionate acceptance in which what is recognized can rest. It investigates experience inclusive of the aspects of self that naturally arise in our experience.

Inquiring deeply is based on the idea that in order to fully penetrate a problem we must make sense of it within the broad context of relatedness to others in which it is embedded. In this relational framework, therapeutic empathy becomes the basis of greater self-acceptance and compassion for oneself.

Inquiring Deeply: Some Clinical Examples

In the vignette that follows, I describe my work with a patient, Bethany, to whom I recommended mindfulness as a strategy for exploring and managing certain difficulties. I would highlight that mindfulness was used as a way of investigating what was going on with Bethany rather than as a cognitive behavioral intervention *per se*:

Clinical Illustration 3.3: Bethany

Bethany was a 35-year-old single mother I saw in weekly psychotherapy primarily for help with parenting her 3-year-old. Early in treatment I referred her to a mindfulness-based stress reduction (MBSR) course to learn some tools to help with stress management (Kabat-Zinn, 1990).

One issue that troubled Bethany was that she awakened almost daily in an uncomfortable state she called her "morning fog." She found it hard to tolerate this experience and was quick to medicate herself with strong coffee. However, the worst part of this pattern from her point of view was that the caffeine use felt compulsive. Bethany's mother had been a drug addict and so she had harsh self-judgments about her caffeine "addiction." Coffee also jangled her nerves, which caused her to be quite irritable and short-tempered with her daughter, and she felt quite guilty about this.

Aided by my empathic inquiry, Bethany was able to see that caffeine helped her to feel more focused and face the day and that it was a well-intended effort to cope with the difficulty of mornings in her household. This helped her feel somewhat more accepting about her behavior, but her negative view of herself as weak (like her mother) remained. I suggested that she might try using meditation as an alternative morning routine, but she repeatedly failed in her efforts to get herself to do it. I then suggested to Bethany that she might try a "morning coffee meditation," bringing mindful awareness to the before-during-and-after of drinking coffee. She found this helpful.

On her own, it occurred to Bethany to experiment with what would happen if she sat quietly for a few moments before she actually drank her cup of coffee. Much to her pleasant surprise, she discovered that the fog started to dissipate even before she had caffeine in her system. At her own initiation, she then decided to "wean herself" [sic] from her caffeine habit by substituting decaf.

Inquiring into the origins and meaning of this problem, we explored Bethany's childhood experiences of having to get herself up and dressed for school when she was much too young to have to do so. I interpreted to her the possibility that the fog was a form of dissociation; an embodied memory of something. I conjectured about what it might have felt like to her as a child: scary to have to take care of herself when she felt so little and helpless. She talked about what she remembered of that experience. Under these circumstances, I interpreted, perhaps her defense had been to split off the feelings; to dissociate.

As our work together progressed, Bethany and I arrived at a shared understanding of her morning fog as a body/mind memory of this early

parental neglect of an important developmental need. After we had spoken of
it this way, Bethany began to experience the anxiety which was wrapped up
in fog; she could feel the anxiety within the fog.

Bethany used caffeine to self-medicate. Though well-intended, and not
without psychological benefits, addiction to caffeine became at the same time
a form of violence against her young and vulnerable self.

In this clinical example, mindfulness was first used to investigate a problematic area of experience. "Morning coffee meditation" came to mind as a creative
clinical intervention that might help illuminate what was going on psychologically. Although Bethany's feeling states in the morning might commonly be
thought of merely as negative mood, I conceptualized them as "self states" that
needed to be recognized and understood. Although the very same intervention
might well be used by a cognitive behavioral therapist, in this instance the clinical
focus was defined psychodynamically. My effort was to help Bethany understand
the developmental origins and "organizing principles" at play in her experience.
In addition to the benefits of mindful awareness, I believe that a large part of the
positive therapeutic outcome came about as a result of our therapeutic relationship. Specifically, my stance of empathic inquiry was helpful to Bethany in reframing and containing her experience.

Because avoidance of pain is so deeply ingrained in us, it is quite natural both
for patients and their therapists to try to utilize mindful awareness as a "solvent"
for dissolving psychological pain. While at times this may be a "skillful means"
in working with a difficult experience, it may also readily become a subtle way
in which aversion to experience is unconsciously expressed. In this therapeutic
approach, emphasis is on fully receiving experience mindfully and relationally, as
well as on gaining deeper understanding of the psychological reactivity that holds
problematic patterns in place.

The next clinical illustration focuses on an experience of reactivity that a
patient, Charles, experienced within the therapeutic relationship. Such upsets present a uniquely valuable therapeutic opportunity because the relational pattern
can be seen and discussed from both points of view in the interaction (therapist's
and patient's). This affords a unique opportunity for experience to be relationally
received. In psychoanalytic language, it becomes possible to work directly at the
"intersubjective intersection," exploring what the patient consciously and unconsciously expects from other people. This allows observation of fundamental and
ubiquitous psychological processes such as *transference/countertransference*,
projection, and other defenses[7] as they arise, which in turn promotes the ability to
recognize these phenomena in ourselves and others.

Clinical Illustration 3.4: Charles

Charles, a meditator in treatment for chronic depression, was beginning to
see that there was much to be learned by being mindful of exacerbations

in his depressed mood. On one particular day, he was telling me about an acknowledgment he had recently received at his work place. As he was relating the events to me, I noticed that his mood seemed to be worsening. When I voiced this observation, I invited Charles to tune into his felt sense of this moment. This introduced a mindful pause in which Charles was reminded to feel into his emotional state. He immediately recognized that he was feeling heavy and sad; he reported that he also felt an aching sensation in the area of his heart.

This in-the-moment mindful investigation and the therapeutic inquiry which followed led Charles to the realization that he was disappointed because he had expected me to be more effusive in response to his good news. We explored this response in relation to his frequent feelings of being unappreciated by others. Charles had a long-standing feeling that no matter what he did it was never good enough. In the present context, though, he saw that the center of his despondency was disappointment and anger triggered by what he perceived as my "flat" response to his news. This was reminiscent for him of repeated failures in childhood to get positive mirroring from his father.[8]

In this clinical example, psychotherapy is both dynamic and mindful. What occurred simply emerged in the course of the therapeutic interaction; I invited Charles to focus on his experience in the here-and-now, and he responded in the ways that he did. Together, we were able to witness and reflect upon his emotional reaction as it was happening.

The intimacy of our psychotherapeutic connection created space for me to call Charles's attention to what was happening between us and for him to receive it.[9] This became an important opportunity to explore a deeply ingrained emotional pattern. Such moments of emotional reactivity arising in the course of therapy are an optimal point of entry for exploring psychological issues. (This is the forte of the psychoanalytic approach.) With deliberate attention, it is possible to develop more refined awareness not only of a particular issue but, more generally, of the relational paradigms that are the underlying matrix of psychological pain.[10]

After the "transference enactment" in which he got upset about the way I responded to him, Charles had the opportunity to practice over several weeks and months noticing and reflecting upon his angry reactions in daily life. He tried to mindfully investigate every instance in which he had an angry reaction to things in everyday life; and then he and I inquired into the patterns in therapy.

In Charles's case, for example, one part of the story was the unfortunate, repeated occurrence during his childhood of lack of adequate mirroring. An equally important part of the story, as we came to understand it, was the fact that Charles typically reacted to disappointments by becoming angry. Charles discovered how he actively held onto anger; further, he saw how his tendency was to "feed" his grievances in a way that blocked out support that *was* being offered. Some months later, we are still engaged in this inquiry into the way anger functions in Charles's sense of self.

Over time it simply became quite clear to Charles that when disappointments occurred, they played and re-played in his mind in a way that escalated his resentment and kept him distant from whoever was "to blame." This led to clear seeing of *blaming* as it arose in his experience. But whereas Buddhist inquiry might focus on letting go of the interpersonal story, or perhaps a koan-like inquiry into *"who is blaming?"* here the process was simply to invite elaboration and "unpacking" of the experience. Mindful awareness amplified this process of exploration. Overall, the process helped Charles to recognize and articulate some of the unacknowledged dimensions not only of the present situation but of related formative events in his earlier life and relationships. In my way of thinking about it, this represents an important acquisition of new psychological structure and is the core of personal growth.

The next vignette describes a spontaneous moment that emerged unexpectedly in the psychotherapeutic interaction when a patient, Denise, caught herself "in the act" of being self-effacing and was able to laugh at herself.

Clinical Illustration 3.5: Denise

Denise is a 34-year-old woman recommended to therapy by someone from the Vipassana meditation community in which she has participated for several years. She wants help with pervasive feelings of depression.

The present situation Denise faces is a decision about whether to leave her current job. She finds herself in a familiar paralysis of indecision. As we explore the situation together, it seems that there is a conflict between two desires/values. On the one hand, Denise wants to quit the job because it is very stressful and she yearns for a more peaceful life. On the other hand, she is very invested in being successful and "amounting to something"; she fears that to leave her current job will be giving up an important opportunity to climb the ladder of success.

In our initial work together, Denise and I inquired together into her work life and the kinds of difficulties it presented. A recurrent sense of pressure was the worst aspect of most of her work day(s), which left her feeling stressed out and exhausted. As we explored this together, it became increasingly clear how much Denise's self-critical feelings came into play, both in terms of her feeling pressured and in terms of her mood. She had not previously been aware of this. She was, in effect, caught in a bind of perfectionistic self-expectations.

As we looked at this together, I suggested to Denise that it might be of value to try to "catch herself" in moments when she was feeling pressured in order to see all of this even more clearly. Her spontaneous response was to say "I don't think I'm a good enough meditator to be able to be that mindful." In the very next instant, Denise recognized that she had just "done it again" (disparaged herself for not being good enough)—and, further, that in her ability to observe this she has just proven herself wrong! We shared a deep laugh in the mutual appreciation of the irony and new potential of this moment.

The first observation I want to make about this piece of work is that I did not at this point probe Denise in regard to her investment in success at work. Given Denise's perfectionistic self-expectations, it would be helpful to explore this more deeply.[11] What I am highlighting in this vignette is the experience of new self-awareness which spontaneously emerges for Denise in catching herself in the act of self-deprecation. I would characterize this as *insight*. (I highly prize such moments when they occur in my own life.)

I also conceptualize what occurred as an ***emergent moment***:[12] one in which a new self-recognition unfolds spontaneously in the process of growth. Emergent moments are especially valuable when they occur in psychotherapy because they can be relationally received, articulated, and validated. What stood out to me in the therapeutic moment described in the vignette is that Denise and I co-witnessed something new coming into being in her awareness. This was a turning point for Denise; she was beginning to wake up to the process of self-criticism as it lived in her experience.[13]

The next vignette describes in some detail a psychotherapy session that took place early on in my work with a patient named Elizabeth, a woman with a deep commitment to her path of Buddhist insight meditation. I saw her three times per week in treatment that became deeply analytic. I spotlight this particular session as an example of how I sometimes do psychoeducational groundwork to help orient patients to new ways to think about experience relationally and psychodynamically.

The session which is reported focused on Elizabeth's relationship to her dharma practice. There are many aspects of the clinical material that would have been interesting to follow up on and explore, but here I simply "bookmarked" them in my mind and let them take a backseat to the interpretative themes of interest. (Because this session was so illustrative of what I was writing about in *Inquiring Deeply*, I made a point of taking extensive process notes immediately after the session ended. I paraphrase our dialogue here in a way that is quite faithful to the conversation we had, albeit not verbatim.)

In the interaction which I describe, as in our work generally, my effort was to help Elizabeth understand her feeling states in a deeper way. I did this in part by sharing with her the thoughts that surfaced for me in the course of our therapeutic conversation. The way that I interpreted the pain she was experiencing helped Elizabeth ground her understanding of the dharma in the emotional reality of her feeling states:

Clinical Illustration 3.6: Elizabeth

Elizabeth has a longstanding history of depression and agoraphobia. Although she was not clinically depressed when she came to see me, she nonetheless struggled painfully with depressive tendencies within herself. She hoped that psychotherapy would help her without being at odds with what she was learning in her dharma practice.

Feeling depressed has been a lifelong struggle for Elizabeth, in different ways at different times. After her parents divorced when she was still quite young, Elizabeth's mother moved her and her brother from city to city many times in order to pursue this or that relationship with a man.

The following session took place fairly early on in our work together. It illustrates the difficulty that Elizabeth was currently having and the psychotherapeutic exploration we engaged in together. At the time the session occurred, Elizabeth's husband ("Norman") had been out of town for two weeks and would not be returning for an additional two weeks.

E. *This morning was a bad one ...*

Mostly I have been enjoying the time alone, but some moments are really difficult. I knew I should get out of the house, do something, but there wasn't anything that I felt like doing. I knew I definitely did not want to exercise, which probably would have been the best thing for me. I did manage not to binge on cookies though, so that was one good thing.

Elizabeth then describes the sequence of thoughts and feelings she had been experiencing in the morning, feeling lost and uncertain about what she should do that day; how unworthy she feels because she isn't accomplishing anything in the outside world; what a terrible failure she considers herself to be.

M.S. *It sounds like you were trying to stay very mindful of your feelings and to modulate them as best as you could without using food as an escape.*

[This was something we had focused on previously and I was referring to the deliberate intention that Elizabeth had generated.]

I notice though that among all the thoughts and feelings, you didn't mention the fact that Norman is away ... Were you feeling lonely this morning?

E. *[long pause] ... yes, that feels right ... I have been feeling lonely.*

M.S. *Perhaps feeling lonely triggered the depressed mood you were in this morning.*

[I then gave a somewhat lengthy and empathic summary of the themes Elizabeth had been talking about: her loneliness, indecision, and lack of self-worth. As I articulate aloud what I am understanding about Elizabeth's experience; in essence I am reflecting back what Elizabeth said to me, with the addition of my own "spin" on what she may be feeling.

Clinical observations of this kind are the raw material of analytic listening. Sometimes I offer these kinds of observations to a patient as a kind of "clinical evidence" supporting a therapeutic hypothesis I am making.

Elizabeth's response to my input seemed to strongly confirm my hypothesis: She seemed softer, more vulnerable and available; I experienced a deepening of the intimacy between us.]

E. *Yes ... Loneliness and depression.*

[Long pause ensues which I sense as deepening presence[14] in the room]

Anyway, what I eventually did was to go looking on my bookshelf to see if I could find a book that maybe would help me get out of the space I was in ... [names several]. None of them resonated until I picked up Pema's book [Pema Chodron, When Things Fall Apart*]. What I read gave me an immediate sense of relief. [Described passage from book in which Pema talked about the fallacy of searching for refuge outside of ourselves.] But this looking in books. I dunno ... I'm always trying to figure things out. I know from my dharma practice that's not the right way to go about it. I'm not going to get any help by immersing myself in my mind.*

M.S. *It's true that there are some things that you have to live through rather than figure out ... But it's also understandable though that you would want to get away from those painful feeling, isn't it?*

[long pause] I just had another thought I'd like to share: it seemed like you experienced a sense of relief from Pema's book, but then you seemed to make some kind of negative judgment about what you had done. Do you have the idea that reading Pema's book was somehow not a good thing to do?

E. *No, it's not that reading Pema was bad; I love Pema! It's just that I feel like I keep getting stuck in my head trying to figure out the "why?" Knowing why I'm in this state is the booby prize! What I want is not to be found in my head!*

M.S. *I think I understand what you mean, you are aware when you get "caught" in a mental loop trying to figure things out ... but there's another way to look at it too.*

It seems to me that you looked to Pema to help you understand your experience and that what you read gave you an experience of relief. I imagine in part you felt relief because Pema writes about the very thing you were experiencing ... about "wanting relief" ... and she conveys the possibility of living in a different way that could get you off the hook with those difficult feelings.

E. *Yes!!! [apparently resonates very strongly]*

M.S. *The meditative path can provide something like that, it's true. It can help you to soften into your experience.*

I think there's another aspect of this to consider too: I think Pema's book gave you a sense that there is someone who deeply understands the kind of anguish you experience, and that was comforting.

Sometimes we need a relationship with someone else to uncover a particular quality of being within ourselves. That's how we learn a lot of things in life ... You wouldn't find relief in reading Pema unless it resonated with something that is already inside of you.

These comments as well as those that follow later in the session have the flavor of an elaborate interpretation.[15] They essentially re-frame Elizabeth's experience in terms of relational needs in a way that was new to her. I think of this as "planting seeds" of emotional understanding that hopefully will take root as new psychological growth.

So when you said that you can't find what you're looking for in your head, I think maybe what we could say instead is that, while you can't figure out a way to get past your problems, you can use your mind to locate a bridge to something inside yourself that would bring you relief.

E. *Yes ... I have a lot of those moments ... [Deep silence and long pause]*

I want to feel more often the way that I do when I am gardening [describes the feeling of being deeply present in the simple pleasure she takes in gardening]—but then I get lost in thoughts of what I should be doing (how I should be accomplishing something, etc.)

M.S. *Yes, those kinds of simple pleasures are very deeply nurturing.*

I'm guessing that when you are gardening sometimes an experience of anxiety comes up which takes you away from the moment and leads you in the direction of all that list-making. You feel a moment of spaciousness and then something stirs a moment of agitation ... then one thought leads to another and you start to spin out into your "to do" list.

Before we go on, though, I just want to acknowledge something that happened a moment ago, when you were speaking about gardening ... it seemed like you touched something of the experience of calm spaciousness that we have been talking about.

E. *Yes. [long pause]*

M.S. *I think maybe it's hard for you sometimes to find ways to soothe yourself. That's when you go looking for help from the bookshelf.*

You could think of it as quite skillful, actually; you are trying to find a bridge to a space of self-soothing inside yourself. Pema provides a "balm" of words that comfort you. That's what you're hoping to find here with me, too.

[Long silence ensues.]

You know, the next time you feel the way you felt this morning I think it may be useful for you to tune in more deeply to whether you are in need of some kind of soothing.

E. *Yes ... I was just thinking about how I've never been able to soothe myself.*

When I was a child I never felt safe at home … it wasn't peaceful there somehow. I always preferred to be at someone else's house [described the experience of visiting the home of a childhood friend because it felt so cozy and safe there]

But the irony is that now there isn't any safe place I can think of except inside of my house!

M.S. *That's really quite a predicament! You are looking for somewhere you can feel connected and safe, but you don't feel safe enough to search out that comfort from other people.*

[E. begins to cry soft but very deep tears … very poignant silence followed]

There are a number of different topics that came up in the above dialogue, too many to discuss at any length here. I would summarize them as follows: first, Elizabeth's experience of depressed mood. Second, her attempt to find a way to use her dharma practice as a way to cope with this difficult mind state. This included—third—her awareness of and frustration with her own tendency to get caught in thinking, coupled with self-judgment. A fourth theme, which I introduced into the therapeutic dialogue, was Elizabeth's unmet needs for contact and soothing. This was associated with a lot of childhood history.

I would underscore several points about what unfolded in this and our subsequent clinical work:

First, Elizabeth became clear about the various factors that were dynamically involved in her depressed mood, including especially unmet psychological needs. (In psychoanalytic terms, it was helpful for her to discern her selfobject[16] needs more clearly.) It became apparent to Elizabeth that her emotional pain was made worse when it was misdirected into a need to be productive. The self-criticism that was associated with that was especially toxic.

Second, my therapeutic function implicitly supported Elizabeth's capacity to soothe herself. It was reinforced by my highlighting the qualities of calmness and spaciousness in her experience and its importance in the overall goal of modulating painful affect.

Third, by providing deep empathic understanding of Elizabeth's experience I both met her needs in the present situation and helped her to be more compassionate toward herself. Discriminating awareness of her relational needs also helped Elizabeth see how the dharma served her as a refuge against long-standing experiences of pain and longing. This supported her in wise understanding of her dharma practice.

This kind of therapeutic work—which I describe generally as "deepening of emotional understanding"—provides a narrative framework which invites possibilities for new experience. In addition to this narrative aspect, I also want to call the reader's attention to the therapeutic aspect of the clinical *process* in my work with Elizabeth (including the transference). This was apparent in the qualitative change in her mental state which occurred in the session as we focused on the calmness and spaciousness of her experience and as our interaction deepened.

The next and last clinical vignette for this chapter summarizes the phases of inquiring deeply in a patient, Frank, who I saw for several years several times a week:

Clinical Illustration 3.7: Frank

Frank was a 48-year-old university professor and Zen practitioner who sought me out after reading a book about Buddhist psychotherapy which he resonated with.

Frank's presenting complaint was chronic depression. He often wondered if life was worth living and not infrequently had suicidal ideation and fantasy. He had a daily practice of meditating with the breath.

In the first year of our work, Frank was quite consistently depressed on a daily basis. As we examined what was involved, it became clear that he felt increasingly lonely in his marriage now that his children were grown and married. He loved his wife but didn't know how to connect with her. The strongest bond between them had been a very active sexual life, but this had dwindled since his wife had entered menopause.

The other major psychological theme was Frank's anger. He was chronically irritable and did not "suffer fools gladly." He was regularly cross with his wife and often lost his temper at home over small "infractions." He also had a pattern of repeatedly engaging with strangers, e.g. customer service representatives, which provided an opportunity for him to "dump" his anger. Although he was mad at himself that he did this, he continued to do it.

Rather than go over my clinical work with Frank in the detail of the other vignettes already given, I will instead summarize the different phases of treatment that evolved over several years of treatment:

Phase 1: Description and delineation of problems
Depression and anger were quite conscious from the outset of treatment. As we opened these topics to inquiry, Frank also became aware of malignant tendencies of self-criticism; marital and intimacy problems.

Problems with emotional intimacy had "hidden beneath" sexual activity, and now that sexual intimacy was less available, emotional intimacy issues stood out quite strongly.

Phase 2: Alcohol abuse
It came to light that Frank was dependent on alcohol.
After several enactments in which he phoned me when he was drunk,

Frank came to acknowledge that he had likely been an alcoholic for many years (which he had denied and rationalized up until the present time). As a consequence, he eventually decided to give up drinking.

We explored alcoholism along with other "addictive" tendencies, including being a "rage-oholic" (my terminology) and "sex-aholic" (Frank's description).

Phase 3: Clinging

Initially, Frank used his meditation practice to investigate a wide range of topics that I would suggest during the course of our sessions. For example, he focused mindful awareness on urges to drink; on feelings of separateness and loneliness; on varying sense of connection to his wife and children.

As the above issues became increasingly clear, Frank became interested in extending mindful awareness into a practice of inquiry about grasping and clinging (dharma concepts) as these manifested in his life more generally. He found it especially helpful to see how he was clinging to various aspects of self-representation: himself as a virile man, loving husband, professor, meditator.

After three years of twice weekly psychotherapy, Frank has been clean and sober for more than a year and has entered marital therapy with his wife in order to enhance the intimacy of their relationship during this new phase of life. He still suffers from depressed mood but is more aware now of how much anxiety lives just beneath the surface. He remains very self-critical, but very seldom engages in rationalized abuse of others (in customer service roles, etc.) and overall is very much less irritable and depressed. For example, he has not felt seriously suicidal in a long time.

The Place of Narrative in Inquiring Deeply

As I hope the above clinical vignettes have shown, inquiring into the plot-lines of our inner drama can help to reveal how the experience of self and other is organized in the mind. By inquiring deeply into these, we become much more aware of the ideas, beliefs, and unmetabolized emotion which bind us. Ultimately, the goal of mindfulness in both inquiring deeply and Buddhist mindfulness practice is to enable us to get disentangled from the web of unconscious and disavowed experience which manifests in our lives as painful feelings and personal problems. When we can bring mindful awareness to bear on these experiences, repetitive themes and inter-related elements become more clear, allowing insight into the core issues which give rise to pain and hold it in place.

Some narrative structures are conscious: they are associated with explicit stories, thoughts, or images that occur in the course of daily life and/or during sitting meditation. However, it has been my experience that even when a narrative is quite conscious, its meaning is often poorly understood; at the very least, there are usually blind spots in what someone can see of their own problems. Some areas of difficulty are so unconscious that they might escape notice entirely were it not for the presence of painful affect. In regard to these "shadow" areas of the psyche, enactments that arise in psychotherapy (such as in the example of Charles given above) provide an important opportunity to illuminate and heal psychic wounds (Stern, 2010).

Not all stories in the mind are created equal. Some stories, it is true, reinforce emotional patterns in the mind which are dysfunctional and have the effect of keeping us stuck in old ways of being. Some stories, in contrast, illuminate where we have been stuck and open the possibility of new ways of being. As David Loy (2010) beautifully articulates in a recent book, the world is made of stories; when our accounts of the world become different, our world becomes different. Stories codify and teach us what is real, what is valuable, and what is possible. Without stories there is no way to engage with the world because there is no world, and no one to engage with in it.[17]

Present-moment reactivity is always embedded both in a psychological history and particular narrative context. A further point is that we can't simply let go of, or wake up from, or transcend our stories, because we are made of stories. Narratives of understanding (and this includes Buddhist narratives) hold important keys to understanding who we are. Re-constructing the narratives we live by and articulating what may previously have been unformulated is the work of psychotherapy. The telling and re-casting of our stories is an essential part of the process of psychological healing.

Conversely, by ignoring the story line, which is how many people construe Buddhist practice, we may miss the opportunity to see the deeper structure of our psychological knots. Much of what is "sticky" and problematic in our minds is embedded in our developmental history and the relational patterns which underlie much of our experience. New psychological understanding re-frames experience, highlights what needs attention, and helps in the development of wise intention and action going forward.

In Buddhist-informed psychotherapy mindful attention and investigation are brought to bear on highlighting how the mind is dynamically organized with respect to basic psychological needs for love, approval, and acknowledgment as well as self-regulatory functions.[18] Psychoanalytic ideas about how self and other are represented in the mind, and how these internal schemas are enacted in experience, point our attention to things in daily life in ways that might otherwise not be recognized. This is quite analogous to the process by which studying the dharma points our attention to the truths of basic Buddhist teachings that we can discover in our own experience.

Notes

1 "Felt sense" is defined and discussed in Chapter 4.
2 Open, receptive awareness is similar if not identical to the idea of "reverie" in the work of the psychoanalyst Bion, a state of consciousness in which the mind functions as much as possible "without memory or desire" (Bion, 1967).

3 For me, writing is a reflective process of this kind.

4 In this way, I sometimes think of it as an impromptu and very personal koan practice.

5 Kornfield described this method and its acronym, crediting Vipassana teacher Michelle McDonald with having developed it.

6 In psychoanalytic language, our "self-representations" and our "narcissistic investments" in those self-concepts.

7 Fragmentation, denial, dissociation, pathological accommodation, splitting, etc.

8 The process of inquiring deeply described here unfolded naturally within psychotherapeutic conversation and did not involve any directed process apart from suggestions which may have been implicit in my questions, comments, and interpretations. In this clinical illustration, emphasis is placed only on the psychodynamic theme that seemed most salient in my work with Charles. There are many other ways that one might think about this clinical material; for example, I did not explore whether, in the countertransference, there were *real* ways in which Charles was not good enough for me, just as he was not good enough for his father.

9 See Chapter 5 for a discussion of how mindful awareness participates in creating intimacy in the therapeutic connection.

10 While in this instance the focus was on the patient's "issue" with what I had done, in other instances patient and therapist become co-participants in relational happenings or *enactments* that have to get sorted out. Such events provide the opportunity to develop skills in working out relationship issues.

11 In inquiring deeply, this might be investigated with respect to "selfing," the defense of a particular self-representation (see Chapter 8).

12 Emergent moments are discussed further in Chapter 5.

13 Although here I am narrating this moment in psychological terms—a psychotherapeutic moment—it could also be described as a moment of dharma practice; a moment of mindfulness of mind.

14 The concept of "presence" will be discussed at length in Chapter 5.

15 It is calling attention to the selfobject functions that were served by reading Chodron's 1997 book.

16 See Chapter 8, Note 8.

17 Chapter 8 takes up at length the role of story in the creation of self.

18 In clinical language, needs for mirroring, validation, and *affect regulation*.

References

Bion, W. R. (1967). Notes on memory and desire. *Psychoanalytic Forum, 2*, 271–280.

Boorstein, S. (2012). Spirit Rock Meditation Center e-News. Spirit Rock Meditation Center, www.spiritrock.org.

Chodron, P. (1997). *When things fall apart: Heart advice for difficult times.* Boston, MA: Shambhala Publications.

Kabat-Zinn, J. (1990). *Full catastrophe living.* New York, NY: Delacorte Press.

Kornfield, J. (2008). *The wise heart.* New York, NY: Bantam Books.

Loy, D. (2010). *The world is made of stories.* Somerville, MA: Wisdom Publications.

Stern, D. (2010). *Partners in thought: Working with unformulated experience, dissociation, and enactment.* New York, NY: Routledge Press.

Stolorow, R. (2007). *Trauma and human existence: Autobiographical psychoanalytic and philosophical reflections.* New York, NY: Analytic Press, Taylor & Francis Group.

Sumedho, A. (2007). *The sound of silence.* Somerville, MA: Wisdom Publications.

Uchiyama, K. (2004). *Opening the hand of thought.* Somerville, MA: Wisdom Publications.

Chapter 4

Questions for Clinical Inquiry and Self-Reflection

What to Inquire Deeply About

Psychotherapeutic inquiry begins with problems. It examines the direct experience of problems; the felt sense of problems; their story line; their developmental origins; and the narrative meaning we give to them. In this kind of psychotherapy, there is no attempt to follow any pre-conceived path or model, apart from the underlying clinical assumption that what emerges in psychotherapy is always co-created and is engendered by the patient-therapist relationship.

As a therapeutic approach grounded in contemporary psychoanalysis, inquiring deeply endeavors to show the patient how experience is organized in the psyche, including how the mind relates to itself.[1] The relational dimensions of experience are emphasized. As a Buddhist-informed psychotherapeutic approach, inquiring deeply also focuses attention on how the mind gets stuck in grasping, clinging, and aversion. The two theoretical frameworks are interwoven but come together in a focus both on the stories in the mind and on the functions of storytelling. This exploration also highlights subjective beliefs, values, and world view.

Buddhist and Western psychology have been likened to different lenses through which we may view the mind (Rubin, 1996).[2] Despite differences in how wide or how narrow the angle of view, and despite differences in the "depth of field", both psychologies are concerned with similar phenomena. Relational therapy emphasizes an understanding of how our minds function psychodynamically, but, similar to Buddhist practice, its overarching goal is finding a wise and harmonious relationship to our experience.

The Process of Inquiring Deeply

The core of inquiry is commitment to deep introspection: looking repeatedly and deeply within for answers to questions or the path through problems.[3] Inquiry consists simply of holding a problem in reflective awareness and examining it from different perspectives, deliberately and repeatedly, and then listening inwardly for the answer. Listening can be made deeper by engaging inquiry during meditation (in which case it can be called "contemplative meditation").

The act of questioning itself breaks open the unexamined and stagnant shell of the present, revealing the hidden and stale surfaces of the way we think about things. Asking probing questions opens up fresh options to be explored (Peavey, 2003).

When inquiry is done as a self-guided process, it may take its shape from a specific intention to inquire about something, or it may simply emerge organically as a matter of curiosity about something. Something happens—an event or an experience—which is painful and which intrudes itself strongly into the stream of consciousness in a way that seems to beg to be investigated. Or, one may deliberately choose to reflect upon a "problem area" where one feels stuck or where one gets recurrently upset. In this sense, inquiry runs in parallel with emotional life.

In the context of psychotherapy, inquiry can be co-created in the process of therapeutic exploration. It may follow a trajectory which is based on the psychotherapist's input (and in turn, may be influenced by theoretical models).

One key aspect of inquiry as a process is the *depth* of self-reflection. The dictionary suggests two meanings of "deepening." The first, based on a spatial metaphor, is the idea of extending from the surface downward or inward, from top to bottom, from front to back, or away from the edge. The second meaning is "profound." With respect to the mind, both definitions imply a subjective change in the scope and depth of what is noticed.

"Inquiring deeply" implies a particular quality of awareness in self-reflection which is cultivated through mindfulness practice. Subjectively, the effort is to settle the mind until it becomes quite spacious, clear, unified, and collected (as it does in concentration practice, for example). With the clutter of the normal waking state in abeyance, intuitive awareness is quite keen and insights tend to emerge. A commonly used metaphor is that of looking beneath the surface of a muddy pond. As the mud settles, we can see further into the depths below. In such deep states, consciousness may become transcendently reorganized[4] and insight is facilitated.

Notwithstanding the fact that inquiring deeply is aided by a meditative frame,[5] it can also be done in an "ordinary" state of mind. It is not essential to "meditate" in the moment nor to hold a single-minded focus. In fact, once it has begun, inquiry may continue rather unconsciously—much like what the mind does when it is searching for a word that is felt to be on the tip of one's tongue. This has been likened to the process of throwing out a question like a boomerang and waiting to see what answer will return.

Most simply, to inquire deeply means to hold the *intention* to become more fully aware of thoughts and feelings, and of the web of narrative meaning in which experience is embedded. Although in psychotherapy the explicit focus is on the experience of the patient rather than the therapist's, optimally it will also be understood that dyadic experience is by nature ***intersubjective***: both people participate in what unfolds between them (Bass, 2001).[6] The therapist's job is to listen from a perspective which is inclusive of the patient's experience as well as his or her own self-awareness (***countertransference***).

In inquiring deeply, we focus not only on the content of thoughts, feelings, and narratives, but also, at various levels, on *process*. Feelings give rise to thoughts, which in turn give rise to more feelings, and so forth. In the kind of psychotherapy I do, I see it as my responsibility to track the interwoven layers of the patient's associations, to "connect the dots" and to provide a container of theory for the dialogue. This kind of listening is a complex skill. On the one hand, it is the therapist's role to listen deeply and openly, as much as possible without bias or preconception (Epstein, 1995).[7] On the other hand, what emerges as salient for the therapist is necessarily shaped by theoretical orientation as well as personal characteristics.

Moreover, this dynamic process of mind looks different at different moments and from different depths of awareness. Depending on the state of mind of one or both participants in the moment, awareness may be relatively spacious and "wide-angle" or relatively narrow and focused on some particular aspect of experience. The importance of the quality of *presence* and the interaction between the states of mind of both participants is discussed at some length in the next chapter.

In sum, inquiring deeply is mindful awareness of mind, or, as we may say, "minding the mind". To repeat the definition set out in the earlier chapters of this book, it can be defined as *a stance of mindful reflection that arises in the therapeutic process as a function of shared psychotherapeutic intention*.

The next sections of the chapter present a series of questions which are valuable for inquiring into psychological issues and problems. These questions have been culled from thousands of hours of clinical inquiry in my several decades working as a psychotherapist and psychoanalyst. They are not intended as a guideline for self-help, but rather as points of orientation for investigating and exploring experience in psychotherapy (or for self-reflection during the course of everyday life[8]).

On another level, I have found it interesting to also examine how inquiries pattern themselves over time. My own reflections, both personal and professional, often seem to follow in the wake of whatever theories and ideas have currently engaged my interest (including the dharma, which is a constant backdrop). A lot of what I discuss in this book has emerged from these inquiries.

Basic Questions for Inquiry and Self-Reflection

There are several "generic" questions one can ask oneself (or someone else) in regard to any experience; they can be applied in dharma practice or in psychotherapy. Several such questions are described here which can be offered to patients for self-reflection.

Is it true?

The first is the question, "*Is that true*" and several variations:

- *What is true here? What story am I (are you) believing now?*
- *Is it true?*

- *Is that really true?*
- *How do I (you) know that's true?*

Our notions about what is true often change as we come to understand something more deeply. Also, people may bring themselves to believe almost anything they are inclined to believe, unconsciously selecting for confirming evidence. For this reason, when we examine our thoughts it is very valuable to continually hold the underlying question "*is that true?*" as a basic frame for inquiry (Katie, 2002).[9]

A simple inquiry about what is true can be used as a very basic cognitive psychotherapy intervention to help a patient recognize thoughts, beliefs, and judgments that are implicitly present and to highlight the difference between thoughts and feelings. For example, the following brief dialogue took place one day between me and a 65-year-old depressed man named Aaron about his angst over "running out of time" in his life. In the session prior to the one in the illustration, we had discussed Aaron's concerns about death, and I had suggested the idea that how comfortable we are with the idea of dying often has a lot to do with whether we feel that we have lived fully.

Aaron told me the next time we met that he had reflected on this idea and had concluded that he did not consider his life to have been well spent. Our exchange went something like this:

Clinical Illustration 4.1: Aaron

M.S.   *Your life has not been well spent—is that true?*
A.   *Well no, not entirely*
M.S.   *Your life has been well spent—is that true?*
A.   *Well no, that's not entirely true either*
M.S.   *What would you say is true?*
A.   *I don't know … I guess they're both true. Some moments have been well spent and some haven't been*
M.S.   *I imagine most anyone could say the same, wouldn't you think?*
A.   *Yes, I suppose so. I just wish I could get to the point where I could feel like in the balance I've done a good job with my life*
M.S.   *So you're making the judgment that you haven't done a good job in life?*
A.   *I suppose so, yes.*
M.S.   *That seems to be a conclusion you draw when you are feeling sad … maybe it serves to explain to you why you feel sad.*
        [Long pause]
        I'm reminded of what you've told me about how your dad would get so punitive when he was displeased with you.
A.   *Yes, it is kind of like that. I'm displeased with myself and at the same time I feel like a child who has displeased his dad.*
        I just wish I could figure out what to do so I didn't feel that way.

Aaron's intractable sadness always seemed in his mind to boil down to the idea he wasn't doing it (life) right: If he were, he thought, he wouldn't feel so bad. In Aaron's life, bad feelings were construed as a punishment for being "bad", as often he had felt himself to be in his father's eyes. This deep belief and an unconscious identification with his father kept him trapped in a vicious cycle of thought and feeling in which negative feelings led to self-critical judgments which perpetuated the bad feelings.

The exercise of mindful awareness in itself is a simple form of inquiry about truth: we look in order to see what is so in this moment (objectively and/or subjectively). Applied to ordinary experience—that which is grounded in a personality-based view of the world—mindful inquiry examines What is my truth about this? What am I believing to be true of myself, of others, or about life in general?

Aaron had a life narrative, a story about himself which he had formed in identification with his father's behavior toward him. Although calling it a "story", it needs to be understood as a relational *paradigm* that functions automatically to generate Aaron's negative feelings about himself and his life. This set of cognitions is a common "depressogenic" framework for experience: negative view of self and future. It is this set of core beliefs that most needs to be addressed in Aaron's psychotherapy going forward.

(This in no way denies that it may be important for Aaron to recognize regrets he has about the past. This is an important part of the ability to make better choices in the future.)

We can expand the inquiry "what is true?" specifically to psychological narrative by asking the question "what story am I believing now?"[10] In the very act of asking this question, we have already taken a stance of observation which changes the way that we are relating to "storyteller mind". This inquiry invites disidentification from belief: it creates space in which we can reflect upon what we may previously have *assumed* to be true.

Examining what is true applies not only to the way we are construing life events—the spin we place on things—but even to the veracity of the events themselves. It may sometimes happen that we discover that a story we have told repeatedly did not in fact actually happen the way we remember.

Clinical Illustration 4.2: Victor

A clinical example is that of one man I worked with, "Victor", who had grown up on a farm and had an emblematic childhood story about a family gathering that had occurred when he was about three years old. As Victor remembered it, an aggressive chicken had chased him around the yard while the family stood around laughing. In remembering this event, he described himself as terrified and we speculated together that this joke at his expense must also have felt humiliating.

An unexpected twist in the plot occurred when an old home movie re-surfaced in which this event had been recorded on film. As it turned out, it was not the chicken which had been chasing him, but the other way around! Moreover, the family did not appear to have been laughing at him. It was disconcerting [though therapeutic] for Victor to discover that the "formative event" had not happened the way he remembered it.

Notwithstanding the historical accuracy or inaccuracy of the life events depicted, there is much we can learn from our narratives. We can gain insight from them about the way we see ourselves, what we feel (or felt, historically), and the psychodynamics which gave rise to the narratives and/or which hold them in place. In the case of the patient just described, the narrative condensed a rich store of feelings about aggression and fear ("being chicken").

"Why?"

The question "why?" (and questioning in general) is very basic in the functioning of the mind. From earliest life, questions are an essential part of mental development ("why is the sky blue, Daddy?"). It is important to ask wise questions, since the seeds of answers are contained within them.

All inquiry contains an implied "?". We can also pose questions as a formal inquiry process. For example, we can engage a process of inquiry by asking the question "why?" serially and repeatedly to each "answer" that arises in the mind. I learned about this process from a patient of mine, Leonard, who was in psychotherapy for chronic depression. At a meditation workshop, the inquiry "Why?" was introduced as an exercise, and he recorded the following in his journal:

Clinical Illustration 4.3: Leonard

Question for Inquiry: What is salient in your experience right now?
I am sad.
Why?
Because I have nothing to look forward to.
Why?
Because I have no friends.
Why?
Because nobody likes me.
Why?
Because I am so negative.
Why?
Because nothing makes me happy.
Why?
I don't know why.

The reader will note that this brief inquiry did not uncover the "cause" of Leonard's sad mood, nor what had triggered it. It did reveal some beliefs close to the surface of Leonard's mind that were associated with the sad feeling;[11] and, in the end, it led to his making an assertion, "nothing makes me happy" that turned out to be quite generative.

As we were discussing this exercise and his experience of it, I asked Leonard if it were actually true that nothing made him happy. He had not really considered this, so I suggested that it might be useful for him to investigate in the ensuing days whether he was actually devoid of happy feelings. (He discovered he was not. To the contrary, he had quite a lot of happy moments.) As this inquiry unfolded in his psychotherapy over the following couple of weeks, we focused clinical attention on the fact that Leonard's happy feelings tended to go un-noticed and we explored why this was so.

Quintessentially, inquiry is none other than the process and serial unfolding of "?" in the mind. But questions can also be problematic to the extent that they selectively engage the mind in a process of trying to figure out answers. Many questions have to be lived through rather than thought through, so the effort to figure things out tends to ensnare us in mental traps. To the contrary, wise answers to questions generally involve feeling as well as thinking, and they evolve out of intuitive awareness. Cultivating the ability to rest in not knowing, creating a generative space from which answers can emerge, is one of the primary goals of inquiry both in meditation practice and in inquiring deeply.[12]

Inquiring into Storyteller Mind

As has already been stated, inquiring deeply begins with the premise that it's not helpful (at least for psychotherapeutic purposes) to simply dismiss ideas, thoughts, and stories in the mind because they are fundamentally "empty" of substance.[13] Unlike Buddhist practice, Buddhist-informed psychotherapy *prizes* psychological narrative, both for its content and its process. In my experience, being attentively receptive to the storytelling mind often leads to increasingly subtle truths and insights. This kind of inquiry helps us to achieve deeper contact with what is true for us personally and to anchor our experience, thoughts, and beliefs in our own wisdom.

This psychotherapeutic approach explores psychological experience as it naturally presents itself, including (or even especially) the ordinary experience of "being me."[14] Narratives encode subjective experience and create meaning in the psyche. They reveal the way we see ourselves and others. For good or for ill, they are one of the principal influences on the way our lives unfold.

While narratives can serve a variety of functions, generally speaking they make sense of what has happened to us and comprise a blueprint in the mind for what we can expect in the future. In this way, they create the structure we live by. This gives psychological narrative a position of great importance.

It is especially useful to be aware of storyteller mind with respect to the way that problems are constellated. This connects to the basic idea that it's never the problem that causes suffering; it's how we think about a problem—the narrative in which the problem is embedded—that creates suffering. Similar to dharma practice, Buddhist-informed relational therapy calls attention to our tendency to get caught up in (identified with) the stories of the mind. However, contrary to the implication that we can solve this predicament by simply "waking up" from the stories we live in, psychotherapy recognizes the complex functions of psychological narrative. "Letting go" of stories may be simple in concept, but it is not an uncomplicated act!

One question which usually arises for meditators in psychotherapy concerns how to be skillful vis-a-vis the present moment. The first rule in mindfulness practice has to do with being "here and now". But as soon as we invite awareness of narrative, "there and then" begins to proliferate in our minds.[15] As we all know, many of our beliefs, ideas, thoughts, and feelings can be traced to childhood origins, and the dimension of time is tightly woven into the fabric of our associations. Although Buddhist psychology lacks an explicitly developmental dimension, the fact that experiences can be traced to past causes and conditions in our lives is well understood in Buddhism. Psychodynamic/relational psychotherapy provides a narrative framework which allows us to understand these causes and conditions more fully. Memories and new experiential discoveries alike can be assimilated into this elaborated framework of autobiographical narrative. Coherent narrative is essential for the temporal continuity which allows for a grounded experience of self.

The key to inquiry is the ability to be deeply introspective, holding complex thought in reflective awareness so that we can examine it. We examine the entire stream of consciousness (as best we are able) within a framework of mindfulness and with sustained intention directed toward the changes we want to make.

As has been previously stated, one factor which distinguishes Buddhist-informed psychotherapy from Buddhist mindfulness practice is its receptiveness to the content of experience (including narrative). Dharma practice, on the other hand, tends to emphasize the ***background field*** of awareness from which experience continually arises and in turn disappears, like waves emerging on the vast ocean of consciousness.

Personal Truth and the "Felt Sense"

Inquiry in both spheres is facilitated by inviting attention to the felt sense of experience: the internal knowing which is directly experienced but which has not yet been formulated in words ("implicit", "unformulated", or "undifferentiated"). This way of attending to our inner experience—sensing into it and feeling it directly—is the foundation of mindfulness practice.

Felt sense was first identified by the psychologist Eugene Gendlin (1978), who noticed that it was one of the key elements in successful psychotherapy. He described this experience as the composite body sensation, often visceral, which carries the emotional meaning of something—for example, the jittery feeling in the stomach when we stand up to speak in public, or a heaviness in the heart when we think of a distant loved one. The felt sense, as he described it, was often (but not always) elusive, vague, subtle, and hard to describe in words; paying attention to it facilitated change in psychotherapy. Gendlin went on to create a therapeutic process or method, "focusing", for helping patients learn to pay attention to the felt sense. This method could be used to invite deeper awareness of our feelings and thoughts as they were emerging.

Simply defined, focusing is a self-reflective process for attending to the inner knowing that speaks to us through the body. We can "focus" when we are "stuck" or want to discover what is true for us at a deep level (Cornell, 2013). Focusing is a useful process within the psychotherapeutic hour or at any time that we want to get more clear about something. A clinical illustration will perhaps make the psychotherapeutic relevance of "felt sense" more clear. It was an instance in which I used the language of "felt sense" to clinical advantage with a patient for whom I thought the language of "mindfulness" would have been off-putting:

Clinical Illustration 4.4: Catherine

Catherine was a 72-year-old patient who had enormous difficulty making decisions, among many other problems with daily living. Even minor choices were associated with considerable anxiety. My first clinical efforts focused on helping Catherine expand her framework of understanding of the problem: she was very concerned with making the "right" decisions, but she had trouble figuring out what the "right" decision was. In our work together, she discovered that she feared that if she made the wrong decision others would disapprove of her, reject her, or—at the very least—that she would be exposed as inadequate.

One day, as she was in the middle of describing one of her decision dilemmas to me in obsessional detail, I said to Catherine that in addition to how scared she felt about making the right decision (which had been the focus of our recent work), I imagined that obsessively "ping-ponging" back and forth between the various options might itself contribute to her feeling nervous. She wasn't sure what I meant, so I suggested that she might find it interesting to just pause for a moment and get a felt sense of her predicament. I then guided her through a very brief focusing exercise: what did her current indecisiveness feel like? As she turned her attention inward and began to sense into her experience (following upon some guiding prompts from me) Catherine first experienced how anxious her body felt. Then something shifted and she began to feel much more calm and quiet.

Catherine was both impressed with and puzzled by this experience. It surprised her that her inner sense could change so rapidly. The calm and quiet feeling was a new experience for her. As we discussed all of this, I highlighted the difference between the feeling of trying to figure something out vs. just looking at/ being with the feeling of indecisiveness. (This could be considered implicit mindfulness training.)

> *A flood of associations followed in the wake of this brief inquiry. We talked about childhood experiences in which Catherine had had to make decisions which were way beyond her developmental capacity at the time and for which she had had little or no support. As she put this together for herself, she saw that she had never really learned how to make decisions. The idea that there was an alternative to figuring things out had never occurred to her.*

Focusing on felt sense is especially useful with patients like Catherine who are unsophisticated about introspection. In addition to being a new experience for Catherine, it naturally unfolded into an opportunity for her to take a more compassionate view of her difficulty with decisions, so understandable in terms of her developmental history. Focusing is a "neutral" psychotherapeutic intervention which I describe to patients as turning inward and tuning into intuitive awareness. It is very useful even in those patients who have little or no interest in mindfulness or meditation. It serves to help patients get in touch with and articulate their feelings, and it develops the habit of pausing in the midst of experience in order to self-reflect.

Questions for Clinical Inquiry

This section lists several categories of questions which can be used as starting points for either psychotherapeutic inquiry or self-reflection. The primary goal of these inquiries is to invite deepening of one's experience rather than to find "the truth". The questions that are posed are primarily focused on unpacking the nature of our personal problems. "Answers" that come to mind will tend to unfold with repeated inquiry and over time.

The questions are divided into four categories: I. Delineating the problem; II. Problematic aspects of self-experience; III. Relational dimensions; and IV: Existential dimensions. (Note that problems often have different layers of meaning which need to be explored.) The specific questions listed are intended as suggestions; in no way do they comprehensively define all of the relevant and important ones.

Delineating Problems

A first set of questions in inquiring deeply has the goal of unpacking the presenting problem or situation and delineating the experience more clearly. I liken this to the process of locating a splinter: first we have to probe the inflammation to find out what is sharp and psychologically painful. The focus of inquiry includes sensations in the body as well as "objects of mind" as they are called in mindfulness practice: thoughts and images, emotions, moods, attitudes and states of mind.

The assumption in this set of inquiries is that emotions or affects underlie every problematic state of mind. Feelings may be blunted, confused, or missing. Therefore, the emphasis is on finding, feeling, and articulating them. Inquiry provides a space which invites feelings to come into awareness.

I A. What is the problem?
- What *specifically* is the problem?
- What is problematic about that?
- What is at stake?
- What are you trying to be, do, or have?
- What do you need to be right about?
- What are you resisting?
- What assumptions are you making?
- What story are you believing?

These various questions can be asked repeatedly, sifting through the descriptions that come to mind until the person feels that they have found its core or center. (This may change and unfold during successive inquiries.)

I B. What is the subjective core of the problem?
- What attitudes, moods, and/or states of mind are associated with the problem?
- What specific body sensations, emotions, thoughts, and images are most salient?
- What is the felt sense of the problem?
- What feeling are you trying to avoid?
- What is the worst of it?
- What *specifically* about the experience feels unbearable?

In exploring the subjective core of problems with patients in this way, the goal is to help the person clearly differentiate the external circumstance or situation that they associate with the problem from the *experience* that is causing them difficulty.

The felt sense of the problem can also be underscored with contemplative practice of the kind taught by Ajahn Sumedho (2007): disappointment is like this, feeling rejected is like this, etc.

Indirectly, many of the questions point to the underlying "dharmic" dimensions of grasping (clinging) and avoidance (aversion). As appropriate, these can be made specific dimensions of inquiry.

Problematic Aspects of Self-Experience

Ordinary psychological experience is organized around the individual's sense of self. The concepts that someone has about themselves—who they take themselves to be (called "self-representations" in psychoanalytic language)—are deeply entwined in most emotional problems. Our identification with our self-representations, and our emotional investment in maintaining them and defending them, is one area touched upon in the following list of questions (II A below).

A second area of focus is self-experience (II B below). Inquiry can help illuminate the degree to which "self-experience" is integrated and coherent: the consistency and continuity of subjective experience over time.[16]

In psychoanalytic self psychology, healthy self-experience is considered to have three major dimensions: positive *affective coloration*, temporal continuity, and structural cohesion (Stolorow et al., 1994). These are reflected in our ability to modulate affect, regulate self-esteem, and navigate transitions smoothly. When these functions are poorly organized, affect becomes dysregulated (resulting in flooding, freezing, or other traumatic states) and psychic fragmentation may occur.

The questions listed in II A and II B touch upon common "garden variety" problems as well as issues which are involved in psychological dysfunctions and personality/self disorders. Indeed, the scope of the questions is so broad that it branches out into virtually the entire territory of dynamic psychotherapy. Nonetheless, the questions have utility as points of focus for therapeutic inquiry as well as for the design of adjunctive self-reflective awareness practice.

Probing disturbances in self-organization is the art and science of clinical practice. In doing this work, it should be borne in mind that deep meditative practice is not without risks in those whose self-experience is poorly organized (as may be true, for example, in those who have been severely traumatized). Self function must be sufficiently cohesive to support deep inquiry. Therapeutic support and guidance—either from a psychotherapist or dharma teacher—may help circumvent the possibility of an adverse response.

II A. Concept of Self[17]
- What concept of yourself are you invested in or identified with?
- What view of yourself are you defending?
- How do you want others to see you?
- Are you seeking recognition? Acknowledgment? Approval? (For what?)
- What view of yourself are you seeking to have validated or confirmed?
- Are you feeling vulnerable or threatened?
- Do you feel shame and or a sense of unworthiness?
- In what way do you believe that you are defective?

II B. Self-Experience
i   Affective Coloration:
- What is the "mental weather" like in your mind at this moment? (Calm or stormy? Emotional clouds? Climate of thoughts?) Investigate your predominant or underlying mood or affect.
- In general, what states of mind (or self-states) are most troublesome for you? (e.g., shame, self-doubt, regret, apprehension, frustration, irritability, boredom, etc.)
- Investigate mood episodes: upsets, melt-downs, or similar experiences ("falling into an emotional hole" and the like).

- Identify underlying core issues or experiences associated with prominent moods or affects: e.g. separations; rejection or abandonment; powerlessness, helplessness, or feeling trapped; fragmentation, flooding; or loss of control; fear of death, annihilation, or non-being.

ii **Temporal Discontinuity:**
- Investigate stability/lability of mood/affect; whether there are frequent abrupt or jarring shifts and changes in mood or state of mind.
- Make transitions in mood a focus for inquiry: what has triggered a noticeable shift or change? What is the felt sense of the shift?
- Investigate possible "flashbacks" to traumatic memories.

iii **Structural cohesion:**
- Investigate self-esteem and regulation of self-esteem.
- Investigate self-states which seem either expansive or contracted; aggrandized ("grandiose") or devalued ("deflated").
- Investigate areas of experience which seem dissociated or disavowed.
- Investigate "splitting" in experience: e.g., tendency to see things as black/white; all good or all bad.

Relational Dimension of Problems

A third general set of questions concerns the role of relationship in the presenting problem or situation. Whether or not it is apparent at the outset, most problems form in response to our attachment patterns and the matrix of relationship in which we live. Mindful awareness and self-reflection can be usefully incorporated into therapeutic exploration of these patterns in order to sharpen focus.[18]

Our various relational needs shape our psychological world: needs for contact, connection, attachment, dependency, belonging, freedom, autonomy, and love. As is well recognized in clinical psychology, secure attachment is a primary foundation of mental health. From earliest infancy, experience is organized by patterns of connection/interconnection: first through physical contact with mother and her attention to our bodily needs; later, through our mental connection to mother and other significant others. In this way, we learn about our own mind and the minds of others. In short, relationships are involved in regulating every aspect of life from infancy on. *Affect regulation/dysregulation* is key (Wallin, 2007).

Along with the need to develop secure attachments, we need to learn how to manage relationships with others and how to handle ourselves in the face of the inevitable disruptions that occur. Intimacy refers not only to the fact of relationship; it is also the set of organizing patterns that govern the way we turn toward or away from others, the way we seek to amplify or dissipate the intensity of connection. We learn to regulate interpersonal distance in a way that finds a balance between the two major relational fears of abandonment, on the one hand, and fear of being controlled, trapped, or smothered on the other.

It is especially important to understand the dynamic and fluid quality of what occurs between ourselves and others, since bonds with others "morph" from moment to moment as a complex function of how we feel and what we say and do (and, of course, the same goes for the person on the other end of the relationship). We need to develop awareness of how relationship affects us in an ongoing way.

The relational dimensions of problems are well-suited to a psychodynamic focus on attachment patterns, and/or they can be directly addressed in conjoint psychotherapy. In addition, inquiry can be useful in exploring painful patterns of reactive experience and in heightening awareness of the vicissitudes of relationship. General areas of inquiry include how connection/intimacy needs are being met or avoided; relationship patterns including fights and conflicts; emotional upsets in relation to disruptions of bonds with significant others; narcissistic injuries; and feelings of rejection or abandonment (among many others). The following are some questions which are useful in inquiring deeply into reactive upsets, either in therapy or as a self-guided process:

- What happened that triggered this upset? What does (did) the other person do that was (is) problematic for you?
- What are you feeling in relation to this person? (sad, angry, humiliated, threatened, guilty, etc.) Apart from what *happened*, what do you *feel* that is a problem for you?
- Did your feelings get hurt? In what way, specifically?
  - Did something make you feel rejected?
  - Did something make you feel neglected, ignored, or overlooked?
  - Did something make you feel invalidated? Insulted?
  - Did you feel criticized? Negatively evaluated? Blamed?
- Did the other person disappoint you in some way? What expectations were thwarted?
- What did you or the other person do that you view as "bad" or "wrong"?
- Is there a power struggle involved?
- Are you holding a grudge or resentment against the other person?
- What do you hope or need to get from the Other? What relational needs can you identify?
- When else have you felt this way in your life? About whom?

Existential Dimension of Problems

A last set of questions which can be productively explored with inquiry are general or existential in nature. They concern broad views and feelings about one's purpose in life and what one deeply values.

Whenever we invest energy in examining our lives, either in psychotherapy or in meditation, an implicit goal is deepening self-reflection. I sometimes describe this domain of activity as developing the inner philosopher. The more aware we become of our implicit assumptions about life, our "operative paradigm" or world view, the better our chances of being aligned with ourselves.

- What do you strive for?
- What makes you happy?
- What are your core values?[19]
- What is your deepest longing?
- What is your heart's desire?
- What would be a good title for the story of your life?

Reflections on Clinical Inquiry

The questions for inquiry and self-reflection presented above are not intended as a "workbook", but rather as a broad framework for exploring the psychological dimensions of problems. It can serve as a guide to some areas for inquiry in psychotherapy but is also suitable for use as a structured process for self-guided inquiry. It works well in combination with the process of journaling. In no way is it implied that these questions are a comprehensive set of questions for inquiry. It is merely one of many possible frames of reference, and is heavily skewed toward a contemporary psychoanalytic viewpoint.

"Questions for Clinical Inquiry" are presented in order to convey the scope of the inquiries I often use in inquiring deeply with patients about their problems. Most often, questions emerge naturally in response to some particular problem. The most important idea is that inquiry is not simply a cognitive tool. A fundamental aspect of the structure of most problems is that the mental and emotional levels of experience have become disconnected in some way. For example, we may understand something clearly in our minds, but emotionally we may still be conflicted about it. Or, something may be so painful that it has become unconscious. It is essential that we bring both feeling and thought (the felt sense of things) into inquiry.

With regard to psychotherapeutic aims, one of the key vectors in mindfulness practice is learning to discern the difference between "external" ("objective") and "internal" (psychological) dimensions of problems. (The basic underlying inquiry here would be: "What part of this problem is internal/psychological/ subjective?") Apart from the external causes of emotional pain, very often we can find one or more "*second arrows*" as they are called in Buddhism: judgments, interpretations, or attributions that add more suffering to an already painful situation. The internal or psychological "second arrow" often includes what one of my patients refers to as "borrowing trouble from the future". Comparing oneself with others is another common pitfall. This part of suffering is optional rather than quintessential. As Buddhist teacher Sylvia Boorstein has quipped, this is the "Third-and-a-half Noble Truth" (Boorstein, 1995).

The Multiple Dimensions of Problems

As has already been stated repeatedly, problems have many layers. Clinically, the overall goal of both inquiry and psychotherapeutic exploration is multi-dimensional understanding of the patient's predicament.

The following clinical vignette will illustrate some of the dimensions of understanding I pursued as I investigated a problem situation brought into therapy with a patient, "Tina":

Clinical Illustration 4.5: Tina

Tina had responded with rage to something "small" her husband had done. She thought he had spoken in a condescending tone to a customer service representative. She perceived him as rude (which it sounded likely he had been). What needed to be empathically examined was the magnitude of her reaction.

The first layer of the problem we explored was what specifically was so upsetting. This was not hard to locate: As she imagined the feelings of the person her husband had been rude to, Tina felt ashamed. She was angry at her husband for having shamed the other person, and for being so unempathic to their feelings.

Although what her husband had done might seem a "small thing"—objectively—it was a big thing to Tina. She recalled that her parents had often acted in ways that seemed to shame other people, and she was "allergic" to that kind of behavior. She herself made it a point to always be polite to everyone. Also to the point, Tina was very shame-prone because of being treated in those ways as a child.

Of equal importance, it became evident that Tina was also upset because she recognized that she was over-reacting. Seeing this in herself was painful. "Over-reacting" was a sore point left over from Tina's childhood, when her mother had dismissed her feelings and shamed her about her emotional intensity. In the current situation with her husband, Tina felt cast back into that all too familiar bind. And as long as she needed to defend herself from recognizing that she was probably over-reacting, she had no choice but to blame her husband.

Another layer of insight that emerged in the light of empathic inquiry was that Tina's behavior toward her husband was itself harsh. She was able to see that she sometimes treated her husband in the same ways that she had been treated as a child. This was a "relational dance" she had experienced again and again. She recognized her "identification with the aggressor" (her mother).

Moreover, this was a two-person dynamic. It was not difficult to see that Tina's husband played an active role in this. This was not the first time she had fought with him over similar things. Perhaps her husband was unconsciously provoking Tina to treat him in ways that his mother had treated him. In any event, she wasn't responding in a vacuum.

In the light of these layers of empathic understanding, Tina's blame and rage dissolved. As together she and I re-narrated the various dimensions of the story, several layers of the "back story" behind a minor incident had become apparent in this session.

Tina now recognized that what she most hated—even more than her husband's behavior—was the fact that she was acting like her mother!

Problems as Koans

We are all born with certain innate qualities of being which precede and become woven into the fabric of our personality structure. Who we take ourselves to be, and how we defend this identity, is the primary factor which determines our psychological well-being (Welwood, 2000). Over the course of a lifetime, the problems that we develop tell the story of this process. Problems express the thematic core both of what is happening in one's life right in the moment as well as the story of one's psychological development. Moreover, the struggle we have with problems also becomes a factor in who we become. When we can find a constructive attitude about—and context for—problems, this creates conditions in which problems are more likely to resolve.

In my therapeutic work, I have found it helpful to apply the paradigm of "koan" to working with problems. Koans are paradoxes or questions for contemplative meditation (for example, "what is the sound of one hand clapping?") which do not have "answers" nor make logical sense, and that is the point of them: to boggle the mind. Sometimes the problems of everyday life have a koan-like effect: they tend to entangle the mind in the search for logical solutions which cannot be figured out.[20] In Zen practice, engaging with a koan involves living inside of the conundrum; sitting with, being with, and repeatedly asking the question as a means of inviting a profound shift in one's experience of the world. This has been described as a profound change of heart (Tarrant, 2004) or inner transformation. A koan creates a kind of mental slope which inclines the mind in a different direction than it might otherwise go—off the beaten track of familiar mental patterns and toward creative discovery which lies outside the box.

There are two explanatory metaphors that I find helpful. In the first, imagine a fish that has been swimming in water but has had no way to become aware of that basic fact; the koan stirs the water, causing the fish to jump and thereby glimpse the water (and, simultaneously, something "beyond" the water). In the second metaphor, think of states of consciousness as configured into stable but in some ways dysfunctional orbits; grappling with a koan may bring about a shift in orbit, however momentary, and with that shift, the possibility of a fundamental reorganization of the structure of experience.

Might the koan "paradigm" be useful in approaching the predicaments of everyday life?

This idea came to me one day in the form of an epiphany in which I suddenly recognized that *the problem was the problem*. I saw that the very notion of having a problem supported the idea that there must be a way out, a solution, and that this tended in turn to lead down a rabbit hole of trying to figure things out. I could also see that this kind of effort was often a waste of energy, or worse. In the first place, many problems could not be "figured out"; solutions were more apt to emerge from unexpected directions. Secondly, ruminating over problems distracted attention away from the feelings which were at the core of most emotional problems. Last but not least, getting stuck in trying to figure things out often became a problem in its own right.

So, the problem was itself the problem. Further, it was evident that what made something problematic was in essence an embedded stance of non-acceptance; it was the way someone was relating to the circumstances in which they found themselves. Instead of engaging in struggling against the problem, perhaps it would be beneficial to relate to it as a kind of koan practice. In doing this, I found, sometimes it might feel at first as if one were getting further tangled up with the problem, but then one might also suddenly find one's way to a new insight, a shift. The following vignette describes how this process occurred in a kind of koan-like predicament in which my patient Darlene found herself:

Clinical Illustration 4.6: Darlene

Darlene's adult daughter, age 27, was living at her parents' home and had overstayed her welcome. She had found it necessary to move back home when she lost her job, but now, a year later, she was still ensconced there, even though she had found a new job and could have managed the cost of living by herself if she limited her discretionary spending. However, she kept "failing" in her attempts to save any money, and it was clear to Darlene that her daughter was reluctant to take this step toward independence. Darlene's predicament was how to encourage her daughter to move out without imposing budgetary boundaries or rules that would have been more appropriate for an adolescent. How could she "emancipate" her daughter if in the process of doing so she treated her like a child?

Making matters more complicated, Darlene had struggled in her own adolescence with separating and individuating from her parents, and there were ways in which the current situation with her daughter repeated the dynamics she had experienced with her own mother years before.

In discussing this predicament in psychotherapy, Darlene was at a loss as to what to do. With the model of koan in mind, I helped her construct a different frame for the problem: instead of imposing an arbitrary solution, such as a timeline, could she simply live with the question of what to do and allow the situation with her daughter to find its own way toward resolution?

The plot thickened. As it happened, an event soon occurred which brought the entire situation to a head. In looking for a misplaced household object,

Darlene went one day into her daughter's bedroom and found herself spontaneously doing something which was very much out of character: looking into her daughter's bureau drawers. There she found some marijuana her daughter had hidden so that her mother would not see it. Now what? Should she tell the daughter what she had done and what she had found? She teetered on the edge of an old experience of shame.

The irony of the situation and the meaning of this koan became clear. When Darlene had lived in her parents' home, she had lived with an unspoken injunction to not acknowledge certain things that were "hidden" in plain view. Here was a situation in which history could easily repeat itself: If she said nothing to her daughter, she would be complicit with her daughter's act of hiding and would be drawn back into her own hiding. On the other hand, she now had an opportunity to create a new path for herself and her daughter.

Without any great deliberation or struggle, Darlene's "koan" practice now completed its unfolding. In place of feeling ashamed of what she had done, she mindfully recognized that her unpremeditated act of "snooping" in her daughter's room had unconsciously created a situation which beautifully expressed the entanglement she felt between her and her daughter. At the same time, it also provided a way for her to resolve an ongoing dilemma.

At what felt like an opportune moment, Darlene decided to disclose to her daughter what she had done and what she had been learning from the process. Rather than shaming her daughter about the "contraband"—which would also have perpetuated the shame that had existed between her and her own mother—Darlene chose to talk to her daughter adult-to-adult. In an act of intimate and vulnerable sharing, she told her daughter what it had been like for her when she was growing up and how she thought this might have influenced the current relationship. She might, she surmised, have unwittingly invited her daughter to go underground in lieu of becoming more independent. This sharing had the effect of deepening their authentic relationship and helped to set them both free.

In Buddhist terms, struggling to solve problems is at best a misguided effort, because there can never be a way around the reality of what's so. For this reason, a premium is often placed on the mental maneuver of *letting go*. However, when we let go without working out the underlying causes and conditions, very often the problem simply re-emerges.

In psychological terms, however, while there may be no way around reality, there may yet be a way through. As one of my colleagues expresses this idea, it's like running up against a door that opens inward: no matter how hard you push against it, it won't open, but the moment you pause and open to it, the door opens and you can pass through (Leggatt, 2014).[21] This is what we seek in psychotherapy. When we can ask the right questions and tackle them with a mind which is steady, focused, and receptive, we can best discover what we need to do next.

Despite the benefit of holding questions or conflicts in "open mind"—what I have termed here the "koan paradigm"—I am not suggesting a one-size-fits-all strategic "formula" for dealing with problems. There are many situations in which sorting things out or thinking them through is essential in arriving at an appropriate course of action. There is a difference between creative thinking/problem solving, on the one hand, and unproductive rumination, on the other. In place of efforting at figuring things out, it is possible to explore the content and meaning of experience by feeling into it and investigating where it came from and where it wants to go. This is a way of paying attention to problems which invites clarity and allows intuitive wisdom to emerge. It is a method of approaching problems which integrates thinking and feeling.

The Path of Problems

Problems express the troublesome side of ourselves. As in the simile of the splinter introduced above, they invite our attention to what is painful and needs attention within us. Struggle is one of the fundamental motifs in the dance of life: we react to something, our feelings get hurt, we strive to get something we don't have, to do something that is difficult to do, or to become something which we are not—to achieve something or to become something. These struggles are among the basic causes of suffering in everyday life.[22]

Problems reflect the struggle we have with the shadow sides of our nature. The "shadow" is the unconscious aspect of the personality which the conscious ego rejects, disowns, or otherwise fails to recognize in itself.[23] Omnipresent as conflict, the shadow can be observed in the interplay of resistance and counter-resistance between different sides of ourselves. It is also revealed indirectly in the form of symptoms, dreams, and the like. What we cannot own within ourselves is projected out and perceived to be external. For example, disowned anger may be experienced instead as a paranoia in which the world is perceived as aligned against us.

The negative aspect of shadow is the dark side of our nature, the devil within (Batchelor, 2004).[24] However, there is also a positive aspect, which is that there are valuable opportunities available through encounters with the shadow sides of ourselves. For example, in the story told above (Clinical Illustration 4.5) of Tina's struggle with her husband's "dark side," Tina became able to see a hidden aspect of her own nature as well as her childhood wounds. What emerges once a shadow is illuminated is often exactly what most needs to be seen. Indeed, in this respect, a *problem is a path* that leads us toward deeper consciousness.

In this way, problems can be seen to have an innate intelligence, leading us to psychological growth, wholeness, and integration. The psychological pain of a problem or predicament in life has a perfection through its ability to reveal what we most need to see. In the light of this awareness, we can often see exactly what we are looking for (even—or especially—when we didn't *know* that's what we were looking for!).

In a broad context, the fundamental challenge of problems is that they require us to accept things as they are. Indeed, part of what makes a problem *a problem* is that there is something we don't *want* to accept. The pain of a problem shows us precisely that we are *resisting* the way things are. By bringing awareness to the process of *struggle* that is part of every problem, we have the opportunity to discover what we have disowned, disavowed, or repressed within ourselves. This dynamic dialectic between different sides of ourselves is a fundamental part of the process of how we come into being. The goal in psychotherapy is to heal these splits within ourselves, to recognize and integrate the shadow sides of our nature.

From a Buddhist view, the liability of couching problems in psychological terms is that it tends to support the view of "me and my problems which I have got to get rid of" (Amaro, 1990, p. 9). According to classical Buddhist understanding, the person doesn't have a problem; ego-centered view is itself the problem. We tend to identify with and define ourselves in terms of our problems. We locate ourselves in that struggle and in that suffering. Moreover, defining ourselves in terms of problems may contribute to an endless quest for self-improvement and a futile, misguided attempt to finally "arrive" somewhere beyond the difficulties of life. In this (Buddhist) view, the fundamental predicament rests on reification of *self* and the idea that there is *someone* apart from the causal chain of being which is Life.

For all of these reasons, wise understanding of the nature of problems is very important both in Buddhist-informed psychotherapy and in dharma practice. Indeed, inquiring deeply about problems can *be* dharma practice—a path of personality (Welwood, 2000).

Summary and Conclusion

As stated earlier, insight often begins with bad news. Our emotional problems provide a very useful door into mindful awareness; an ever deepening opportunity to meet the moment of experience and to discover new truths. One of the basic advantages of focusing on problems in the ways described in this chapter is that it develops the capacity for self-reflection. Especially when practiced in conjunction with mindfulness meditation, states of self-reflective awareness deepen and consolidate.

As I have come to think of it, the basic psychological "move" in the process of inquiry is an experiential frame of "?". "?" is part of the basic grammar of the life of the mind. The difficulties and predicaments of life are natural invitations to inquiry and investigation. Inquiring deeply neither denies nor reifies the self of everyday life, instead engaging exploration of its process.

The fundamental difference between Buddhist-informed therapy and meditation is the importance placed on narrative meaning. In the framework of meditation, engaging with the narratives in the mind can tend to obscure the background field of awareness from which all experience emerges (Siff, 2014).[25] In contrast, in the framework of sustained psychotherapeutic inquiry, narratives are not distractions but rather appropriate stepping stones on the path of awareness. By exploring narratives, we develop awareness of the (unconscious) sources from which stories originate and proliferate. This allows the development of compassionate insight, which ultimately is the goal of both Buddhist meditation and psychotherapy.

We can meet our problems with mindful awareness and without preconception as to whether our inquiry about them is psychological, spiritual, neither, or both. In a Zen koan, Nonquan says to Zhaozhou, "the Way is not about knowing or not knowing. When you know something you are deluded, and when you don't know you are empty-headed" (Tarrant, 2004, p. 49). In inquiring deeply, the "middle way"[26] is the truth of our own experience.

Notes

1 Later chapters in this book (especially Chapters 8 and 9) will take up some developmental perspectives on this issue.
2 Jeffrey Rubin (1996) introduced and explored this metaphor in his book *Psychotherapy and Buddhism*. The natural partnership between psychotherapy and Buddhist practice has also been explored by many writers in what is now an extensive professional literature.
3 In this book, I distinguish between solutions to problems which are figured out and those which are seemingly emergent (a way *through*).
4 The concept of "transcendent subjectivity" will be further defined and discussed in Chapter 8.
5 As in the instruction "*relax, observe, allow*".
6 A very interesting discussion of this issue can be found in Bass's (2001) paper, "Whose Unconscious Is It, Anyway?"
7 Freud famously described this quality of listening as evenly-suspended or hovering attention (Freud, 1912). Wilfred Bion's description "listening without memory or desire", is also frequently cited (Bion, 1967).
8 Readers with similar background may likely recognize the influences of (in alphabetical order) Andreas Angyal (1965); Joseph Bobrow (2010), Brandschaft et al. (2010), Heinz Kohut (1971; 1977), Rollo May (1983), Stephen Mitchell (2000), Mitchell and Aron (1999), Roy Schafer (1976; 1983; 1992), Donnel Stern (2003; 2010; 2015), Robert Stolorow (1980; 1992; 1994; 2007), John Welwood (2000), and D. W. Winnicott (1965a,b,c), among others.
9 The concept of "truth" also has different meanings. In Welwood (2000), *Towards A Psychology of Awakening*, he delineates conceptual truth (truths of the logical mind and science), experiential truth (thinking mind interacting with felt experience), and contemplative truth (deeper order of being beyond both thinking mind and felt experience). This is roughly equivalent to distinction in Buddhist philosophy between Relative and Absolute truth.
10 This method is taught by James Baraz, one of the guiding teachers at Spirit Rock Meditation Center, Woodacre, Calif.
11 "Depressogenic" cognitions.
12 In Rinzai Zen practice, asking paradoxical questions has been elaborated into the form of meditation called koan practice. Koans ("what is the sound of one hand clapping?", etc.) are intended to exhaust the analytic intellect, readying the mind to receive experience spontaneously and intuitively.

13 Emptiness is an ontological construct, whereas inquiring deeply concerns itself with phenomenology and with epistemological questions.

14 In psychoanalytic language, "self-experience" and "representations of self and other". These concepts are discussed and elaborated in Chapter 8.

15 Not to mention unknown layers of memory, etc. which are unconscious or ignored.

16 Both of these aspects—self-representations and self-experience—will be elaborated upon at length in Chapter 8.

17 This set of questions touches upon threats to self-representations: "narcissistic injuries".

18 Important psychological dimensions of relationship and connection are explored at length in Chapter 6.

19 See Moffitt (2012) for a very useful discussion of this issue.

20 In Zen practice, people sometimes refer to these as "life koans".

21 The quality of this experience is also conveyed by the Chinese straw finger puzzles which can be solved only by doing the counter-intuitive thing: pushing one's fingers *into* the puzzle/trap rather than efforting at pulling them *out*.

22 In Buddhist terminology, basic manifestations of "dukkha."

23 This concept is one of the major archetypes in Jungian psychology.

24 Stephen Batchelor takes up this theme in his book *Living with the Devil* (2004) where he explores in depth the mythic story of the Buddha's encounter with Mara.

25 However, a case can be made for the fact that narratives need not be an impediment to the meditative goal of calm abiding if wise attention can be brought to them. The interested reader is referred to Jason Siff's (2014) book about the role of thinking in meditation.

26 Before the time of the Buddha, there were two widely held beliefs: one, the idea that there was an eternal soul that survived death, and the other that Being was extinguished after death. The Buddha taught what became known as "the middle way": neither eternalism nor nihilism. It recommended a stance of moderation which avoided both austerity and sensual indulgence. The middle way refers generally to dharma practice which balances opposite poles and extreme views.

References

Amaro B. (1990). The golden state. In Amaro Bhikku, *Rugged interdependency: A monk's dependency on the American Buddhist landscape 1990–2007* (pp. 8–13). Redwood Valley, CA: Abayaghiri Monastic Foundation.

Angyal, A. (1965). *Neurosis and treatment: A holistic theory*. New York, NY: John Wiley & Sons.

Bass, A. (2001). It takes one to know one; or, whose unconscious is it anyway? *Psychoanalytic Dialogues, 11*, 83–702.

Batchelor, S. (2004). *Living with the devil: A meditation on good and evil*. New York, NY: Riverhead Books.

Bion, W. R. (1967). Notes on memory and desire. *Psychoanalytic Forum, 2*, 271–280.

Bobrow, J. (2010). *Zen and psychotherapy: Partners in liberation*. New York, NY: Norton Professional Books.

Boorstein, S. (1995). *It's easier than you think: The Buddhist way to happiness*. New York, NY: Harper Collins.

Brandschaft, B., Doctors, S., and Sorter, D. (2010). *Toward an emancipatory psychoanalysis: Brandschaft's intersubjective vision*. Psychoanalytic Inquiry Book Series. New York, NY: Routledge Press.

Cornell, A. W. (2013). *Focusing in clinical practice: The essence of change*. New York, NY: W.W. Norton.

Epstein, M. (1995). *Thoughts without a thinker: Psychotherapy from a Buddhist perspective.* New York, NY: Basic Books.

Freud, S. (1912). *Recommendation to physicians practicing psychoanalysis.* In J. Strachey (Ed. and Trans.), *The standard edition of the complete psychological works of Sigmund Freud* (Vol. 7, pp. 109–120). London, England Hogarth Press.

Gendlin, E. (1978). *Focusing.* New York, NY: Bantam Books.

Katie, B. (2002). *Loving what is.* New York, NY: Harmony Books, Random House.

Kohut, H. (1971). *The analysis of the self.* Madison, CT: International Universities Press.

Kohut, H. (1977). *The restoration of the self.* Madison, CT: International Universities Press.

Leggatt, D. (2014). Personal communication.

May, R. (1983). *The discovery of being.* New York, NY: W.W. Norton.

Mitchell, S. A. (2000). *Relationality: From attachment to intersubjectivity.* Hillsdale, NJ: Analytic Press.

Mitchell, S. A. and Aron, L. (1999). *Relational psychoanalysis: The emergence.* Hillsdale, NJ: Analytic Press.

Moffitt, P. (2012). *From emotional chaos to clarity.* New York, NY: Hudson Street Press/ Penguin Group.

Peavey, F. (2003). Strategic questions are tools for rebellion. In Brady, M. (Ed.), *The wisdom of listening.* Somerville, MA: Wisdom Publications.

Rubin, J. (1996). *Psychotherapy and Buddhism: Towards an integration.* New York, NY: Plenum Press.

Schafer, R. (1976). *A new language for psychoanalysis.* New Haven, CT: Yale University Press.

Schafer, R. (1983). *The analytic attitude.* New York, NY: Basic Books.

Schafer, R. (1992). *Retelling a life: Narration and dialogue in psychoanalysis.* New York, NY: Basic Books.

Siff, J. (2014). *Thoughts are not the enemy.* Boston, MA: Shambhala Publications.

Stern, D. (2003). *Unformulated experience: From dissociation to imagination in psychoanalysis.* Hillsdale, NJ: Analytic Press.

Stern, D. (2010). *Partners in thought: Working with unformulated experience, dissociation, and enactment.* New York, NY: Routledge Press.

Stern, D. (2015). *Relational freedom: Emergent properties of the interpersonal field.* New York, NY: Routledge Press.

Stolorow, R. D. and Lachmann, F. M. (1980). *Psychoanalysis of developmental arrests: Theory and treatment.* Madison, CT: International Universities Press.

Stolorow, R. D. and Atwood, G. E. (1992). *Contexts of being: The inter-subjective foundations of psychological life.* Hillsdale, NJ: Analytic Press.

Stolorow, R. D., Atwood, G. and Brandschaft, B. (1994). *The intersubjective perspective.* Northvale, NJ: Jason Aronson Press.

Stolorow, R. D. (2007). *Trauma and human existence: Autobiographical psychoanalytic and philosophical reflections.* New York, NY: Analytic Press, Taylor & Francis Group.

Sumedho, A. (2007). *The sound of Silence.* Somerville, MA: Wisdom Publications.

Tarrant, J. (2004). *Bring me the rhinoceros.* Boston, MA: Shambhala Press.

Wallin, D. J. (2007). *Attachment in psychotherapy.* New York, NY: Guilford Press.

Welwood, J. (2000). *The psychology of awakening.* Boston, MA: Shambhala Press.

Winnicott, D. W. (1965a). The capacity to be alone. In Winnicott, D. W. (Ed.), *The maturational processes and the facilitating environment: Studies in the theory of emotional development* (pp. 29–36). Madison, CT: International Universities Press.

Winnicott, D. W. (1965b). The theory of the parent–infant relationship. In Winnicott, D. W. (Ed.), *The maturational processes and the facilitating environment: Studies in the theory of emotional development* (pp. 37–55). Madison, CT: International Universities Press.

Winnicott, D. W. (1965c). Ego distortion in terms of true and false self. In Winnicott, D. W. (Ed.), *The maturational processes and the facilitating environment: Studies in the theory of emotional development* (pp. 140–152). Madison, CT: International Universities Press.

Chapter 5

Present Moments, Moments of Presence

Moments of Meeting in Psychotherapy

Verbally understanding or narrating something is not, in and of itself, sufficient to bring about change. The premise of relational psychotherapies (including the Buddhist-informed approach described here) is that change comes into being as a function of special moments of communication between psychotherapist and patient. The psychoanalyst Daniel Stern (2004) terms these "moments of meeting." The defining quality of such special now moments is the profound sense of mutual connection. It is on this stage of the therapeutic here-and-now that change most readily unfolds.

The prototypical "moment of meeting" is the one that occurs in the first moments after birth, when the new baby looks into the eyes of a mother who is looking back. Important moments of meeting occur in psychotherapy every time something is said and received in such a way that the patient feels deeply seen, felt, accepted, and understood. Dan Siegel (2010) describes this as a process of interpersonal attunement in which the Other experiences "feeling felt" by us. Such moments of deep contact, "mutual now moments," are what the philosopher Martin Buber understood as the essential meeting of "*I-and-Thou*" (Buber, 1958).

The therapeutic encounter provides an opportunity for a unique and vivid kind of connection. Patient and therapist participate together in the mutually-lived experience which takes place between them and, in addition, in the creation of a healing narrative which describes that shared experience. Such therapeutic moments of meeting involve more than just an exchange of information; both participants engage in co-creating the mutually lived story between them. This is the secret of the relational here-and-now (Stern, 2004).

The importance of Now Moments is widely recognized in the literature of relational psychoanalysis. Of many relevant descriptions, I especially like the phrase *fertile mutuality*, referring to the field of unseen emotional action within and between people.[1] The descriptive term "intersubjective" is also broadly useful, carrying the general meaning that two (or more) minds come together in a space of shared thought and feeling. So in this language, we can define therapeutic now moments as experiences of deep intimacy at the intersubjective intersection.[2]

Deep "now moments" have also been termed blood moments (Shafer, 2010), a description which derives from the native American ritual in which two members of a tribe mixed their blood in celebration of bonding as brothers. By this metaphor, we can understand an intersubjective now moment as one in which two individuals co-mingle their most vital essence. The idea of a blood moment also carries the meaning that real feelings and actions are taking place between real people in real time (Stern, 2004). Last but not least, because blood is a quintessential element in birth, the term "blood moment" is also well suited to express the meaning that something new is being born. From my point of view, psychotherapeutic blood moments are those in which new aspects of self come into being.[3]

The following vignette briefly describes an extended series of therapeutic moments of meeting that occurred in my work with one of my patients, "David."

Clinical Illustration 5.1: David

David came for help at age 40, reluctantly, when his wife left him unexpectedly and he fell apart. He spent much of the time in our early sessions sobbing deeply for the first time in his adult life and got in touch with wounds from his early life that had been opened up by this new loss. I didn't say much, at first, but I felt deeply moved by his pain—sometimes to the point that I found myself welling up with tears. We worked together for about a year and then he moved on. On a return visit recently, David told me that he could see from the perspective of time passing that he had been sealed off and compartmentalized for most of his adult life. His emotional shut-down was what had allowed his marriage to slowly die without his even being aware of it happening. My deeply felt response to his pain had moved him, he said. It was pivotal in his taking the risk to open up and gave him hope that it might yet be possible to find real connection with a woman.

This vignette conveys the importance that cumulated "now moments" can have in psychotherapy. It is important to emphasize, in addition, that such moments of meeting occur as a function of *two* subjectivities, therapist's and patient's, both immersed in the present moment as a lived experience. The important implication here is that the therapist, as an individual, is intimately connected to and radically engaged in moments of meeting. His or her emotional responses, personality, and state of awareness are all integral parts of the unfolding mutual experience—in positive as well as in limiting ways. In this framework, clinical detachment is a hindrance (although this should not be taken to mean that clinical objectivity and neutrality are undesirable).

The Therapeutic Relational Field

Therapeutic now moments can also be defined as the *lived experience of the therapeutic relational field*. "Relational field" connotes the conjoined surface of interplay between therapist and patient; a mingling of minds which occurs at the intersubjective intersection. The therapeutic relational field typically includes many different "flavors" of experience. Some are relatively flat and ordinary: the everyday events that occur in a working therapeutic alliance. Others engage a deeper intimacy which makes possible the emergence of "blood moments."

One way to describe the intersubjective field in relational psychotherapy is in terms of its content: what is talked about and the insights that arise from that conversation (Stern, 2010, 2015; Atwood and Stolorow, 2012).[4] In effect, a new chapter in the patient's life story gets written, adding new episodic memories to the patient's ongoing autobiographical narrative. This shift in narrative is well illustrated by David's story about what happened in his psychotherapy and its significance in his emotional life.

But in addition to what *happens*, equally important is the patient's *felt sense* of the psychotherapy relationship. In relational psychotherapy, this non-verbal dimension of experience is an important area of focus. It is taken up in the context of ***implicit memories*** of relationship: the distillation in the patient's mind of how they were treated and how they felt with significant others in their lives. Implicit memory refers to the compartment of memory which remembers things in a way that doesn't involve thinking about them; it is the common sense we live by even though we may be unaware of it and may not be able to put it into words. This "unthought known" (Bollas, 1987) may be likened to the water unseen by the fish which is swimming in it. It lives within us as our intuitive sense and automatic set of assumptions about people and situations.

An important premise in relational psychotherapy is that implicit memory is often acted out in relationship without awareness (or with distortion of its impact). Such ***enactments*** re-create the psychological themes and patterns of our lives in living color: present moments with romantic partners, family members, and friends. When this happens, two people may find themselves stuck in repetitive, painful "knots" of entangled emotion and behavior (often in the form of fights) which are determined by the emotional baggage each one carries.

The opportunity in psychotherapy is to shine a light on this baggage— i.e. implicit relational patterns—by exploring the repetitive roles that get acted out in interpersonal relationships and the corresponding roles that are induced in others. In clinical language, enactments express and represent implicit memory—what I refer to in this book as "non-experienced experience" (Rhinehart, 1976)—through transference onto others and projection of the past into the present.

Therapeutic now moments have the potential to become building blocks of significant change. This takes place on several different levels. First, as previously mentioned, the lived experience of the therapeutic encounter itself may constitute a set of new experiences. Second, the psychotherapeutic dialogue elaborates upon the connections between what is happening now, what has happened in the past, and how the person is acting upon it; it builds new structures of understanding and meaning. Third, therapy cultivates the capacity to reflect upon and relate to feelings and mind states in more skillful ways. In all of these ways, by exploring the here-and-now of the therapy relationship, new relational possibilities come into being. Both the implicit relational field and the personal narratives that organize our lives have the opportunity to be re-shaped and repaired in therapeutic moments of meeting. (This is what happened in my work with David.)

Therapeutic Presence in the Relational Field

One important dimension of therapeutic now moments is the quality of being which in Buddhism is called *presence*. Although hard to define, to be Present means to be aware in a way which is open, attentive, balanced, and flexible. Therapeutic presence is a quality of deep listening which has long been recognized in psychoanalytic work. It has been compared with Freud's (1912) "evenly hovering attention" and Wilfred Bion's (1967) idea of listening "without memory or desire" (Epstein, 1995).

The cultivation of presence is one of the hallmarks of Buddhist mindfulness meditation. As previously described, the core meaning of mindful awareness is the ability to *be with* what is; to be intimate with the present moment of experience. The practice of mindfulness cultivates this intimacy and depth of Presence. In the frame of inquiring deeply, the therapist lends his or her mindful awareness and presence to the purpose of illuminating the shared experience of the relational field.

As a therapist, to be Present means to be receptively and empathically aware both of self and other; non-defensive and curious about the experience of the present moment. Our Presence is part of the felt sense someone has in being with us. It is an essential aspect of the clinical atmosphere we provide, an important part of what allows the patient to feel deeply seen, felt, accepted, and understood.

As the therapist speaks from a state of Presence, s(he) has the opportunity to listen deeply to the patient, to be present with what the patient is saying and not saying, and to track the nuances of change in the interpersonal connection. As the patient speaks into the Presence of the therapist, s(he) has the opportunity both to listen more deeply to him or herself and to be transformed by the therapist's listening. Often, as a patient narrates their experience in a therapeutic space of deep presence, a new sense of immediacy, freshness, and transparency is injected into experiences which had become repetitive, stale, and intractable. In this process of sharing, both people change.

Some idea of the impact of therapeutic presence is conveyed in the following brief vignette.

Clinical Illustration 5.2: Evan

Evan has tremendous difficulty communicating about his feelings with his life partner, William. Because William came into the relationship with a history of serious depression and several suicide attempts, Evan fears that to speak about his negative feelings honestly would cause emotional harm to William.

> As a consequence, Evan defers to William's preferences in most of the deci-
> sions in their relationship, from minor ones such as where to eat, to major
> ones such as how to spend vacations, what furnishings to buy, and so forth.
> The more he accommodates, the angrier Evan becomes, and the more diffi-
> cult it is for him to feel comfortable expressing himself honestly.
>
> Despite our repeated discussions of the importance of his speaking up,
> and despite very thorough analysis of the childhood reasons for his inability
> to do so, Evan remained frozen and unable to express himself. My clinical
> strategy was to call Evan's attention to similar inhibitions that arose for him
> in our therapeutic relationship. All of this further frustrated Evan; now even
> in therapy he was finding himself jammed up and unable to express himself.
> He was mad at himself for the fact that he could see so clearly what he needed
> to do and yet felt so unable to "pull the trigger" [sic] by being honest and
> forthcoming with William. I pointed out that his language seemed to suggest
> that he was concerned about the damaging impact of his anger. From my
> side, I repeatedly noticed myself working way too hard.
>
> One day, something occurred between me and Evan which surprised both
> of us: As I started to paraphrase something he was saying, he snapped at me
> in annoyance: "If you'd only let me finish without interrupting me," he said,
> "you'd understand better what I'm trying to say!" Both of us sat in stunned
> silence as we absorbed what had just happened; the atmosphere of Presence
> in the room had palpably thickened. Immediately following, in a poignant
> "blood moment," Evan says "Thank you. I can feel that you really heard me.
> This is what I most need from you: for you to hear what I am saying from
> here [pointing to his heart] and less what I am saying from here [pointing to
> his head]."[5]

The moment of spontaneity described above was one of intimacy, self-awareness,
and growth for both Evan and myself: Evan expanded his capacity to be authentic
and I saw more clearly how my own efforts to be therapeutic could get in the way.

Psychoanalytic work is based on the idea that as therapeutic interactions unfold
over time, echoes of the patient's history will inevitably begin to be enacted
within the therapeutic encounter itself. Deeply embedded interpersonal patterns
(or "transferences") enter the therapy as elements of a lived emotional story which
becomes the story of the psychotherapy. It can even be theorized that when we
are very deeply present in the intimacy of the therapeutic encounter, the implicit
(nonverbal) memories of interpersonal gaze and interpersonal resonance between
mother and baby are evoked in the *transference/countertransference*. It is in this
space of fertile mutuality that healing takes place.

Emergent Moments in the Relational Field

Change comes into being in the therapeutic relational field in the form of
emergent moments: new experiences, relational events, or psychological

developments which arise unbidden and in a way that can be neither predicted nor controlled. The hallmark of emergent moments is that they simply arrive: They feel in some essential way "separate" from us (D. N. Stern, 2004; D. Stern, 2010; D. Stern, 2015). In psychoanalysis, emergence is described in terms of third-person qualities distinct from the subjectivity of either therapist or patient, understood in terms of the interpersonal field.[6] Emergent moments are described as a characteristic of the clinical process itself. It is the role of the psychoanalytically-minded relational therapist to recognize, understand, and articulate what is emergent.

It has often been said that the most important healing factor in psychotherapy is the therapist's state of mind (Diamond, 2011). "State of mind" is a broad description. It includes the capacity for "compassionate attunement" which is the hallmark of the therapeutic milieu, as well as the therapist's psychological traits, such as emotional balance and self-reflective awareness, which provide a living template for the development of healthier self-function in the patient. Perhaps it is useful to think of psychotherapy as a process akin to osmosis in which there is an intersubjective mingling of mind states and in which the therapist's qualities can be absorbed in whatever ways are most needed by the patient.

When therapeutic moments of meeting occur within a field of deep Presence, their emotional impact is amplified and the sense of experience as emergent is more vividly felt. Mindful awareness registers both what is enacted and what is emergent. This mindful attention to what is emerging in the relational field feels like (or perhaps is) a kind of meditation practice, in which relational emergent moments are felt to arise against a backdrop of a still, heart-centered, receptive listening field (Packer, 2002; Sills, 2009). Emergent moments are facilitated as a consequence of the qualities of alert, focused attention developed through mindfulness meditation practice: deep presence, clarity and its implied wisdom, and centeredness or resilience ("equanimity"). Like other aspects of the therapist's subjectivity, these qualities of mind are shared intersubjectively in the therapeutic relationship as it unfolds through moments of meeting.

Therapeutic presence entails a number of component skills which are facilitated through the practice of Buddhist mindfulness meditation. The core capacity on which it is based is the ability to sustain focus of attention in the present moment—the ability to bring awareness repeatedly back to a chosen object of attention. Such "whole-hearted attention" is a wonderful frame for psychotherapy. It allows therapists to listen and observe more acutely. It also amplifies the sense of person-to-person connection between patient and therapist.

Mindfulness meditation may be thought of as a process of *intra*personal attunement: in essence a process in which we learn to empathically receive and accept our own experience. Analogously, *inter*personal attunement is facilitated when we bring mindful awareness to the relational field. It amplifies awareness of subtle cues in body language, facial expression, and language and heightens empathic sensitivity to how the patient is feeling in a particular moment. It helps capture the emotional gestalt of the interaction that is occurring, creating space for feelings to be felt more deeply. Such attunement involves the "reading" both of the text and subtext of communication; both left and right brain (Siegel, 2007, 2012).

Mindful awareness highlights nuances of both the patient's responses and the therapist's own (countertransference) responses. In the continual dance that takes place between any Self and any Other, there is much that can be observed about the way "self" (therapist's or patient's) defensively protects itself.[7] In the process of relational psychotherapy, mindful attention heightens awareness of this—and other relational happenings—at the boundary of Self and Other.

Therapeutic presence is the foundation of *relational mindfulness*: awareness of the felt sense of connection and relatedness as it shifts and changes from moment to moment (Surrey, 2005). It fosters the therapist's capacity to respond spontaneously in a way that matches what the patient needs. The therapist's compassionate acceptance—the "unconditional positive regard" described by Carl Rogers (1995)—also gives the patient a sense that they are not alone, which is the essence of hope. One of the themes in this book is the idea that the therapist's presence is one of the raw materials used in building this "*corrective relational experience.*"[8]

The Transcendent Relational Field

In mindful psychotherapy, there is a dimension of experience which may spontaneously emerge in the relational field: "*transcendent subjectivity*" in the transference/countertransference. Transcendent subjectivity is a state in which awareness is heightened, clarity is sharpened, and things are deeply felt. It can be further characterized in terms of the experience of acceptance, harmony, and flow and the felt sense that everything is okay just as it is. Subjectively, this feels like the emergence of another *dimension* of experience, a shift in depth of field. This may be conveyed by analogy with "Magic Eye?" computer graphics: appearing at first to be flat two-dimensional images, the pictures have a third dimension embedded in them, so that when we gaze at them at length, all of a sudden they become three-dimensional. The mental landscape changes (Schuman, 1998). Analogously, inhabiting the present moment with mindful awareness, a new dimension of expanded subjectivity can emerge. Sometimes this shift carries a felt sense of "epiphany," but whether or not it feels profound, things seem to take on a new dimension. Subjectivity shifts in a way that *feels* transcendent. Such states are part of the allure of meditation practice.

Transcendent subjectivity gives an intuitive glimpse of a state of being without the felt sense of limitation that typically defines problems. Ultimately, this can also yield the insight that a problem and its solution are interpenetrating, two sides of a single coin.

When we are deeply present with another, transcendent subjectivity can also occur as an emergent aspect of the relational field. This can be termed a *transcendent relational field*; it involves an experience of *transpersonal* awareness. We may think of such experiences as "blood moments" in which the usual boundaries between self and other are temporarily relaxed, yielding an interpersonal experience of belonging, connectedness, and deep intimacy unbounded by the sense of separate self. This quality of relatedness can emerge intersubjectively in the transference/countertransference when mindful awareness is brought to bear on the experience of the relational field. This subjective state cannot be said to "belong to" either patient or therapist. It is felt to be emergent: arising of its own accord in the mysterious alchemy of the therapeutic relationship.

The intersubjective qualities of the transcendent relational field were described by Alfano (1995) in the context of Buddhist-informed psychoanalysis. She wrote about what she termed *transcendent attunement*: a state of deep reverie in the countertransference in which the therapist experiences a transient suspension of duality between self and other. She delineated its qualities as *mental flexibility* (fluid transition between somatopsychic experiences), *negative capability* (capacity to dwell in an experience of uncertainty and not knowing), *unconscious reception*, and *intuition*.[9]

Transcendent attunement can also be understood as a state of interpersonal resonance. In my experience, states of mindful awareness and deep presence tend to emerge naturally in the process of sitting with and deeply listening to another. These qualities resonate intersubjectively between therapist and patient, permeating the relational field. This should not be thought of as one particular experience but rather a spectrum of experiences with varying degrees of depth.

In the transcendent relational field, the focus of attention shifts from the foreground of ordinary relational experience to an expanded awareness of the *background field*, which is felt to be a space in which we *are* connected. Such transcendent attunement is one of the hallmarks of the transcendent relational field, and, indeed, is the sine qua non of inquiring deeply with others. I do not know if a state of consciousness is actually "shared," but it does *feel* that way; transcendent attunement occurs in the process of inquiring deeply with another (Kramer, 2007). I believe that this shared "space" of mindful awareness can contribute to psychological healing.

When there is a deep sense of subjective Presence in psychotherapy, transformative possibilities for change emerge. Designating the dimension of Depth as an aspect of the relational field, Donnel Stern (2015) describes it this way:

> Depth is our awareness of the possibility that relations we have not yet imagined will emerge, and it appears only when those possibilities, like three-dimensional perspective, are already present and alive in our experience.
>
> (Stern 2015, p. 7)

Quoting from earlier work by others, he goes on to say:

> Some process is going on which they (patient and therapist) have not initiated or energized. There is a remarkable experience of being carried along by something larger than both therapist and patient: A true sense of an

interpersonal field results. The therapist learns to ride the process rather than to carry the patient.

(Stern 2015, p.14)

This description is fully congruent with the concept of the transcendent relational field presented here. When subjective depth of Presence expands into an experience of transcendent subjectivity, new transformative possibilities emerge.

Sometimes—not always—transcendent subjectivity in the relational field includes a direct experience of the fundamental inseparability between Self and Other. In a spiritual context, this might be called "non-dual awareness," a direct experience of the unity of all being. I suspect that such states of awareness are especially likely to occur when therapist and/or patient are familiar with them from meditation practice. In my experience, such moments tend to arise when shared silence is deep and when the need to know is suspended;[10] when we hold a question without immediately seeking an answer.

In psychotherapy, we can see non-dual experience as a deep well of potential wisdom and compassion; what has been called the *fertile void*. This has been described as a state of generative, non-defensive silence (Bobrow, 2010).

One practitioner described her amazement about such "moments of presence" this way:

> Ever so slowly, I am learning that the Present moment contains everything I need. It contains the next step on my path. It contains just what needs to be realized or spoken. Yet, trusting what the present moment wants to tell me is one of the hardest things to do. Compared to my intelligent, analyzing, complex, problem-solving active mind, the information contained in the present moment seems naïve, simple, and not enough, somehow. After all, what can a few body sensations (and/or subtle feelings), floating on a bed of silence, possibly know? Talking, describing, relaying, and analyzing my story must be infinitely more valuable than sitting quietly in the moment and waiting for what wants to arise from the silence.[11]

As therapists, we can invoke moments of deep Presence through our own states of being as well as through clinical suggestion. Such states are an intersubjective container, a place to hold suffering while the tangles of our psychological world of lived experience unwind. This expands the *intimate edge* of interpersonal connection (Ehrenberg, 1992) and opens psychotherapy into a space of cooperative mutuality which is deeply healing.

Inquiring Deeply: Mindfulness in the Countertransference

Therapists who have the aspiration to deepen their clinical work in the ways described in this chapter will do well to recognize that cultivating depth of Presence is a *practice*; it is something which develops rather than something we acquire. It deepens gradually and over time.

Although the shared experience of psychotherapy has the explicit purpose to be of service to the patient, by its very nature this practice also confers benefit to the therapist. It may be thought of as a form of compassion meditation: time and attention exclusively devoted to being open to the experience of the suffering of others. In this way, the therapist has the opportunity (as well as responsibility) to become aware of his or her personal defenses against staying open in the face of suffering. A concomitant benefit for the therapist is greater awareness of his or her *own* suffering, previously defended against.[12]

By highlighting the background field of awareness, inquiring deeply can help the patient learn to "embrace the moment": relax into experience rather than exclusively focusing on how to change it. At the same time, this helps to highlight how the patient tends to relate to his or her experience, for example with habitual judgments or the effort to be in control. In other words, we can use the opportunity of psychotherapy to help the patient explore opening to the Unknown and resting with What Is. This develops the capacity for greater trust, surrender, and acceptance. While these dimensions of experience are probably implicit in every good psychotherapy,[13] inquiring deeply makes them explicit as an aspect of how the patient relates to the problematic experiences of life. This frame for psychotherapeutic work is quasi-meditative as well as radically relational: it expands focus beyond interpersonal intimacy to include what the famed Zen master Dogen called "intimacy with all things" (Dogen and Tanahashi, 1995).

In sum, inquiring deeply can be understood as a form of mindful awareness practice; a meditation-à-deux practiced within a framework of relational psychotherapy. In this practice, Present Moments are received as Moments of Presence in order to cultivate psychological insight. This is the essence of inquiring deeply as contemplative relational psychotherapy.

Notes

1   A similar concept is Bobrow's "fertile void," a "deep cooperative mutuality into which pieces can gather and out of which surprises, discoveries, and new movement unfolds" (Bobrow, 2010, p. 11).
2   What happens at the intersubjective intersection between two people, and why, is a fascinating question, although one which is substantially beyond the intended scope of this discussion. Intersubjectivity theorists and relational psychoanalysts have elaborated upon the developmental and psychodynamic processes which are involved; see for example Mitchell (2000) and D. N. Stern (2004). In this book, I place special emphasis on depth of relatedness as discussed throughout this chapter.
3   See also discussion of "Coming Into Being" in Chapter 10.
4   The psychoanalytic literature is replete with many different points of view about how best to understand and respond therapeutically to such unconscious content.
5   In my view, my responsibility as a therapist in this moment is to understand the developmental needs that were engaged and to try to help foster Evan's self-reflection about these aspects of himself.
6   The so-called "analytic third."
7   This relates in turn to the Buddhist views of self, which are taken up in Chapter 8.

8 In classical psychoanalysis, the term "corrective emotional experience" originally meant that the emotional atmosphere of psychoanalysis could reverse the effects of early childhood trauma or neglect. More broadly and pragmatically speaking, "corrective relational experience" also refers here to any relational event in the therapist-patient relationship in which the therapist recognizes misattunements, misinterpretations, or mistakes on their part and apologizes or otherwise attempts to repair the intimacy in the therapeutic connection. Such repairs deepen the therapeutic relationship by demonstrating the possibility of attuned emotional responsiveness in relationship.

9 Alfano's transcendent attunement is based on the concept of reverie in the work of the psychoanalyst Bion (1967): the analytic frame of mind of being receptive, relaxed, and open; without memory or desire. Alfano integrates her own experiences as an analyst within the matrix of intersubjective object relations, Buddhist psychology, and perinatal research.

10 Such moments might also be described as the edge of the unknown.

11 Unidentified source.

12 By extension, this is also dharma practice, in that it helps us recognize more clearly the quintessential features of suffering that are emphasized in the teachings of the Buddha.

13 Are the *essence* of good therapy as described in the psychoanalytic literature.

References

Alfano, C. (1995). Traversing the caesura: Transcendent attunement in Buddhism and psychoanalysis. *Contemporary Psychoanalysis*, *41*(2), 223–247.

Atwood, G. E. and Stolorow, R. D. (1984). *Structures of subjectivity: Explorations in psychoanalytic phenomenology.* Hillsdale, NJ: Analytic Press.

Bion, W. (1967). Notes on memory and desire. *Psychoanalytic Forum, 2,* 271–280.

Bobrow, J. (2010). *Zen and psychotherapy: Partners in liberation.* New York, NY: Norton Professional Books.

Bollas, C. (1987). *The shadow of the object: Psychoanalysis of the unthought known.* London: Free Association Press.

Buber, M. (1958). *I and thou.* New York, NY: Scribner Press.

Diamond, M. J. (2011). The impact of the mind of the analyst: From unconscious processes to intrapsychic change. In Diamond, M. J. and Christian, C. (Eds), *The second century of psychoanalysis: Evolving perspectives on therapeutic action* (pp. 205–235). London, England: Karnac Books.

Dogen, E. and Tanahashi, K. (Eds) (1995). *Moon in a dewdrop: Writings of Zen master Dogen.* New York, NY: North Point Press/Farrar, Straus, & Giroux.

Ehrenberg, D. (1992). *The intimate edge: Extending the reach of psychoanalytic interaction.* New York, NY: W. W. Norton.

Epstein, M. (1995). *Thoughts without a thinker: Psychotherapy from a Buddhist perspective.* New York, NY: Basic Books.

Kramer, G. (2007). *Insight dialogue: The interpersonal path to freedom.* Boston, MA: Shambhala Press.

Mitchell, S. A. (2000). *Relationality: From attachment to intersubjectivity.* Hillsdale, NJ: Analytic Press.

Packer, T. (2002). *The wonder of presence and the way of meditative inquiry.* Boston, MA: Shambhala Publications.

Rhinehart, L. (1976). *The book of est.* New York, NY: Holt, Rinehart & Winston.

Rogers, C. (1961). *On becoming a person: A therapist's view of psychotherapy*. New York, NY: Houghton Mifflin Co.

Schuman, M. (1998). *Suffering and the evolution of subjectivity*. Paper presented at a conference on Psychotherapy, Spirituality, and the Evolution of Mind. Santa Monica, CA. May 15–17, 1998.

Shafer, R. (2010). Personal communication.

Siegel, D. J. (2007). *The mindful brain: Reflection and attunement in the cultivation of well-being*. New York, NY: W.W. Norton.

Siegel, D. J. (2010). *The mindful therapist: A clinician's guide to mindsight and neural integration*. New York, NY: W.W. Norton.

Siegel, D. J. (2012). *The developing mind, second edition: How relationships and the brain interact to shape who we are*. New York, NY: Guilford Press.

Sills, F. (2009). *Being and becoming*. Berkeley, CA: North Atlantic Books.

Stern, D. N. (1985). *The interpersonal world of the infant*. New York, NY: Basic Books.

Stern, D. N. (2004). *The present moment in psychotherapy and in everyday life*. New York, NY: W.W. Norton.

Stern, D. (2010). *Partners in thought: Working with unformulated experience, dissociation, and enactment*. New York, NY: Routledge Press.

Stern, D. (2015). *Relational freedom: Emergent properties of the interpersonal field*. New York, NY: Routledge Press.

Surrey, J. (2005). Relational psychotherapy, relational mindfulness. In Germer, C. K., Siegel, R. D. and Fulton, P. R. (Eds), *Mindfulness and psychotherapy* (pp. 91–110). New York, NY: Guilford Press.

Chapter 6

Reflections on Connection

When I work with patients who suffer from painful feelings of separateness—perhaps the majority of people who come to see me—I am frequently reminded of the biological imperative underlying our yearning to belong. We are social creatures by nature. Both the need to connect and the pain of not feeling connected are embedded in our biology.

Relationships with significant others throughout the life span are the primary regulators of emotional equilibrium, as well as emotional (and physical!) health. To feel affirmed, accepted, and loved is the basic impetus behind psychological development. The pain of feeling separate, insufficiently appreciated and understood, unworthy, or unloved lies at the core of the experience of most suffering.

Inquiring deeply can be described as a contemplative relational psychotherapeutic approach[1] that is psychoanalytic in emphasis. Its basic aim is to explore the dynamics of the patient's intimate relationships: both those with significant others in the patient's life, and those that unfold within the therapeutic relationship. The latter is especially useful because it gives the therapist an opportunity to experience firsthand how the patient relates. There are two interrelated goals here: first, to illuminate the problematic relationship patterns that the patient tends to get tangled up in; and second, to help create new ways of relating.

Inquiring deeply is similar to other psychoanalytic psychotherapies in its focus on what is emotionally compelling at the intersubjective intersection between therapist and patient. It is different in that it strategically incorporates mindful investigation, inquiry, and various reflective practices into its exploration of relationship. Mindful awareness and self-reflection expand upon the relational emphasis in contemporary psychoanalytic work. This dimension of inquiring deeply is its defining feature as a "contemplative relational psychotherapy."

Basic Aspects of Connection

Relational psychoanalytic psychotherapy explores the various dimensions of connection between therapist and patient, on the one hand, and between the patient and other people, on the other. This can be described as a triangle of connectedness (Figure 6.1).

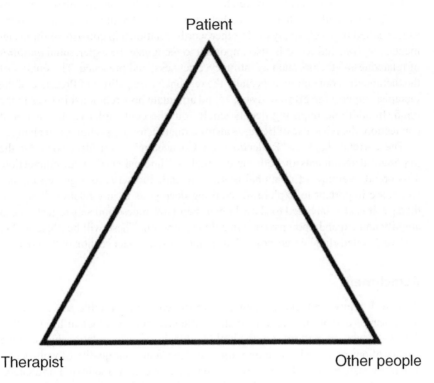

Figure 6.1 Triangle of Connectedness.

Each side of the triangle also has two different aspects: an *external surface of the relationship*—what is occurring in the "real world"—and an *internal surface of the relationship*—how it is held in mind.

As will become clear later, the internal surface of relationship constructs the external surface, and vice versa, so the two are closely interrelated. Although relationship is by nature a two-way connection, it is of course asymmetric with regard to the roles of therapist and patient. Be that as it may, the therapeutic relationship is mutual and co-created; it is always a product of both minds.

Psychoanalytic theory further distinguishes between two aspects of relationship, especially of the therapist–patient relationship. One aspect is the "real relationship" between the two people, and the other is its transferential aspect. "Transference" is the dimension of relationship that repeats what was important in the person's childhood, now reflected in how relationship is represented in the mind.[2] Be that as it may, both the internal and external surfaces of relationship in psychotherapy are necessarily asymmetric given the basic purpose to explore the *patient's* experience of relationship.

Each of the basic surfaces of relationship can also be conceptualized in terms of Self, Other, and the shared space between—the "intersubjective intersection" as it is called in psychoanalysis. In other words, relationship consists of three elements: *me*, *you*, and *we*. It is also important to recognize the experiential *qualities* of relatedness—factors such as intimacy, openness, and presence. The quality of the therapeutic connection, especially the responsive empathy and Presence of the therapist, support the effort to discover and articulate how relationship lives in the mind. In addition, inquiring deeply singles out the contemplative dimension of connection, the felt sense of Being as an important factor in psychological change.[3]

The current chapter—"Reflections on Connection"—considers some of the important determinants of both the external and internal surfaces of connection. This broad overview of relational issues is intended to serve as a guide to issues which are important to explore in inquiring deeply, as in any relational psychotherapy. It is also intended to show how mindful awareness and self-reflection can amplify and expand upon psychodynamic exploration. These will be illustrated in the two detailed clinical transcripts that are included in a later section of the chapter.

Attachment

As is well known, attachment patterns are forged in the crucible of our earliest relationships and are the main formative influence in psychological life (Wallin, 2007). Attachment patterns are the building blocks of every relationship, and the quality of our relationships, in turn, directly determines our quality of well-being. The most basic relational needs are for contact, connection, and love. Fortunately, when early development doesn't lead to healthy attachments, we can form new connections that have the potential for repairing these patterns and healing relational wounds.

Fanning out from core attachment needs are a myriad of other relationally based needs: needs for dependency and belonging, for separateness and togetherness, for freedom and autonomy (among others). These themes are woven into the fabric of every intimate relationship and comprise the warp and woof of human life. They create a dynamic dance of movement *toward* and *away from* others.

Developmentally, experience is organized through patterns of connection/ interconnection: first through physical contact with mother and her attention to our bodily needs; later, through our mental connection with mother, father, siblings, and others. In this way, we learn about our own mind and the minds of others.

Our ongoing subjective experience in life carries these imprints of our early attachment figures and our relationships with them. Our needs and how significant others do/do not meet them also create the template for personality to form. This becomes the blueprint for how experience gets organized and who we become.[4]

When we inquire deeply into problems, it is most often this personality level— our patterns of attachment and our defenses against attachment-related pain—that is salient. Therefore, if we are to live productively with our personalities and with our problems (and other people!), it is of paramount importance to develop a deep emotional understanding about the relational dimension of experience.

The more clearly we can see where we are stuck, the better we can untangle our psychological "knots." By reflecting on what happens in our lives and looking into ourselves, we can discover a great deal about how we organize our experiences. Often, however, we can see our patterns most clearly in the mirror of another. For this reason, exploration of relational (or other) problems is optimally accomplished within a psychotherapeutic framework. And so, we inquire deeply, together.

As a preliminary to looking more deeply into this method, I will first review some of the key dimensions of relationship as they are understood in contemporary psychoanalysis. This synthesis of psychoanalytic and intuitive ideas provides a useful narrative foundation for understanding relationships, and it will also help orient the reader as to where I am coming from in the clinical work described in subsequent sections of the chapter.

Becoming Separate

In clinical terms, one preliminary distinction which may be useful is between *separation* and the experience of *separateness*.

Becoming separate—achieving separateness—is a developmental process. The conceptualization of separation and its correlative, individuation, first came from the work of the psychoanalyst Margaret Mahler in the 1950s, who believed that the original state of mind of a baby at birth is undifferentiated from the surround and lacking in any essential separateness. In Mahler's view, a sense of self emerges only after complex developmental events that she described as "hatching" from an original experience of symbiosis (Mahler, 1965).

Naturalistic studies of infancy have since made it very clear that Mahler was wrong in some of her primary assumptions. There is an innate experience of self present from the earliest moments of life (Stern, 1985),[5] not the primary state of symbiosis that Mahler presupposed. Be that as it may, separation and individuation are very important processes psychologically. Differentiation, based in the similarity and differences between ourselves and others, is a closely related process.

Taken together, these give rise to the development of a differentiated sense of self-identity.[6]

Along with differentiation, the progressive mastering of separation challenges is an essential aspect of becoming separate. "Separation" describes the state of being apart from, or the act of separating from, someone or something that we are attached to. Separations are an intrinsic, constant, and unavoidable feature of human life. But why is separation so challenging?

This question circles back to the crucial importance of connection, attachment, and relationship. Connection is essential to a felt sense of safety and security; to basic trust. In the absence of a needed connection, anxiety arises, signaling danger. Therefore, anxiety over separation is fundamental and prototypical. Additionally, the anxiety that arises from being separate can itself feel threatening, so that separation anxiety readily feeds on itself. It may progress to panic, or generate phobic reactions to being alone. It may push someone into problematic connection to others and all manner of dysfunctional behavior.

As emphasized in previous chapters, psychological development depends upon the presence, empathy, and attuned soothing of an Other. It is in relationship that we learn to modulate feelings.

This entails the development of highly complex functions of self-regulation, which is often understood in the metaphor of digesting and metabolizing experience. Optimally, we develop this capacity in childhood with the nurture of secure attachments, but it can also be developed in adult life—in love relationship, friendships, or in psychotherapy. Be that as it may, until these capacities are acquired, there can be little sense of safety. To the degree that one cannot manage separation and other anxieties, one remains psychologically reliant on the other.[7] (This is discussed further below in relation to the capacity to be alone.)

In summary, separateness is a psychological capacity that requires the support of secure attachment bonds in order to mature. We can only be comfortably separate to the degree that we have individuated and mastered the anxiety of separation. Managing separation stress allows the development of a healthy and confident experience of autonomy; without this capacity, there is difficulty with separation and psychological distress results. Coping with separation gives rise to structures of mind that house a comfortable experience of being separate, as well as the capacity for connection and intimacy.

Separation and separateness are processes I emphasize in inquiring deeply with others. Separations large and small are often triggers for emotional reactions and it is useful to bring mindful awareness to them. It is also useful to notice transitions— they mark the separation between different "chapters" of our experiences with others (such as the loss of an old relationship or the beginning of a new one); different epochs of time (such as graduation from school); changes in place (such as vacation or moving); or even simple transition points in time (such as the rhythm of mornings and evenings, weekends and weekdays). Inquiring deeply also focuses on ruptures in relationship: events in which connection to a significant other is disrupted. Often such events are construed as problems, or even felt-catastrophes. From the perspective of inquiring deeply, they are opportunities, key moments for insight and growth.

People suffer from the lack of secure connection to others in a myriad of ways. In this chapter, I delineate several different varieties of problems with separateness and separation:

1   *Painful experiences of separateness.* These range from loneliness to commonplace social anxiety (self-consciousness, social awkwardness, and similar insecurities) to debilitating shyness. Feeling painfully out of place, not fitting in, or not belonging are other common themes.
2   Separation anxiety *per se* (inability to be alone, anxious clinging to attachment figures, fear of abandonment, and the like).
3   Problems with *establishing and/or sustaining intimate connections.*

These three "kinds" of separation-related problems tend to occur in tandem with deep-seated relationship and attachment issues. Although I am conceptualizing different types of problems, in actuality they tend to be intermingled rather than clearly delineated. They vary in many ways: in different diagnostic groups, different people, and even in the same person at different times. Each of the following clinical "sketches" presents a brief (fictive) example of a "presenting problem" which revolves around separateness or separation. Each vignette describes a fictive narrative "history" but is a composite of real experiences with real people that I have come to know in my consulting room. (In a later section of the chapter, I will present some actual clinical examples in considerable detail.)

Prototypical Presentations of Relationship Problems

6.1   Social Anxiety: *A 25-year-old woman feels painfully awkward, separate, and out-of-place in groups. She reports having been shy as a child, embarrassed by her alcoholic mother whom she experienced as loud, obnoxious, and socially inappropriate. She carries a lot of shame, which manifests in current-day social inhibition. In groups she often feels like she has nothing to say.*

6.2   Intimacy Anxiety and Avoidance: *A 43-year-old woman is very high functioning and has a satisfying life in most respects, including a lot of friends. She feels generally comfortable socially in both small and large groups of people. Yet she feels paralyzed when it comes to dating. Whenever there is a prospective love interest in the picture, she becomes agitated and unsettled; anxiously checking her phone for messages, she finds it difficult to focus on her work. Because of this discomfort, she prefers to remain single.*

6.3   Attachment Hunger: *A 21-year-old college student came to treatment at the behest of her parents, who were concerned about her academic performance at school. In a phone conversation with the mother prior to my first meeting with the patient, she described her daughter's problem as attention deficit disorder. In the clinical work, it quickly became apparent, however, that the real problem was how much time the patient spent compulsively engaging with her Facebook friends. During the course of treatment, she came to understand that she had a kind of "internet addiction," and that this "attachment hunger" was fed by an undercurrent of anxiety about how she would be able to navigate in her adult life once she graduates from school (separation anxiety).*

6.4   Separation Panic/Agoraphobia: *A 54-year-old man lives a very limited life ostensibly because of a heart condition. He feels comfortable only when at home with his four cats. The anxiety he experiences whenever he goes out tends to cause palpitations, which validate his fears and keep him trapped in an agoraphobic lifestyle.*

6.5   "Love Addiction"[8]: *A 44-year-old gay man is troubled by the serial sexual encounters he has with men he meets on the internet. Because he has little tolerance for being alone, he repeatedly and rather indiscriminately "hooks up with" any available partner. The pattern of "one-night stands" is increasingly unsatisfying to him. Despite his wish to have a long-term partner, he has little idea of what underlies his inability to form a lasting intimate relationship or why this pattern persists.*

6.6 "Commitment Phobia"[9]: *A 35-year-old woman asks for help with her love life. She is stuck in a pattern of serial relationships with men. Each is initially exciting but none leads successfully to a lasting connection. The pattern is the same each time: following an early phase of idealization, the patient discovers flaws in the potential partner that she considered to be "deal breakers." She can't bring herself to "settle" for any of these men and keeps hoping the next one will be "the one." Her wish to have children makes the predicament increasingly urgent.*

6.7 Detachment: *A 58-year-old woman comes for help with chronic depression that began following the death of her dog. She is a successful professional who lives a life exclusively focused on work; she keeps her distance from other people. Her dog was her significant other. In the process of psychoanalytic psychotherapy, a profound intimacy developed in the therapeutic connection. The patient came to understand that—contrary to what she had initially described—she does bond to people, but with bonds of avoidance. She evocatively described this as "tethering by non-tethering."*

Typically, the narrative picture of a person and his or her problems, such as the ones given here, comes into clear focus only after a process of psychotherapy. Once the leading edge of the problem has been understood, and as a way of understanding it more deeply, I often prescribe questions for contemplative or reflective inquiry, as will be shown in the clinical examples given below.

Creating opportunities to practice with problems as mindfulness "homework" between sessions is one of the things that patients seem to appreciate most about the way I work.

This creative aspect of applied mindfulness is also one of the things that *I* have appreciated about the way I work. "Prescribing" questions for contemplative or reflective inquiry often provides "data" that help me in my clinical understanding of a particular person. Experimenting creatively with this process has been one of the major catalysts for the reflections that have gone into the writing of this book.

Some case examples follow below. Before giving those examples, however, I will first present some clinical reflections that show how I conceptualize problems with separateness and separation.

Fusions and Confusions

One important dimension of emotional experience that I emphasize in psychotherapy is the need for soothing, merger, and fusion. Most basically, the "urge to merge"—as I describe it in shorthand—is the striving to join with another in a way that provides a feeling of comfort and safety. One searches for the perfect other: a soul mate.

The most archaic forms of merger experience are states of drifting and floating first felt in the womb, and then, after birth, during nursing; the baby relaxes into an experience of safe unity with mother. Later, merger needs are expressed in the wish to be held by others, expressed in many different forms, both literally and figuratively. Most often, the urge to merge is expressed in sexual and other aspects of love relationships. With or without merger experience, the need for soothing and self-soothing remains primary throughout the life span. Unmet needs for merger may be seen in the search for fusional experiences through the use of drugs or alcohol (or meditation). Alternatively, they may be expressed in dysfunctional relationship patterns such as dependent-clinging or promiscuity. "Love addiction," the clinical example described in 6.5 above, gives one example of a difficulty that can be understood in these terms. In place of healthy connection, the person seeks confluent experiences, the experience of fusion with the Other.

Frustrated needs for connection, including attachment hunger and the urge to merge, often result also in unclearly delineated boundaries between self and other. We may think of this blurring of boundaries as a literal "confusion" between self and other—needs for fusion that are not worked out and therefore create a problematic surface in the relationship. Enmeshment of this kind is one of the most common sources of problems in intimate relationships. However, participants are typically unaware of it, as it tends to have been learned within the family of origin and, as such, is accepted and not recognized as problematic. Moreover, enmeshment patterns tend to be perpetuated from one generation to the next.

Relationships based on the urge to merge don't have a good probability of working out very well, for a number of different reasons. When the intersubjective intersection is confused or enmeshed, it may be difficult for the two people involved to discern clearly who is doing what, to whom: for example, each person may be angry but may see the anger as originating in the other. When such confusion operates in both directions at once—which it typically does—each person is likely to defend being right and a fight may often ensue. This tendency toward blaming is one of the most common and stubborn sticking points in interpersonal conflict. It is often the source of "irreconcilable differences" in couples.

Another common source of difficulty is the tendency to make unwise concessions to the wants or needs of the other. To the extent that it is felt as essential to maintain a relational connection at all costs, pathological accommodations may result (Brandschaft et al., 2010). For example, it is common in couples for one person to engage in rote forgiveness in response to betrayals by the other in order to protect the survival of the relationship. In essence, the person who accommodates effectively renounces his or her authentic feelings, which may be pragmatic in the short run but which breeds resentment or other difficulties over time.

A full description of the kinds of psychological problems that can be traced to problematic needs for merger and fusion is beyond the scope of this book, but several are illustrated in the sections that follow.

Core Intimacy Fears

Inquiring deeply focuses mindful awareness on the dynamic exchange that is continually unfolding at the boundary between self and other (the "intersubjective intersection"). The fundamental themes about separateness discussed in the present chapter are an important and basic facet of our connection with others. Psychologically, it is helpful to notice the balance between needs to feel connected, on the one hand, and needs to be autonomous and separate, on the other. This dynamic is a major choreographic theme in the dance of relationship.

When one or both partners have strong fears of intimacy, toxic relationship patterns often result. Primal fears and strong affects are involved in issues of connection to and disconnection from others. On the one hand, core fears of abandonment propel a movement *toward* others (or, in extreme form, desperate efforts to generate experiences of fusion). Conversely, claustrophobic anxieties fuel the need to stay separate and move *away from* others (or push others away). As a result of these anxieties, relationships will tend to become either enmeshed (too close or fused) or, conversely, distant or detached. Moreover, when separation anxiety, fear of abandonment, or fears of getting trapped are too great to be effectively modulated, they may instead be *acted out* in destructive ways. The kinds of problems that result are among the most common reasons people seek psychotherapy.

The essential predicament may be conceptualized as a core conflict between approach and avoidance: a struggle between fears of being alone, on the one hand, and fears of being interpersonally suffocated, on the other. When someone feels too afraid of being alone, he or she is likely to pathologically accommodate, doing whatever is felt to be necessary to sustain the tie that is needed with the other. On the other hand, when someone is motivated by the need to avoid being dominated or overwhelmed by the other, this may result in a pattern of disengagement or pathological self-sufficiency.

The dynamics of core intimacy fears are most clearly seen in love relationships, where the two poles of this core intimacy conflict often comprise a kind of relational teeter-totter. Sometimes the roles are polarized, with the partners on opposite "sides"; for example, one person pursues while the other person distances. It is as if one person carries the fear of being alone, while the other carries the fear of being dominated by the other.

Inquiring deeply into these patterns, awareness can be brought to bear on how connection and disconnection are experienced at different times or in different relationships. I have found it especially fascinating to observe in conjoint therapy how, when one person shifts their usual pattern of behavior, this will often engender a shift in the partner also, or even result in a complete reversal in the dynamics between the two. In one couple I worked with, for example, one partner initially appeared to be the more secure and aloof of the two, but as his wife asserted her independence, his own underlying jealousy and insecurity became apparent.

Deep emotional understanding of how these relational and attachment patterns came into being during childhood provides a narrative context for conscious awareness of how they operate in adult life.

As we investigate when and how we seek connection with others, most often we find one of two basic motivations. The first is a core psychological longing for comfort, validation, mirroring, reassurance, and protection; the second is the quest for shared experience. However, the companion piece to these strivings for connection is a deep longing to actualize ourselves, to find an authentic voice to express who we are, and to deepen our sense of vitality and aliveness.

We are vitalized by our relationships with others. Indeed, relationships are among the basic building blocks of subjectivity itself. It is through the interactive interpersonal world that psychological development occurs and that *self* is constituted (Kohut, 1971).[10] This topic will be explored further in Chapters 8, 9, and 10; suffice it to say for now that in relationship with others, needs for connection must be balanced with needs for autonomy. On the one hand, in being connected to others we find the safety of bonds that allow the quintessentially social animal to survive. On the other hand, in being separate we create space for authentic self-expression of our deepest truths.

Relationships Held in Mind

In the previous sections of this chapter, the focus has been on difficulties establishing safe bonds with others that allow experiences both of being connected and of being separate.

The importance of having basic emotional needs met by a primary *Other* has been highlighted. The quintessential point is that a sense of internal security is built on a foundation of having needs ("selfobject needs") met in a "good-enough" manner. This is how people develop comfort in modulating their emotional states and in simply being who they are. Issues with unmet basic needs linger in the lives of many adults, most frequently expressed in the form of relationship problems.

Beyond exploring actual connections with relationship partners, it is equally important to look at how relationships are represented in the mind. In experience-near language, we need to develop awareness of how we "hold relationship in mind"— our point of view not only about particular others, but also about relationship itself. Point of view is inclusively defined here and specifically encompasses awareness of the process of relationship as it changes in the mind from moment to moment.

The capacity to hold another in mind as I am describing it here has two primary components: what one holds in one's own mind and what one imagines is held in mind (or not) by another. These two sets of thoughts and feelings develop concomitantly in early life. The classic example given is that of a toddler who wanders off down the beach away from her mother. Totally absorbed in looking at seashells, the child suddenly becomes dismayed when it occurs to her that she has forgotten about her mother. At the same moment another frightening thought occurs: "If I have forgotten my mother, then perhaps my mother has forgotten me."

We need to feel held in the mind of others in order to assure ourselves that we are safe. This is part of what is called "object constancy." This representation of "held in mind" mediates the experience of relationship.

Holding relationship in mind involves a complex web of subjective thoughts and feelings about self, other, and relationship. It is part of the assumptive framework which underlies all experience: the internal surface of relationship. Every individual's matrix of meanings is different, but regardless of the particulars, how relationship is held in mind tends to be enacted or expressed in relationship and so always has a major bearing on quality of life. Also, having a deep understanding of relationships (and how they are held in mind) invites the possibility of consciously participating in creating better connections with others. This too is an important determinant of quality of life.

The following are some observations that patients have reported to me in the course of their inquiries into how they hold relationship in mind. They reveal a few of the ways in which anxiety about connection can present itself in the mind.[11]

- *I saw that I am preoccupied with whether or not my partner feels connected to me in any given moment.*
- *My whole meditation is usually filled with imaginary conversations with other people.*
- *I'm always trying to figure out what people are thinking about me.*
- *I constantly give myself a grade on my relationship performance.*
- *I notice that I'm always trying to find something to say. I wonder what I am afraid of? What would be in the space if I stopped trying so hard?*
- *It seems like my concern with what I should be feeling—what I think a "normal" person would feel in that same situation—takes the place of what I am feeling.*
- *I think in my family I was taught that it was bad to want to be separate. When I would go out with friends, I always thought my mother would be constantly anxious until I got home.*
- *When I'm not with you, I spend a lot of time trying to figure out where you are and what you're doing. I think that's a way I try to stay connected to you. Otherwise, I imagine that you would never think about me in your regular life.*
- *I noticed that I'm always comparing myself to someone else, even when I'm doing something all by myself. Then I thought it's as if someone else were there in my mind along with me. Maybe that's a way to keep myself company when I'm lonely.*
- *My "inner tyrant" is always criticizing me!*

Framed here as the "inner surface of relationship," these kinds of observations and insights about what is held in mind also reveal a lot about "self-representations" (Chapter 8) and/or concepts about others (Chapter 9). In whatever context, they become the basis for therapeutic narrative about the patient's connections to others. Inquiring deeply about how relationship is held in mind heightens awareness of the *process* of relationship and what it connects to at a deep emotional level.[12]

There is also an underlying agenda in inquiring deeply: to call attention to how relationship is constructed in the mind. When it can be clearly seen that "connectedness" is a subjective state which morphs and changes over time[13]—that it is in fact constructed from the stories we tell—this shines a light on *relationship as process*. Rather than reifying a particular moment or set of moments as the "truth" about the relationship, there is now an opportunity to open that story to retellings, and therefore to the emergence of new possibilities.

Many people unconsciously hold the view that relationship is about "how it turns out" rather than about the journey. By highlighting the folly of that view, inquiring deeply confers leverage in the effort to bring about change. Mindfulness and self-reflection are key elements in creating a constructive context for change (see Chapter 10).

Inquiring Deeply into Relational Problems

There are many ways that mindful awareness and self-reflection can be brought to bear on the exploration of dysfunctional behavior and/or emotional problems, both in individuals and couples. As has been described throughout this book, inquiring deeply takes a psychodynamic approach: it seeks to expand present-centered awareness at the same time as it explores developmental roots of experience and seeks to facilitate deeper emotional self-understanding.

Some of the general topics for clinical inquiry were delineated in Chapter 4, and hopefully the relational "landscape" that can be investigated has become clearer in the current chapter. Questions and issues for inquiry emerge spontaneously in the natural unfolding of the clinical process (as will be illustrated in the clinical vignettes to follow). Generally speaking, important goals in inquiring deeply include:

- *Coming to a deeper understanding of one's relational needs and patterns.*

    It is important to learn to recognize core relational fears, such as feeling trapped or suffocated, fears of abandonment, etc., and to see how one defends against them.

    This involves both the conceptual understanding of how one reacts and responds, as well as mindful awareness of patterns as they arise.

    To give just a couple of examples that have come up in recent days, someone may be unconsciously organized around getting others to take care of them, or may organize themselves around keeping the upper hand with their partner in order to stay safe.

- *Learning to recognize the relational triggers for one's emotional upsets.*
    Becoming aware of areas of relational "dysjunction."

It is important to recognize points at which one's relationship with another becomes entangled due to mutual areas of enmeshment/confusion. (The "cue" that a dysjunction has occurred is emotional upset in one or both people.)

• *Attuning attention to how relationships are being "held in mind."*

Two Different Modes of Listening:
Close Process Attention vs. Mindfulness of Connection

It may be instructive for the reader to distinguish two kinds of clinical focus. Here, I will describe them; in a later section of the chapter, they will be illustrated in two detailed clinical vignettes. Both modes of listening are interwoven in psychotherapy; both involve the therapist listening with the "third ear" to what is said, as well as to what is *not* said. Listening in this way helps uncover currents of the mindstream that lie beneath the surface of awareness. As was described in Chapter 5, the therapist listens to the patient and also listens to the listening of the patient.

Close process attention is the exploration of psychotherapeutic content and process with interpretive focus on anxieties and the way the mind defends against them (Gray, 1994).[14] Close process attention can be applied to anything the patient talks about, but in the psychoanalytic paradigm, emphasis is placed on the interpersonal encounter in the therapeutic here and now. Awareness of what goes on *interactively* in psychotherapy reveals the internal surface of relationship in the mind.

Inquiring deeply as a psychoanalytic approach focuses close process attention on what Darlene Ehrenberg (1991) calls in the title of her book "the intimate edge" of experience. Roughly equivalent to what is referred to elsewhere in this book as the intersubjective intersection, the intimate edge between self and other is defined as "the nature of the integration, the quality of contact, what goes on between, including what is enacted and what is communicated affectively or unconsciously … it is the point of maximum and acknowledged contact at any given moment in a relationship without fusion, and without violation of the separateness and integrity of each participant" (Ehrenberg, 1991, p. 33). It is the living surface of our relationship with others.

Awareness of the intimate edge of experience is valuable therapeutically because each time something is identified and explicitly acknowledged, it also changes what is occurring. Over time, new experiences that happen in the therapy relationship become incorporated into an evolving process of change and growth.

Mindfulness of connection is the second of two basic aspects of clinical attention in inquiring deeply. It is the process of paying mindful attention to the living reality of relationship with the other in the moment: body sensation, breath, feelings, body language, facial expression, words, and thoughts. These comprise the patient's lived experience of being in relationship. An especially important focus in inquiring deeply is the *felt sense* of the therapist–patient relationship and the shifting quality of connection or disconnection between.

Mindfulness of connection as I use the term does not necessarily entail any specific category of experience or explicit meditative focus. It refers to conscious awareness of *any* aspect of the experience of being with someone else: the experience of connection, plus the *knowing* that this is one's experience, moment by moment as it is occurring.

Mindful awareness of connection encompasses the entire spectrum of experience that arises in the mind. It includes sensations, feelings, and mind states ("objects of mind" familiar from Buddhist mindfulness practice), but also *psychological awareness*, inclusive of the narratives and psychological explanations that are generally eschewed in Buddhist practice.

The scope of mindful awareness gradually deepens as we bring conscious attention to the interwoven threads in the rich fabric of subjective experience. Because the therapist is a relationship partner in this work, his or her mindfulness has a big influence on the deepening of the shared experience.

Mindfulness of connection in inquiring deeply is somewhat distinct from relational (interpersonal) mindfulness practice *per se*. Whereas the latter is a form of Buddhist-based mindfulness meditation (sometimes taught in MBSR format), mindfulness of connection focuses instead on psychological awareness rather than dharma practice. This difference can be further delineated by contrast with "Insight Dialogue," a form of relational dharma practice developed by Gregory Kramer and now widely taught (Kramer, 2007).

Though secular in language and format, Insight Dialogue is deeply rooted in Buddhist psychology. It is a process of contemplative inquiry with another (or others) in which attention is focused on each of the four foundations of mindfulness, facilitated by meditative guidelines (instructions) for relaxing, allowing, and observing what comes up during the process. Essentially, Insight Dialogue is a process of meditating out loud with a partner, focusing in parallel on various topics of contemplation.

In contrast, inquiring deeply unfolds as a process of *interaction*, a deep conversation about what is happening between us, as it is happening. It is more interactive than Insight Dialogue and emphasizes the personal experience of the relationship between self and other in the moment.

In inquiring deeply, psychotherapeutic awareness may gradually deepen to include the various phenomena of "Buddhist mind" that comprise the third and fourth foundations of mindfulness (mindfulness of mind). For example, inquiry may be expanded to include attention to experiences such as greed, aversion, delusion, and other aspects of the mind which are described in Buddhism. Among the most important areas of inquiry are various aspects of self-experience and self-identity, discussed under the heading of Subjectivity in the next chapter.

Mindful Clinical Attention

Mindfulness of connection and close process attention are two elements of mindful clinical attention. They are not distinct dimensions of clinical focus but are, rather, interwoven threads in the clinician's *experience* of the patient and of the therapeutic interaction.

In seeking to clarify the essential components of mindful clinical attention in inquiring deeply, several additional points come to mind.

First, mindfulness of connection and exploration of relational suffering come together in inquiring deeply in the framework of relational psychotherapy. It should be emphasized that mindful clinical attention encompasses many layers of the *felt sense* of being with another, not only the bare attention of mindfulness meditation. It is inclusive of the experience of intimacy or distance, the complex texture of the feelings evoked by the other, and the mental representations of Self and Other. This focus on the experience of connectedness helps illuminate the dynamics of relationship and illuminates the mechanisms by which we get entangled in interpersonal suffering. Mindful clinical attention also helps the patient develop the capacity to self-reflect on the nuances of emotional life. Both process and content of what emerges can be valuable points of focus.

Second, I want to address the question often raised by skeptical clinicians as to whether mindfulness of connection really adds anything new to close process attention. Psychoanalysts, in particular, often tend to think that mindful awareness is already implicit in process of clinical work: isn't *every* good clinician necessarily mindful, just by virtue of the conscious and self-reflective work of psychoanalysis?

I do agree that dynamic psychotherapy (and relational therapy in particular) entails a kind of home-grown mindfulness. The *felt sense* of clinical process is not dissimilar to the intuitive awareness cultivated in mindfulness meditation. However, the reader is reminded that mindfulness is a dimension of awareness, not a discrete *state*. Mindfulness meditation practice hones the clinician's capacity to attend with depth and clarity of focus to the here-and-now of the therapeutic relationship.

Inquiring deeply begins from the premise that the human mind is relationally organized. Relationships are the hub around which each person's life revolves; they are the fundamental point of reference used to make sense of experience. One bottom line in inquiring deeply about relationship which derives from dharma practice is an emphasis on discerning the difference between subjective experience and external (so-called "objective") reality. Inquiring deeply highlights how the external world is *constructed by* the internal one (and vice versa); man's mind mirrors a universe that mirrors man's mind (Pearce, 1971).

In the clinical vignettes which follow, the reader will be able to see how mindful noticing, investigation, and self-reflection about interpersonal life can be incorporated into the process of working with emotional problems (within relational psychotherapy or by oneself). Sometimes, inquiry arises spontaneously; sometimes the therapist guides the process as a psychotherapeutic intervention or strategy.

Clinical Illustrations of Inquiring Deeply

The frame for the psychotherapeutic dialogue in inquiring deeply is provided by the patient's relationalship or emotional problems. As with any psychoanalytic approach, special emphasis is also placed on what is occurring in the therapeutic here and now. In this section, two clinical vignettes are presented in some detail to show the overlapping of close process attention and mindfulness of connection.

Clinical Illustration 6.8: Allen, Part I

Allen was a 35-year-old mortgage broker who was having trouble control-ling his anger. He reported problematic outbursts of temper both in the work-place and with his wife. He was referred to psychotherapy for further help after completing an MBSR-based anger management program.

Allen was socially pleasant and mild-mannered, but seemed tense and rather depressed and had what struck me as a sullen edge.

In the session excerpted here, Allen has just shared a nightmare in which some violent and awful things happened. He found the dream quite disturbing and wanted my help sorting out its meaning. His surface associations were to a movie he had recently seen that was quite upsetting. Based on material discussed in our recent clinical hours, I suggested that perhaps the dream also expressed Allen's fears of what could happen if he allowed himself to deeply feel his own anger.

M.S. *I noticed that just now when I was sharing my thoughts about your dream that you looked sort of uncomfortable. Were you aware of feel-ing uncomfortable?*

A. *No, not really. I thought your interpretation was probably correct. I am afraid of what might happen if I really let my anger out. Umm, well now that you mention it, it did cross my mind that maybe you thought only a very angry person would have a dream like that.*

M.S. *You were concerned about my judgments of you … that perhaps I might think you as some sort of monster, like the criminal in your dream …*

A. *Yes.*

M.S. *You might consider the possibility that there is a part of you that makes those kind of judgments about yourself.*

A. *Yes, I think you are right about that. I don't like it that I have such vio-lent dreams. It must mean that deep down I am a violent person.*

In this first part of the session, I touched on some implications of the psy-chological content of the dream Allen had presented. Taking note of feel-ings expressed on his face, I brought his attention to what he was feeling. I also interpreted what I presumed might be beneath the surface: con-cerns about my judgments about him. This is the essence of "close process attention."

At this clinical juncture, I might have taken up Allen's narrative of himself as a violent person, but I chose instead to focus further on the psychothera-peutic connection in the here and now:

M.S. I wonder if there was anything you perceived or sensed in me, or between us, that made you feel that I might be judging you ...

A.   Not that I'm aware of ... that's a familiar feeling though. I often worry about how others are perceiving me ...
      [Allen looks down, apparently uncomfortable]

M.S. Yes. I'm reminded of what we've talked about regarding your older brother; your concern with how he views you ...
      Do you consciously worry about how I perceive you?

A.   [pause, re-engages with intense eye contact] Sometimes ...

M.S. [pause] How about in this moment?

A.   No, I don't think so. Just for a minute there when we were talking about my dream ...

M.S. Okay. I'm still wondering, though, about what is coming up for you with me right now.

A.   I don't know exactly. I'm not sure I understand what you're asking ...

M.S. Nothing specific. I'm just asking about how you are experiencing our relationship in this moment ... whatever you're aware of ... maybe a feeling ... maybe just the underlying attitude in your mind right now.

A.   [closes eyes and looks inward] I am aware of feeling tense, my teeth are kind of clenched and my jaw feels tight ... [long silent pause]

M.S. Maybe check out what it feels like with your eyes open ...

A.   I feel very exposed.

M.S. What are you concerned that I might see?

A.   I don't know. I just don't like the feeling of being looked at.

As we had this exchange, I became aware, not only of Allen's initial discomfort, but also of the fact that my probing seemed to exacerbate the feeling. Shifts in his gaze alerted me to the fact that our exchange was highly charged for him. When I went on to ask him directly how he was experiencing our connection, my sense was that he avoided the interpersonal moment by "performing mindfulness" (perhaps in a manner he learned in MBSR) rather than engaging in a more connected and authentic way. In hindsight, I thought that I had perhaps been too direct and confronting. In any event, I made an effort at this clinical juncture to steer the conversation in a more comfortable direction. I spoke empathically about his feeling exposed, framing it as a kind of self-consciousness or shame reaction, and suggested that it might be useful for Allen to pay closer attention to these kinds of feelings when they came up in daily life, to see what he/we could learn from them (therapeutic suggestion for strategic inquiry).

In ensuing weeks, this turned out to be a very generative area of investigation. Allen discovered that there were several people at work with whom he felt quite self-conscious and exposed. Mostly these were people in positions of authority over him, and mostly they were people he disliked. This led to some important discoveries about the way reactive anger and dislike covered over and protected against feelings of vulnerability.

In the work with Allen described above, for instance, I called attention to something which I had just observed in the therapeutic here and now. Using close process attention, I interpreted the feelings I read on Allen's face and speculated aloud about what his inner experience might be. But I also tried to focus clinical attention on Allen's *experience* of the therapeutic connection. I had hoped this would open up into deeper mindfulness of connection, but things didn't happen that way (perhaps because I had triggered a defensive response).

In some subsequent work I will now describe, I sought to help Allen open further to the therapeutic relationship by using a meditative/hypnotic induction for deepening mindfulness of connection:

Clinical Illustration 6.9: Allen, Part 2

> M.S.   *I have an idea ... would you like to try a little experiment?*
> *[He nods agreement]*
>
> M.S.   *Just relax your gaze ... no need to look directly at me, just let your eyes go softly out of focus ... just putting yourself in a receptive frame of mind ...*

[pause to allow him to absorb this instruction]

Nothing special that you need to do, just noticing how you are feeling right now ...

[pause]

Bringing gentle attention to the experience of the two of us sitting here, in this room, here and now ...

[pause]

Aware of the sensations of your own breathing ... and of me sitting across from you, also breathing ...

    And now allowing yourself to become aware of the space around us. Perhaps imagining how the molecules of breath expanding outward into the entire space of this room ...

    So now there is a sense of both foreground and background: each of us in the foreground, then the background space that contains us ...

[pause]

See what happens with that experience of figure and ground as you sit with it. Just relax into the experience and see how it changes from moment to moment. Notice if your perception of figure and ground is steady, or if it shifts back and forth ...

[pause]

M.S.   What's that like for you right now?

A.   It's very relaxing. I feel so much more comfortable than a few minutes ago! So here!

M.S.   You sound surprised.

A.   Yes ... it really shows me what I miss out on by being so uptight all the time.

I do not often use guided meditation (or hypnotic induction, as the case may be) in psychotherapy, but this process emerged naturally in this therapeutic moment and I decided to "go with it."[15] My felt sense of our connection and of Allen's state of mind told me intuitively that Allen was available to opening and deepening in that moment. There was no premeditation about this on my part, simply a spontaneous responsiveness to what was emerging and what suggestions would invite that deepening. The figure/ground metaphor is one I often use; it calls attention to the "space of connection" or to the flow of energy at the intersubjective intersection.

The next vignette illustrates another way that dharma practice and psychotherapy may overlap. It tells part of the clinical story of Tom, a patient who sought my help for problems feeling connected to others.

Clinical Illustration 6.10: Tom: Alive or Dead?

Feeling painfully separate was the presenting complaint of my patient Tom, a pervasively depressed man who suffered with a chronic sense of isolation and separateness from everyone and everything. He expressed feeling as though he were living life through a gauze curtain. For a period of time prior to the work described in the following vignette, we had deeply explored the relational underpinnings of his feelings of disconnection and isolation. He had experienced a very lonely early life. Although reasonably content in a long marriage, Tom had few relationships apart from his wife and grown children.

Tom experienced great relief in feeling empathically understood and formed an intense, dependent transference connection to me. But apart from this, his global sense of disconnection from life remained quite intractable.

Tom had been doing sitting practice at a Soto Zen temple for more than 20 years. Although he had no experience in the Rinzai tradition or in koan practice, he read about a koan that intrigued him and which became the subject of much discussion between us.

The koan in question tells the story of a Zen student accompanying his teacher on a condolence call.[16] The student, much concerned with existential issues of life and death, bangs on the coffin and asks his teacher imperatively, "Alive or dead?" but the Master replies only, "I will not say alive or dead." Despite repeated and escalating entreaties, the Master refuses to answer and won't even say why he won't answer (see Appendix 6.1).

Tom identified with the student in the story—both with his concern about ultimate truths of life and death and with his urgency. I understood from our several years of work together that Tom often felt rather dead himself. He was in urgent need of finding his own aliveness. This is what had motivated him to begin Zen practice in the first place.

As we explored his thoughts and feelings about the koan, I also speculated that perhaps Tom resonated with the frustration of having needs go unmet by a significant Other—moreover, withheld for reasons which felt both arbitrary and incomprehensible. These themes were familiar from Tom's own childhood experience. The koan was a good fit for his life narrative, and highlighted the emotional core of his despair.

At our next session, Tom reported the following dream:

I was visiting a monastery. In order for me to practice the virtue of patience, the monks wanted me to climb into a coffin and proposed that they would lock me in. This was a terrifying prospect and I said that I would agree to get in the coffin only if they would promise not to lock it. They said okay, but once I was inside they did lock it. Somehow I broke free and I ran away in a state of great anger.

It was apparent to both Tom and me that the dream was an association to the theme in the koan, "Alive or Dead?" Overall, I found it hopeful that in his dream Tom had escaped ("lived"). Also, in our work together, we had been talking about how introverted Tom tended to be. "Withdrawal from life" is one of the basic aspects of depression—turning inward (Morgan, 2005)—and I thought this was perhaps one of the meanings of this dream visit to the monastery. Most importantly, the dream represented important relational themes, especially betrayal of trust.

As Tom continued to be engaged with the koan (and as we engaged with it together in psychotherapy), I spontaneously began probing him during sessions with the question "Alive or dead?" at various moments when I noticed changes in his affect. I often chose to ask at moments when I experienced him turning inward and away from contact with me; or, at other moments, when I experienced him shining out toward me, often with a broad smile.

Exploring mindfulness of connection in the therapeutic here and now with the probe "Alive or dead?" served to alert Tom to shifts that were occurring in his affect state. This began to have an impact on Tom's self-experience. Whereas previously he had tended to reify the state of being "dead" or damaged (a state of imprisoned isolation behind a gauze curtain), Tom gradually began to see that "dead" was a feeling state constructed moment by moment through the psychodynamic movement of withdrawal or contraction. He felt alive when he felt relationally connected to me during the hour, or "dead" when his attention turned inward toward the experience of feeling isolated, left alone with sad thoughts and feelings. "Alive or Dead?" turned into a psychodynamic inquiry and opened up insight about the way Tom's feelings were conditioned by the moment-to-moment experience of being in relation.

Intimacy with Self: The Capacity to Be Alone

For the most part, this chapter has consisted of various reflections about connection and the difficulties people have in creating and sustaining intimate relationships with others. This section focuses on a related topic: intimacy with oneself.

Capacities for connection/intimacy with oneself and with others are two interpenetrating dimensions of relationship.[17] How we relate to ourselves reflects how others have treated *us*. (In addition, it also shows how we have observed them treating themselves and others.) In this way, all relationship, including relationship to self, is constructed of elements of self and other.[18,19]

Chapters 8 and 9 will explore in greater depth what can be learned from the template of Self and Object (self and other) in psychoanalytic theory. The most basic idea, already addressed repeatedly in the present chapter, is that Self and Other comprise an intersubjective ensemble, each of which creates conditions essential for the other.

We need to be loved and cared for by others in order to develop a well-integrated sense of self; conversely, we need a well-integrated sense of self in order to have good relationships with others. Relationship with self and relationship with other are two sides of the same coin.

Putting aside until later chapters the question of what defines a "well-integrated sense of self," we can summarize the situation in this way: healthy self-experience is built upon a foundation of inner security; and inner security, in turn, depends upon having good-enough attachment experiences. The mind is based on relationship.

A good indicator of inner security—of healthy relationship with oneself—is the capacity to be comfortably alone. Some people enjoy the ability to rest easily within themselves, others not so much. In dharma talks, Jack Kornfield often illustrates this point with a quip he credits to the novelist Anne Lamott, who likens her mind to a bad neighborhood where she prefers not to go alone! In any event, in order to cultivate a more comfortable relationship with ourselves—in order to learn to enjoy our own company—it is helpful to have interests and rewarding activities. We need to be able to inhabit solitude without too much anxiety.

The development of the capacity to be alone was made famous in a classic paper by the psychoanalyst D. W. Winnicott (1965a). Winnicott was the first to articulate the idea that being comfortably alone was contingent on internalizing experiences of being alone in the presence of another.

The capacity to be alone is conferred by the experience of being held from earliest life onward (including intra-uterine life). Holding, including holding in mind, means the provision of a safe, secure, and non-impinging environment. This is one of the primary psychological roles of the m(othering). The capacity to be alone is essential in learning to tolerate separation, and without it, the development of autonomy is impeded. Moreover, the experience of being alone provides an essential emotional foundation for a sense of belonging with others.

The significance of the ability to be alone cannot be overstated; it is an essential aspect of intimacy with self. In the framework of the present chapter, the issue loops back yet again to the fact that self and other are interwoven: the capacity to be alone and the capacity to be with others are two sides of the same relational coin. Relationship with Self co-emerges along with relationship with Other(s). This idea will be unpacked in the next chapter.

Our twin needs for connection and autonomy can present a dilemma in interpersonal relationships as we try to strike a comfortable balance with another person who struggles in their own way with the same issues. To negotiate those struggles builds intimacy in the relationship. In the context of relationship with oneself the issue becomes: how can one develop an experience of a deeper intimacy with self?

It is only when we can be sufficiently intimate with ourselves that we can be comfortable both alone and *with* others (or alone with others). Whereas the common definition of "solitude" is the state of being alone, solitude (in contrast to loneliness) paradoxically implies the subjective *presence* of the other (Modell, 1993). From this perspective, loneliness can be thought of as a failed experience of solitude.

The need to connect as well as the need to be autonomous enter into all facets of lived experience, including both meditation and psychotherapy. Fortunately, the capacity to be alone—intimacy with self—can be intentionally cultivated in adult life; this is one of the principal psychological benefits of meditation practice. However, if internal experience is too frightening or chaotic, meditation may be difficult or sometimes intolerable.

Inquiring Deeply: Psychotherapy or Meditation Practice?

Inquiring deeply has aspects of both mindfulness practice and psychotherapy, so what is the best way to define its process? Should it be thought of as psychotherapy, or as awareness practice?

Delineating the basic differences between psychotherapy and meditation is itself more complex than might first appear. One might propose that meditation is a solitary activity whereas psychotherapy is an interpersonal one, but this would be an oversimplification. Buddhist meditation has elements of psychotherapy, and inquiring deeply in psychotherapy has elements of meditation.

In both meditation and psychotherapy, experiences of being alone are interpenetrated by experiences of being with others (Batchelor, 1983).[20] As described throughout this book, relationality is inherent in the organization of the mind, and this results in a dynamic interplay between aloneness (relationship to self) and connection (relationship to other). Relatedness to others is present in both meditation and psychotherapy, although certainly they present themselves differently when we sit down on the cushion vs. when we are communicating with others.

In meditation, attention is focused on the internal world, but there is an implicit conversation that goes on between different parts of ourselves, and there is always a backdrop of "relationship held in mind" (Kramer, 2007).[21] In psychotherapy, attention is focused on relationship with other, but awareness of subjective experience, especially our felt sense of things, is also essential. The autonomy of the subjective "private self" (Modell, 1993) is present even as we relate to others.

Relationships are the hub around which each person's life revolves; they are the fundamental point of reference used to make sense of experience. Relatedness is an essential part of *what's so*—a basic truth about human life—and so it behooves us as therapists to deeply understand how relationship works.

Because psychological wounds are fundamentally relational wounds, relationship is also a natural path of healing. By inquiring deeply into relationship, it becomes possible to begin to understand more clearly what is wounded, missing, or dysfunctional in someone. Deep emotional understanding of developmental psychological wounds, such as childhood trauma and neglect, and recognition of their impact on present-day life, lays the groundwork for psychological healing in psychotherapy.

Psychoanalytic theory has a lot to say about psychological healing and growth. Perhaps the most important thing it teaches us is that psychological healing is a relationally co-created event, one which always involves both people. Healing occurs when *new experience* in one person is met by empathic understanding and compassion on the part of the other. These relational conditions favor emergent moments. Chapter 5 described the dimensions of empathic attunement, resonance, presence, and compassion that contribute to such healing moments. Gradually, *corrective emotional experiences*—more properly *corrective relational experiences*[22]—forge new pathways in the brain/mind, which take the place of older, more dysfunctional patterns of behavior and feeling.

Inquiring Deeply, Relational Suffering, and the Dharma

Relational suffering is basic in human life. Sensitivity and reactivity to how we relate to others—to what others say and do (or what they don't say or don't do)—dominate much of our experience. Feeling painfully separate is frequently at the core of psychological wounds. For this reason, having a clear understanding of relational issues is at the heart of Buddhist-informed psychotherapy.

Although relational suffering is not acknowledged as such in the teachings of Buddhism, it is readily understood within the Buddhist concept of "dukkha"—the primary unsatisfactoriness that permeates our experience as human beings. As we dig down into relational dukkha, what we find there is always the same: in simple terms, not having what we want from others and/or not wanting what we do have.

This fundamental Buddhist reality does not, however, directly address the psychological complexities. Relational dukkha is held in place by layers of psychological meaning. Perhaps this point may be understood by analogy with physics: Buddhism brilliantly illuminates the basic atomic structure of suffering but does not much concern itself with the molecular configurations in which suffering presents itself. Buddhist psychology highlights the universal core elements in suffering—grasping, aversion, and ignorance—but it does not concern itself directly with the matrix of psychological factors that organize those core experiences into *meaning*.

Inquiring deeply fills in some of this territory by investigating the narrative as well as enacted meanings that organize our relational lives. It explores the complex psychological issues of relationship in a way that honors the wisdom and methods of dharma practice. Some of the differences between mindfulness in Buddhist dharma practice and mindfulness in inquiring deeply may become more clear by comparing them to each of the three Buddhist marks of existence: *dukkha* (suffering), *anicca* (impermanence), and *anatta* (no self).

Dukkha (Suffering)

In dharma practice, the experience of suffering calls attention to the fact that we have become attached to something and then investigates what we are attached to i.e., what we are holding onto, resisting letting go of, or trying to push away. The frozen ice of dukkha melts under the heat of mindful awareness until the water of experience flows smoothly. Part of this melting is the experience of letting go.

In Buddhist-informed relational therapy, by contrast, we investigate suffering with respect to the psychological needs that hold it in place. As has been emphasized throughout this chapter, relational wounds are a primary source of dukkha, and the effort in inquiring deeply is, therefore, to deeply understand as well as *feel our way into and through* the dukkha of our wounding. This may be likened to a process of untangling knots in the fabric of the psyche. Although sometimes a large area of tangle can get undone in a moment of clear seeing, more often we have to keep working with our relational knots in order to see strategically how best to loosen them. We do this by inquiring deeply into psychological problems.

Buddhist-informed psychotherapy shares with mindfulness meditation practice the aim of discerning when the mind is engaged in spinning stories ("storyteller mind"). However, in most Buddhist practice, the agenda is to notice that the mind has been "hijacked" by a story and then let it go. In contrast, inquiring deeply stays with and delves into story for the purpose of becoming aware of its impact and arriving at more constructive narratives.

There is great power simply in seeing how experience is based on story, *made of* story. Relating wisely to the stories in the mind is more nuanced than simply "letting the story go." It also entails recognizing the story; feeling it more fully; finding what has activated the telling of it; tracing its roots; and looking into what the story *means* or expresses in psychological terms. Also, the latter is constantly evolving, so seeing into the storyteller's mind is an endless process. As Hokusai says in the poem that opens the book, there is no end to seeing.

Anicca (Impermanence)

Many of the psychological dynamics described in the present chapter revolve around issues of change and loss in relationship. Nowhere is impermanence more evident. As Buddhism teaches, we are of the nature to lose everything and everyone that we hold near and dear. Apart from loss through sickness, old age, and death, life is a succession of conscious and unconscious losses as we grow from childhood to old age: the loss of the mother–child connection, the loss of youth, the loss of friends, the loss of opportunities, etc. As Judith Viorst (1986) proclaimed in the title of her well-known book, *Necessary Losses*, losses are necessary in order to develop positive identity and sense of self. Loss is the price of living.

Anatta (Non-Self)

The Buddhist view is that we suffer because we conceive of "selfhood" in ways which are fundamentally misguided. *Feeling separate* reflects a fundamental ontological error: the self is not separate from the universe of which it is a part. A remedy for this problem of reifying the self is prescribed in Buddhism. It calls for insight into **anatta** and a radical change in self-identity. Indeed, one of the purposes of Buddhist meditation practice is to generate direct experience of anatta so that this transformation can occur.

In contrast, inquiring deeply emphasizes relational experiences within the framework of ordinary self. It is a psychotherapeutic approach which highlights the defensive functions served by misguided views of self and other ("mistaken identities"). Self-identity is held in place by psychological needs. As reflective awareness is brought to bear on the various psychological layers of experience, psychological structures of self gradually become reconfigured.

In both Buddhist mindfulness practice and inquiring deeply, one goal is to develop increasing clarity about the constructed nature of self and the "personality view" that holds it in place.[23] Gradually, such experiences penetrate and transform the suffering inherent in psychological selfhood. An important part of this transformation is the reconstructing of psychological narrative, sometimes including the narrative account of self itself.

It seems fair to say that for most of us, most of the time, life is lived within the domain of ordinary self-experience.[24] And so, relational problems—human problems—tend to be pervasive and universal, even among dharma practitioners. This leads me to the conclusion that dharma practice is not "complete" with respect to the task of addressing psychological suffering.

People often object to this conclusion, sometimes strongly so. They argue that since the Buddha taught that the end of suffering was possible, if suffering has not ended in a particular instance, that speaks only to lack of mastery of the practice (Kearney, 1999). There may be some truth in this; be that as it may, it is also important to recognize that the "end to suffering" which the Buddha taught is not the same as psychological healing. Causes and conditions of psychological suffering—emotional problems—are embedded in the structure of personality and are therefore persistent, often unconsciously so.

The experience of "awakening" or "liberation"—the end of suffering promised in the Buddha's four noble truths—entails a radical shift in self-identity on another level entirely: direct experience of the truth of non-self (*anatta*). Personality does not get enlightened (Sumedho, 2007).

Inquiring Deeply vs. Dharma Practice: Reprise

Regardless of whether we are inquiring deeply in psychotherapy, meditating, self-reflecting, or engaging in dialogue with someone else at the time, experience arises when and if it does. Something comes up in the mind and we notice it. Something spontaneously "volunteers" to be noticed and/or we make some intentional choices about what path in the mind we want to follow. We can decide to inquire more deeply into something; to deepen our internal conversation.

As we continue looking, what arises includes what is "experience-near" in a psychological sense—the ordinary "stuff" of thoughts and feelings; in addition, if we are oriented to the dharma, we also see the arising of the various "objects of mind" identified in the third and fourth foundations of mindfulness in Buddhism.

Consider: the same experience can be looked at through different lenses; it doesn't "belong" to any a priori category in the mind. Psychoanalytic constructs, such as those described in this chapter, are one context of meaning for understanding experience; Buddhist concepts are another (Rubin, 1996). Both are valid frames for experience.

Consider: experience simply arises when and if it does. However, specific orientations or expectations color our experiences differently from moment to moment. Along the same lines, whether someone is deliberately inquiring deeply, meditating, or neither, an insight is an insight is an insight. So in this respect also, inquiring deeply cannot be clearly delineated from Buddhist meditation practice.[25]

One of the major points emphasized throughout this book is that a major distinction between inquiring deeply and dharma practice is its narrative context of meaning. But even the narrative context of inquiring deeply varies from moment to moment, and it also deepens as it unfolds over time. The narrative contexts of psychotherapy and dharma practice are overlapping; both shine a light on the stories that entangle and entrap us.

Summary and Conclusion

As was defined in Chapter 1, inquiring deeply is an integrative psychotherapeutic framework that honors the wisdom and methods of the dharma while, at the same time, recognizing patterns of psychological function in the relationally organized human psyche. This chapter elucidated the importance of the relational dimension of inquiry. A relationally wounded self feels itself to be at odds with its network of relatedness and its ground of being. Therefore, inquiring deeply begins with a focus on relational wounds. It invites a deeper lived experience of psychological pain that may have been disavowed or repressed altogether.

Mindful awareness of the psychological experience of connection can play an important role in psychological healing. The therapeutic relationship both builds a foundation of interpersonal trust and heightens psychodynamic understanding of relational experience. At the same time, deep experiences of relaxing into *right here, right now*—both in meditation and in psychotherapy—help to instill a sense of being at home in the present moment, with ourselves and with others. Such experiences can provide a profound sense of safety and belonging, of being held by the world.

Intimate sharing of deep presence with another is a truly corrective relational experience—an essential experience of being with another. As awareness deepens, the felt sense of this relatedness can expand to include wider and wider circles of connection: being with others, being with nature, and, ultimately, the unity of all being. Buddhism creates the understanding that you *inter-are* with every other thing; you cannot actually *be* just by yourself (Nhat Hanh, 1998).

Mindfulness of connection at the intimate edge of experience is not simply the boundary between self and other; it is also the boundary of self-awareness (Ehrenberg, 1992). In Chapter 7, I will discuss further how our experience of the space we share with Others is involved in the construction of Self. The intersubjective intersection is the surface of expanding self-discovery at which one comes to know one's own experience through the evolving relationship with the other, and then to become more intimate with the other as a function of greater attunement to oneself.

The intimacy and compassion of the therapeutic relationship is arguably its most important therapeutic dimension.[26] At the same time, the relational encounter in psychotherapy can also be a doorway into the wisdom and compassion of the dharma. As the therapist brings contemplative awareness into his or her relationship with the patient, this provides a healing experience of connection *interpersonally* and also an experience of non-separate being *intersubjectively*. This experience, which my colleague Concetta Alfano (1995) calls **transcendent attunement**, is a natural outgrowth of mindful therapeutic presence and interpersonal resonance, as discussed in Chapter 5.

From there, self-awareness can evolve toward deeper and deeper inquiry into the very experience of self, who we take ourselves to be, and how we came to constitute ourselves in that way. And for some, this inquiry naturally dovetails with deepening experience in meditation, leading eventually toward inquiry into the nature of being itself. In this way, psychotherapeutic exploration and Buddhist mindfulness become harmonious partners (Bobrow, 2007, 2010). Both participate in the "evolution of subjectivity" (Schuman, 1998).

Appendix 6.1

Condolence Call: Daowu Won't Say (Loori, 1998)

Priest Jianyuan Tan once accompanied his teacher, Daowu, on a condolence call to a family funeral. When they arrived, he tapped the coffin and said, "Is this life, or is this death?"

Daowu said, "I won't say life, I won't say death."

Jianyuan said, "Why won't you say?"

Daowu said, "I won't say, I won't say."

On their way back Jianyuan said, "You should say it quickly for me, teacher, or I will hit you."

Daowu said, "Hit me if you will, but I will not say." Jianyuan hit him.

After returning to the monastery Daowu said to Jianyuan, "You should take leave for a while; I'm afraid if the head monk finds out about this he will make trouble for you."

After Daowu passed away, Jianyuan went to see Daowu's successor Shishuang, told him the story, and asked for guidance. Shishuang said, "I won't say life, I won't say death."

Jianyuan said, "Why won't you say it?"

Shishuang said, "I won't say, I won't say."

Jianyuan immediately realized it.

Notes

1   "Contemplative relational psychotherapy" is a term invented by the author and her colleague Concetta Alfano in 2006. The delineation of relational and other psychoanalytic approaches goes beyond the scope of this book, but the basic frame of reference will hopefully be inductively clear from all of the material that follows in this chapter.
2   The analyst's response to the transference is conceptualized as "countertransference."
3   These qualities were defined and discussed in Chapter 5. The contemplative quality of relationship was well captured by the concept of the *I–Thou* relation, posited by the philosopher Martin Buber (1958). *I–Thou* connotes an intimate quality of immediacy and aliveness that we may experience to someone or some*thing* when we perceive it as participating in unity of all Being (in distinction to the objectification of someone or something in the relation that Buber termed "*I–It*").
4   Psychoanalytic object relations theory, self psychology, and intersubjectivity theory provide many illuminating insights into the complex process of psychological development.
5   Daniel Stern delineated five stages in the development of the self: *emergent self* (birth–2 months), *core self* (2–6 months), *subjective self* (7–15 months), and finally *verbal self.* See Stern (1985).
6   Differentiation, the process of self-delineation, is an essential element in cohesive self-experience. See Chapter 8.

7 In psychoanalytic parlance, the presence of others who can serve selfobject functions will continue to be required.

8 Patient's self-description at intake.

9 The importance of the Other in the formation of the self was conceptualized and described in Kohut's *Self Psychology*. This concept will be described in some detail in Chapter 8.

10 In Chapter 8, these observations will be discussed in regard to how subjectivity is constructed.

11 For many patients, this amounts to psychoeducation about relationships.

12 Awareness of the vicissitudes of subjective experience is a key insight in its own right, which in a Buddhist narrative would be interpreted as insight into *impermanence*.

13 The process I call here "mindfulness of connection" is quite similar to "relational mindfulness" or "mindfulness of self-in-connection" as summarized well by Jan Surrey (2005) and by Gregory Kramer (2007).

14 A related and parallel question that I have reflected on is what, if anything, is the essential distinction between the function of a Buddhist psychotherapist and that of the dharma teacher.

15 This undoubtedly bears the stamp of my training in clinical hypnosis as well as many hundreds of hours both leading and being on the receiving end of guided meditations over my years of dharma practice.

16 The koan in question appears as an appendix to this chapter.

17 There are more than two! More inclusively, also relationship to place, relationship to nature, and relationship to music, among many others.

18 This is the province of objects relations theory in psychoanalysis, as well as self psychology, intersubjectivity theory, and relational psychoanalysis.

19 By extension, relationship takes place within the framework of culture, transmitted interpersonally and transgenerationally.

20 In existential philosophy, these are two essential and interrelated characteristics of existence: being essentially alone yet at the same time bound together in the world with others.

21 In *Insight Dialogue*, Kramer emphasizes the essential relationality implicit in both dharma practice and meditation.

22 See Chapter 5, Note 8.

23 This conflates "personality" in the psychological sense with "personality view" or "self-view" in Buddhism, but there is some validity to this assertion nonetheless. It is important to bring clarity to the construction of self in both frames of reference.

24 In Buddhism, this is the realm of what is considered Relative (vs. Absolute).

25 To the extent that the therapist has themselves integrated Buddhism into their world view, they will tend to create a seamless blend between the two processes, participating in deep dialogue with the other in a way that hopefully leads to greater wisdom and compassion.

26 Chapter 10 presents some further reflections on the process of psychological change and how healing occurs.

References

Alfano, C. (1995). Traversing the caesura: Transcendent attunement in Buddhism and psychoanalysis. *Contemporary Psychoanalysis*, *41*(2), 223–247.

Batchelor, S. (1983). *Alone with others*. New York, NY: Grove Weidenfeld.

Bobrow, J. (2010). *Zen and psychotherapy: Partners in liberation.* New York, NY: Norton Professional Books.

Brandschaft, B., Doctors, S., and Sorter, D. (2010). *Toward an emancipatory psycho-analysis: Brandschaft's intersubjective vision.* New York, NY: Routledge Press.

Buber, M. (1958). *I and thou.* New York, NY: Scribner Press.

Ehrenberg, D. (1992). *The intimate edge: Extending the reach of psychoanalytic interaction.* New York, NY: W.W. Norton.

Gray, P. (1994). *The ego and the analysis of defense.* New York, NY: Aronson.

Kearney, P. (1999). *Still crazy after all these years: Why meditation isn't psychotherapy.* online blog published by Dharma Salon. http://www.buddhanet.net/psyche.htm.

Kohut, H. (1971). *The analysis of the self.* Madison, CT: International Universities Press.

Kramer, G. (2007). *Insight dialogue: The interpersonal path to freedom.* Boston, MA: Shambhala Press.

Loori, J. D. (1998). Daowu won't say dharma: Case 300. *Mountain record of zen talks.* www.abuddhistlibrary.com, Mountain record 16.4, featured in Summer 1998.

Mahler, M. S. (1965). On the significance of the normal separation-individuation phase. In M. Schur (Ed.), *Drives, affects, behavior* (pp. 161–169). New York, NY: International Universities Press.

Modell, A. (1993). *The private self.* Cambridge, MA: Harvard University Press.

Morgan, S. (2005). Depression: Turning toward life. In Germer, C., Siegel, R. D. and Fulton, P. R. (Eds), *Mindfulness and psychotherapy* (pp. 130–151). New York, NY: Guilford Press.

Nhat Hanh, T. (1998). *The heart of the Buddha's teaching: Transforming suffering into peace, joy, and liberation.* Berkeley, CA: Parallax Press.

Pearce, J. (1971). *The crack in the cosmic egg.* New York, NY: Julian Press.

Rubin, J. (1996). *Psychotherapy and Buddhism: Towards an integration.* New York, NY: Plenum Press.

Schuman, M. (1998). Suffering and the evolution of subjectivity. Paper presented at a conference on Psychotherapy, Spirituality, and the Evolution of Mind. Santa Monica, CA. May 15–17, 1998.

Sumedho, A. (2007). *The sound of silence.* Somerville, MA: Wisdom Publications.

Surrey, J. (2005). Relational psychotherapy, relational mindfulness. In Germer, C. K., Siegel, R. D., and Fulton, P. R. (Eds), *Mindfulness and psychotherapy* (pp. 91–110). New York, NY: Guilford Press.

Stern, D. N. (1985). *The interpersonal world of the infant.* New York, NY: Basic Books.

Viorst, J. (1986). *Necessary losses.* New York, NY: Simon and Schuster.

Wallin, D. J. (2007). *Attachment in psychotherapy.* New York, NY: Guilford Press.

Winnicott, D. W. (1965). The capacity to be alone. In Winnicott, D. W. (1965). *The maturational processes and the facilitating environment: Studies in the theory of emotional development* (pp. 20–39). Madison, CT: International Universities Press.

Chapter 7

Reflections on Thinking

The previous chapters of *Inquiring Deeply* have provided some primary layers for systematic inquiry into experience. Before going on to explore deeper layers of inquiry into how self and other live in the internal world, it will be important to elaborate a bit about the nature of the thinking mind and how it functions.

The mind is essentially dynamic, always moving and changing. Its rhythms of mental energy comprise a complex musical signature for each person, interwoven with rhythms of mood, reactions to life events, and repetitive melodies that reflect our life narratives and personality.

How the mind creates experience presents an important question that sits at the heart of both psychotherapy and Buddhism. This is a complex question, one with many layers and more than abstract significance: without a clear understanding of the mind, we lack a clear and valid view of what causes suffering; and without understanding the cause of suffering, there can be no clear strategy for alleviating it.

So it is essential to understand "mind" and its functions. Although Buddhist and Western psychologies have important differences, there is common ground too. Both recognize that the mind is involved in constructing the world; both recognize conscious and unconscious components of mind; and both conceive of the mind's basic functions as sensing, perceiving, thinking, and feeling. Moreover, there is a shared understanding that experience by its very nature is "in" the mind—or *is* the mind (Merleau-Ponty, 1945/1961).[1] Many differences between Buddhist and Western psychological ideas follow from the fact that contemporary psychoanalytic views about how the mind functions (as with most other contemporary psychologies) are informed by cognitive neuroscience.[2]

Dharma practice addresses how experience is held in the mind and the suffering that results. It gives a theoretical account of how the mind gets entangled in the world it creates, with particular reference to mental processes of clinging and resistance. Psychoanalysis addresses some of the same issues but through a very different lens. It gives a theoretical account of internal dynamics and how these tend to get enacted in the outer world.

The human predicament is that we often are not aware of what is going on in our minds until it takes form in who we have become and the situations we find ourselves in. Both mindfulness practice and relational psychotherapy illuminate the role of mental process in the "dance of life" (Moffitt, 2008) and how our individual lives unfold.

This chapter concerns the importance of the thinking mind—both conscious and unconscious—in determining experience. It presents a series of reflections about cognitive organization that blends psychodynamic and Buddhist views.

Where Does Experience Come From?

Metaphysical questions aside, thoughts and other experiences originate from the multiple layers of cognition active in the mind at any given moment. As modern cognitive science makes clear, some basic aspects of the organization of brain and mind are part of the mind's "design function," its operating system as it were, and as such may be intrinsically beyond the scope of conscious awareness. Both Buddhist and Western psychology also posit the existence of an unconscious mind: one or more compartments of mental process that under the right circumstances are able to become conscious.[3]

What emerges into consciousness is merely a wave on the surface of an unseen ocean of potential experience. Each new moment of "now" arises within us as an upsurge of fresh present that crashes upon us like a wave, or appears almost without notice only to slip away like a sea swell. We are unaware of how it got there because it was formed unconsciously, intuitively. Each new perception, thought, or memory emerges with an all-of-a-sudden quality, out of "nowhere" (Now, Here). Moments are porous, flowing into each other in the ongoing transformations we call experience (Merleau-Ponty, 1945/1962).

We can conceptualize this process further: the background state from which experience arises is unformulated, undifferentiated, and inchoate. It remains ambiguous until it is organized—i.e. until it takes form (Stern, 1997).[4] This results in a spectrum of experience that ranges from direct/immediate, on the one hand, to highly symbolized/abstract, on the other. This process can be pictured as a dynamic equilibrium between figure and ground, in which experience emerges into consciousness and then recedes again into unconsciousness. Regardless of whether experience becomes conscious, it always entails largely unconscious processes. The "cognitive unconsciousness" is enormously complex and cannot be accessed through introspection.

Consider a partial list of the processes that are going on in your cognitive unconscious as you are reading this:

- *you are comprehending language: identifying the structure of sentences in accord with the vast number of English grammatical constructions, picking out words and giving them meanings appropriate to context, making semantic and pragmatic sense of the sentences as a whole;*
- *you are constructing mental images where relevant;*
- *you are filling in gaps in the discourse;*
- *you are accessing memories relevant to what is being said;*

- *you are forming appraisals and judgments about what is being said;*
- *and so on.*

In sum, discursive thought depends on highly complex cognitive processes which are unavailable to consciousness. Thinking is a symbolically organized experience; the capacity to symbolize underlies self, language, and culture and, accordingly, stands out as the quintessential human characteristic. We can visualize this complex process as a continually unfolding Mobius strip of experience, cognitively organized within the brain/mind in accordance with countless individual differences. Each moment of lived experience organizes itself into psychological patterns that, in turn, become embedded in the organization of the next moment. In this way, life becomes a complexly woven fabric composed of a series of happenings, our intimate experience of those events ("subjective reality"), plus how we then react and respond to what happens.

As experience occurs in this continually unfolding and ongoing sequence of events, it is also neurochemically encoded into a complex construction which Gerald Edelman (1989) evocatively terms "the remembered present." What we call "the present moment" is a composite of current conditions and similar past experiences the mind remembers. There are two basic forms in which experience is recorded: as implicit memory (which is largely unconscious) and as episodic (narrative) memory. So the "present moment" is a collage of sensation, perception, feeling, cognition, implicit memory, and story.

Part of the relevant associative network that constitutes the present moment are the ***organizing principles*** in the mind: deep beliefs, mental schemas, and psychic structures—largely unconscious—that influence what becomes conscious and orchestrate our customary ways of seeing ourselves, others, and the world. Of particular interest in psychodynamic therapy are the "structures" that organize the mind's various processes and functions: ego, executive function, self, etc. One of the basic goals of psychotherapy includes reorganization at this level of experience.

Organizing principles include concepts and belief systems assimilated through language and culture. These are important elements of the paradigm of meaning that shapes future experience. Both psychoanalysis and mindfulness meditation are fundamentally concerned with uncovering these.

One of the principles of dharma practice is called "right view." The word "right" implies what is correct and appropriate, but it is important to recognize that "right view" doesn't mean *without* view. Experience is *inherently* biased by the organizing principles, ideas, and views in the mind; indeed, this is precisely why "right view" is so important. The implication of this idea is profound: *no experience can ever be completely objective or "just as it is."* As the philosopher Heisenberg posited in his famous "uncertainty principle," the process of observation itself intrinsically affects the nature of what is observed.

From this perspective, we can posit that even the Buddha's awakening arose from the particular nature of his own inquiry: the questions he asked and the way he went about his inquiry.[5]

Lens of View

With this basic caveat in mind, we can examine some basic differences between mindful awareness in the practice of Buddhism and mindful awareness in Buddhist-informed psychotherapy.

In his classic book on the subject, Jeffrey Rubin introduced the idea that psychoanalysis and Buddhism are two different lenses of view about experience, each focused on only one part of the whole picture, each world view a by-product of its method of investigation (Rubin, 1996). Buddhism, Rubin says, is nearsighted, biased toward an overly narrow focus on the building blocks of experience. It ignores the developmental dimension of experience and misses the power and nuance of subjective states. Psychoanalysis, on the other hand, is farsighted: it gets caught in big picture concepts to the exclusion of important particularity and detail.

When people engage in both psychotherapy and Buddhist practice, it becomes more difficult to delineate differences between the two lenses of view. A "mixing of minds" (Jennings and Safran, 2010) occurs: the same experience can often be framed by both sets of narrative concepts, and experience does not sort itself neatly into one category or the other. Moreover, the clarity and depth of awareness honed in the practice of meditation amplifies many aspects of the experience explored in psychotherapy and enhances the *capacity* for self-reflection in a way that is highly prized in psychotherapy. In turn, self-reflection in psychotherapy begins to "feed forward" into meditation practice and influences the way that subsequent meditative experience unfolds.

One valued fruit of practice—psychotherapeutic or meditative—is insight: something new emerges, or something shifts that allows us to see something in a new way. Some insight is shallow and barely registers as insight; some may feel profound, even awesome. Some—called "epiphany"—is sudden, striking realization. Regardless, it doesn't really matter whether insight comes from meditation, psychotherapy, in a formal practice of inquiry, or in a moment of ordinary living. The fruit falls when it ripens. Insight is not something that can be bidden.

On the other hand, one of the benefits of meditation is that it favors the emergence of transformative insight. Long periods of meditation or meditative retreat can result in transcendent or spiritual insight, states of consciousness in which one experiences the unity of being. In such transcendent states, suffering disappears as a function of directly experiencing that there is a way of being in which nothing feels missing and there is no problem to solve. Such insight is highly prized in Buddhism and other spiritual practices.

Be that as it may, experience arises when and if it does, and insight is insight regardless of whether it comes from everyday life, in psychotherapy, or during dharma practice. Perhaps there can't be any fundamental difference given that, as the meditation teacher/scholar Jason Siff has said in another context, the mind that one experiences in meditation is the same as the one that presents itself in psychotherapy (Siff, 2012).[6]

Buddhism and psychodynamic work share the aim to become intimate with experience, expand the scope of what we are aware of, and, in so doing, resolve pain and suffering.

Meditation: It Isn't What You Think

It is a function of the mind to think; the mind makes thoughts like water makes waves. A clear understanding of the process and function of thinking is helpful in elucidating differences between psychotherapeutic and Buddhist perspectives on the causes of psychological suffering.

One of the first things noticed in mindfulness practice is that thoughts constantly arise in the mind. The simplest thought branches off in many directions in rapid succession, distracting attention away from the present moment of embodied experience, and carrying it off into thoughts of past and future. This quality of subjective experience is often termed "discursive thinking" (*papanca*, in the language of the Buddhist sutras). As the Buddha described it, it was as if thoughts were like mud continually spun off some great flywheel in the mind. A colloquialism for papanca, based on the way monkeys swing from branch to branch among the trees, is "monkey mind."

Papanca can be defined in neutral and inclusive terms as *the experience of the subjective world elaborating itself in language and concept.* Experience is named and then elaborated into a labyrinthine network of concepts. In this circuitous process, concepts condition the continual unfolding of reality. The Buddha described this as a kind of conjurer's trick, where the mind creates the world through a process of illusion (Nananada, 1971). As one modern writer put it, man's mind mirrors a universe that mirrors man's mind (Pearce, 2002).

The recurrent process of discursive thinking is in some ways well described by the term "monkey mind": the mind feels restless; it rambles and digresses. However, as Buddhist psychology and psychoanalytic theory both recognize, associations in the mind are highly determined events—not random. A network of "causes and conditions" in the mind gives rise to cognitive activities of various kinds.

The underlying intention in mindfulness practice is to not get caught up in papanca in a way that takes attention away from the present moment of embodied experience. As relaxation increases during any particular session of mindfulness practice, the backdrop of proliferating thoughts tends to become more subdued. States of awareness in which the mind is highly focused and less restless can be developed through mindfulness practice.[7] Papanca is a function of arousal in the body/mind; the mind *can* reorganize itself into states that are calm, steady, and quite still. States of concentrated focus—*samadhi*—can be developed through the practice of Buddhist meditation.

It is important to recognize that discursive thinking has a range of qualities, textures, and energy. For example, deep thinking *about something* is quite different from "monkey mind."[8] Experientially, we can discern a wide variety of cognitive activities that are subsumed under the term *thinking*: reasoning, planning, remembering, fantasizing, speculating, judging and evaluating, worrying and ruminating, etc. The mind generates endless ideas about our daily activities, our relationships, our projects, our problems, or any current topic of concern. Generally speaking, it engages a full-time program of problem solving. As it responds to constantly changing inputs, it constructs cognitive models of each particular issue or problem "space," integrating information from past experience (memory), and generating possible solutions for the future. In this way, potential courses of action are assembled and conscious experience emerges. This sort of problem solving seems to be one of the primary "design functions" of the human mind.

Two important categories of thinking that can be generally distinguished from one another are analytic thinking—"figuring things out"—and "intuition," in which processes beneath the level of awareness lead to conclusions without the need for conscious reasoning. While this is an important distinction, it would be oversimplifying to say that psychotherapy is analytic while mindfulness practice is intuitive. Psychotherapy is not *merely* analytic; it involves a great deal of intuitive awareness. Conversely, despite the fact that mindfulness practice is fundamentally about the felt sense of things, there is analytic thinking involved in study and practice of the dharma. In a simile used by the Buddha, concepts can be utilized in a wise way to undermine "unwholesome ideas and views" just as a carpenter may drive out a blunt peg with a sharper one (Nanananda, 1971).

To function smoothly, the body/mind develops strategies to maintain its homeostasis and support coherent behavior in the world of lived experience. These strategies are organized into stable schemas and patterns, the "structures" of ego, self, character, and psychological defense in Western psychology. It is not the purpose of the present discussion to describe these, but simply to state the generally accepted view that the overarching purpose of psychic structure is to regulate stimulation and arousal, including protecting the brain/mind from the dysregulating effect of emotional reactions. This function is both interpersonal and intrapsychic (Siegel, 2012).

In overview, the mind can only respond to experience in one of several fundamental ways: (1) It can initiate action; (2) It can think about experience by representing ("re-presenting") it in symbolic form and then further elaborating this symbolization (thoughts). Thinking can be verbal—the mind essentially talking to itself in implicit language—and/or mediated by visual or other sensory images; or (3) It can defend against the experience by excluding it from further cognitive processing. This way of thinking about the mind provides a useful context for understanding the role of narrative.

Narrative and Papanca

One basic feature of verbal thought is the proliferation of story and narrative (the hallmark of papanca). Modern cognitive science explains "why": the left hemisphere of the brain functions as an "interpreter module" (Gazzaniga, 2011), which looks for order in chaos as it tries to integrate everything, including activity in the emotional sphere, into a coherent narrative. This becomes the "episodic memory" of our life experience, encoded as explanation, story, and narrative. Narrative capacity also underlies the capacity to create meaning. Other neural activity remains instead in the form of implicit memory, much of which is believed to be encoded in the right brain, and only a small portion of which ever reaches conscious awareness.

One important dimension of thinking that should be highlighted concerns the role of "executive function" in the mind (including the capacity for stable attention). As the brain/mind matures, it acquires the (executive) ability to direct its own problem-solving functions. This organizational capacity varies a great deal from person to person and is also quite vulnerable to disorders of emotional attachment during development. Although this complex topic is well beyond the scope of the present discussion, it is of interest that executive function is a frontal lobe function, closely related to areas of the brain that subserve self-reflection (Siegel, 2010). Of further interest, the practice of mindfulness meditation stimulates the development of these same brain areas.

In experience-near language, the essence of mindfulness meditation is how we *relate to* papanca: how mind is held in mind, moment by moment ("minding the mind"). The essence of mindful awareness is our capacity to notice the *process* of mind. Mindfulness practice instills the ability to differentiate a thought from the actual experience of something, so that we can be less caught up in thinking. This is the art of meditation: it is fundamentally less concerned with what we think than the tendency to become entangled in the web of thought (and how to get disentangled).

Mindfulness meditation highlights the constant activity of the "storyteller mind" with the goal of "waking up" from its spell. It develops awareness of how thinking relates to the background quality of mind, such as how settled or how restless the mind is, how spacious or how contracted, how sharp or dull, how clear or confused. There is also an underlying energy in the thinking mind that can be directly sensed.

Relational psychotherapy also takes notice of how we relate to thinking; however, its focus is somewhat different, in that it is concerned with thinking as a window into underlying psychological processes. How and what we think reflects the history of our experiences with others and carries the imprint of unmet psychological needs. The narrative themes in the mind can be examined as a means of deepening our understanding of the relational paradigms in which the process of thinking is embedded.

The re-frame of thinking in inquiring deeply is an emphasis on "wise relationship to narrative." In inquiring deeply, the story lines in the mind are considered important in their own right, not merely plot content that we label as "thinking" and then pejoratively dismiss as "monkey mind" (as sometimes seems to be implied by dharma teachers). As will be elaborated in the chapters to follow, story and metaphor are an essential part of how the mind processes experience and they provide an important window of insight and understanding.[9] It is, in any event, impossible to simply "drop the story"; story-making is one of the design functions of the mind. Investigating psychological narrative is one of the fundamental activities in relational psychotherapy. We seek to understand the narrative content of the mind in the developmental context of our early attachment history.

It is important to emphasize that "understanding narrative" is not merely a cognitive undertaking; it is an emotional and a relational one. Deep emotional understanding requires self-reflection, which takes place in the context of the *felt sense* of experience. The therapeutic relationship is the overarching context that allows psychological healing to occur.

Psychodynamics of Thinking

Contrary to the idea that "monkey mind" comes about as a result of random neurochemical activity in the brain/mind, it is helpful to understand, as Sigmund Freud did, that the process of "free association" proceeds along understandable trajectories and has psychodynamic meaning. By exploring the patterns of associations in the mind, we can gain a great deal of insight into how the mind is organized.

As was elaborated in the previous chapter, an essential first principle in understanding how the mind is organized is that attachment bonds comprise the fundamental matrix within which the mind develops (Wallin, 2007). A good attachment is one that supports the capacity to "metabolize experience" (Bion, 1962). For experience to be metabolized, the mother has to understand what her baby is communicating and respond appropriately to restore homeostasis. This occurs both on a gross level, as, for example, when a mother knows that her baby is hungry or wet and provides what is needed. On a subtler level, it also happens through the medium of empathic understanding as the mother resonates with the baby's feelings and responds appropriately. In this way, according to the theory, primal impulses are able to be "contained" and eventually come to be elaborated in the baby's mind into fantasy, dream, and narrative, all of which have self-regulatory functions. This relational dynamic of "container" and "contained" is understood as an essential mechanism for maintaining the psyche in a state of emotional balance. Gradually, the exchange that originally occurred between mother and baby, container and contained, is assimilated into the child's developing mind.

One of the basic functions of relational/psychodynamic treatment is that it provides a container for experience and helps the patient develop the function of containment as a psychological capacity. Dharma practice serves some of this same function, and can itself be conceptualized as a container.

Relational/psychodynamic treatment is based on the idea that understanding and being understood are essential to psychological growth and development. Deep psychological understanding is not merely a cognitive process; it has an emotional quality that is transmitted by accurate empathy. Empathy is important in psychological growth, and it can be especially transformative when it is grounded in deep compassion (Kornfield, 2008). With this in mind, inquiring deeply pursues deep psychological understanding and endeavors to use that understanding to help patients understand both themselves and others. The more clearly we can discern and understand where the mind has gotten "hung up," the better we can evolve through the problematic situations we find ourselves in.

When we look into the content of thinking from a psychodynamic perspective, we find that thinking reveals a great deal about the problems that the mind is trying to solve, the underlying feelings that are present, and the network of meanings in which problems are embedded. By thinking about thinking in psychotherapeutic conversation, we create the possibility for a wiser relationship with the thinking mind.

Feeling states are the operative context for "thinking." These, in turn, can be understood in the context of patterns of self and other that have shaped us. We can see that the particular qualities of mind that we develop, even the way that we relate to our minds and the processes within our minds, are formed by our relationships with others. By learning to notice and by investigating these relationally based organizing principles, the ability to metabolize experience improves and psychological growth is facilitated.

Much of the work of psychotherapy can be understood in this framework: it supports the patient's capacity to metabolize experience. Once it has been recognized and articulated by an empathic therapist, experience that was initially inchoate and unformulated can gradually be assimilated into a narrative of meaning and understanding. How well this can happen depends in large measure on the ability of the psychotherapist to contain—i.e. empathically understand and be with—experience that previously had been chaotic and overwhelming and, therefore, had been maintained in an unconscious state.

Thinking and the Need to Know

Patterns of thinking are held in place, in part, by the need to know. As the preceding discussion has suggested, thinking is part of how the brain/mind metabolizes emotion, restores balance, and creates safety. In the face of any negative experience—when we are anxious or threatened or in pain—we instinctively try to think our way out of the situation. For many people, this becomes a basic strategy for solving problems: "figure out" what to do. Over time, we become reliant on this effort to *know*. This strategy solidifies into an unconsciously held and deep belief that knowing is essential to safety (or at least the illusion of safety). We cling to knowing as a primary source of security. It allows us to feel more in control.

Alongside this attachment to knowing, we can also observe the tendency to defend *what* we know (or believe that we know). We can notice the attempt to prove to ourselves or others that our views are right. At deeper levels, we can also see the extent to which particular views and beliefs come to be invested with a sense of self.

At a yet more fundamental level, we can see how we identify with the *faculty of knowing*: how we *become* the knower, never noticing, much less questioning, the assumption that who I *am* is the one who thinks. This is grounded in the lineage of Western philosophy, which embraces Rene Descartes's famous dictum, "I think, therefore I am." However, the converse statement may be equally valid: I am, therefore I think!

In all of this, we can discern the tremendous cost of this relationship to knowing. As Gregory Kramer put it, "*Thinking we know costs us all we don't know—which is nearly everything*" (Kramer, 2007, p. 144). In the functioning of the mind, the "need to know" impedes the capacity to not-know, the ability to trust a process of not-thinking, not-knowing, of letting go. Many problems are held in place by our inability to let go of what we know in favor of something new: a new thought, a new experience, a new possibility.

The point here is not what remains to be known, but rather to learn how to remain aware in a way that allows the experience of not knowing. The intention to "not know" can be engaged in any moment of experience by reflecting on three simple questions: Am I curious? Am I open? Am I compassionate?[10] Psychotherapy and meditation are both strategies that can help us to be receptive to not-knowing, to the engaging of intuitive wisdom. It is in *being* and *not knowing* in this way that we can best be true to what we feel and who we are.

Inquiry and Mindfulness: To Think or Not to Think Is Not the Question

This discussion has highlighted the fact that the mind is never without ongoing processes of cognitive organization. The question is not whether to think or not to think; thoughts arise when and if they do, and regardless of what emerges into conscious awareness, cognitive processing is always occurring. The question, instead, is how to relate to thinking in a way that optimizes the mind's organization, flow, and balance. This question is fundamental to dharma practice and to meditation. It is also an explicit question in the interpretive frame of inquiring deeply.

The essence of the predicament is this: the effort to *not think* (a strategy wittingly or unwittingly adopted by many meditators) is essentially suppressive (Siff, 2012). It imposes control where the underlying purpose is to learn to *let go* of control and to rest in the experience of not-knowing. Trying not to think is counter to the open and receptive state that leads to generative inquiry.

To clarify the comparison between mindfulness meditation and mindfulness in the process of psychotherapy, it may be helpful to distinguish between open awareness meditation practice, on the one hand, and self-reflection, on the other.[11] Both are processes of receptive introspective awareness, but they are somewhat different.

In open awareness mindfulness meditation practice, we sit and watch the mind with the simple frame of intention to be mindfully present. Various contents of mind present themselves—sensations, perceptions, thoughts, and feelings—and we try to pay attention to them without getting caught up in them. Attention may be stable or it may not, we may be focused or we may be distracted, but the process is to come back again and again to whatever is arising in the moment. The content of what arises in the mind is less important than the embodied experience of the present moment and the context of open, receptive awareness.

Self-reflective awareness practices in inquiring deeply have a different aim: to become aware of the network of associations connected with some particular problem or area of psychological interest. Maintaining relaxed, receptive attention is conducive to this purpose, but emphasis is placed on noticing the content of experience. This is the primary difference from meditation practice.

The capacity for self-reflective awareness is facilitated by the trait of "psychological mindedness." Many people who are attracted to meditation are introspective by nature; they seem to be innately psychologically minded and tend to be organized around their inner experience. I have seen many such individuals in my clinical practice; I think of them as "seekers." For them, there is a two-way street between meditation and psychotherapy: what is discovered in psychotherapy often shows up in meditation practice, and vice versa. This makes the impact of mindfulness conjoined with the impact of psychotherapy; they cannot be neatly compartmentalized.

As the relational field of self-and-other is highlighted in inquiring deeply, psychodynamic and relational awareness are developed in psychotherapy. Each in its own way, both mindfulness practice and psychodynamic awareness enhance the capacity for self-reflection by helping us pay attention to how and what we think. Both generate insight into the way that the mind is organized.

The development of self-reflection and its importance in relational/psychodynamic therapy are explored in the next chapter.

Notes

1   It is not intended here to make any dualistic assumptions about "subjective" and "objective" or material realities.
2   This fascinating subject matter receives only cursory attention in this book. The interested reader is referred, for example, to Hansen and Mendius (2009), Siegel (2010), and Varela et al. (1993).
3   The individual unconscious contains memories, images, and beliefs about ourselves, others, and the world that we are not aware of. Some of these, the "pre-reflective unconscious," are readily accessible to consciousness. Others are dynamically unconscious, disavowed, or repressed, and less readily accessible. Some processes are intrinsically unconscious while others can become conscious under appropriate conditions. In addition, some psychological systems posit a collective or transpersonal unconscious.
4   Stern (1997) has a wonderful discussion of the nature of unformulated experience and its relationship to unconscious process.
5   The Buddha's method also engendered altered states of consciousness, which undoubtedly were an integral part of his "awakening." (And, by the same reasoning, it may be presumed that every Buddha would necessarily have his or her own unique experience of awakening.)
6   This language begs the question of how we could ever say that the mind is the "same." One cannot step in the same river twice!
7   Indeed, this is a primary purpose of meditation in the Buddha's Eightfold Path.

8 This kind of deep thinking seems more aptly suited to the common translation of papanca as "discursive thinking."
9 It is also useful to explore the content and process of thinking as a window into the *relationship* we have to thinking. In the object-relations language of psychoanalysis, the mind can essentially take on relational functions of an Other to whom one turns to for protection, who is harsh and abusive, etc. See Chapter 9 for an extensive elaboration of this idea.
10 I learned this wonderful reflective practice from Bruce Gibbs, a teacher of Focusing (Gibbs, 2012). The practice of Focusing is very briefly discussed in Chapter 4.
11 In Chapters 8 and 9, this delineation will be expanded to include the related concepts of "free association" and "observing ego."

References

Bion, W. R. (1962). *Learning from experience*. New York, NY: Jason Aronson Press.

Edelman, G. (1989). *The remembered present: A biological theory of consciousness*. New York, NY: Basic Books.

Gazzaniga, M. (2011). *Who's in charge: Free will and the science of the brain*. New York, NY: Harper Collins.

Gibbs, B. (2012). Personal communication.

Hansen, R. and Mendius, R. (2009). *The Buddha's brain: The practical neuroscience of happiness, love, and wisdom*. Oakland, CA: New Harbinger Press.

Jennings, P. and Safran, J. D. (2010). *Mixing minds: The power of relationship in psychoanalysis and Buddhism*. Somerville, MA: Wisdom Publications.

Kornfield, J. (2008). *The wise heart*. New York, NY: Bantam Books.

Kramer, G. (2007). *Insight dialogue: The interpersonal path to freedom*. Boston, MA: Shambhala Press.

Merleau-Ponty, M. (1945/1962). *Phenomenology of perception*. New York, NY: Routledge Press.

Moffitt, P. (2008). *Dancing with life*. New York, NY: Rodale Press.

Nanananda, B. (1971/2012). *Concept and reality in early Buddhist thought*. Kandy, Sri Lanka: Buddhist Publication Society.

Pearce, J. C. (2002). *The crack in the cosmic egg*. New York, NY: Simon and Schuster.

Rubin, J. (1996). *Psychotherapy and Buddhism: Towards an integration*. New York, NY: Plenum Press.

Siegel, D. J. (2010). *The mindful therapist: A clinician's guide to mindsight and neural integration*. New York, NY: W.W. Norton.

Siegel, D. J. (2012). *The developing mind, second edition: How relationships and the brain interact to shape who we are*. New York, NY: Guilford Press.

Siff, J. (2012). Redefining Meditation. Blog post on Unlearning Meditation. www.skillful-meditation.org.

Stern, D. (1997). *Unformulated experience: From dissociation to imagination in psychoanalysis*. Hillsdale, NJ: Analytic Press.

Varela, F. J., Thompson, E. and Rosch, E. (1993). *The embodied mind: Cognitive science and human experience*. Cambridge, MA: MIT Press.

Wallin, D. J. (2007). *Attachment in psychotherapy*. New York, NY: Guilford Press.

Chapter 8

Reflections on Subjectivity and the Experience of Self

This chapter has two major goals. The first is to describe subjectivity in a way that clarifies the similarities and differences between Western psychological and Buddhist concepts of self. The second is to define in some detail what psychoanalysis calls "self-reflective function," explain how and why it is an important therapeutic mechanism of action, and describe the role of self-reflective practices in cultivating it.

In general terms, enhancing self-awareness is one of the implicit aims of most forms of psychotherapy. Simply by engaging a therapeutic process (whether psychotherapy, counseling, coaching, "growth work," or psychoanalysis) attention is focused in a way that makes us more aware of ourselves in some respect(s): what we do, how we think and feel, and how that affects others.

In the sections that follow, basic concepts about self will first be presented in order to clarify the use of theoretical language. Self-reflection will be defined and described in a psychoanalytic/theoretical context.[1] The psychoanalytic view of subjectivity will be presented, followed by some reflections on subjectivity within a framework of Buddhist ideas. These various strands will be integrated into a discussion of self and self-experience that is compatible both with psychoanalytic work and Buddhist practice. Interwoven throughout the chapter, a clinical example will show how self-reflection can unfold and deepen within the process that I call inquiring deeply.

Self: Terms and Basic Concepts

The Psychological Self

Being a "self," being "someone," is a given in ordinary experience. We all have some sense of "who we are," some sense of coherent identity in the core of our being. This *psychological self* can be defined most simply as the subjective sense of who I am. It is the center of subjectivity, inclusive of personality, thoughts, beliefs, motivations, and emotions.

Although each moment of subjective experience is a one-of-a-kind constellation of sensations, thoughts, and feelings, through the repetition of many such moments, the psychological self comes to be known to itself in a way that is unique for each person. Part of the essential meaning of "self" is the sense of continuity in the ongoing stream of subjective experience, which gets narrated in language.[2,3] It is what is referenced by the personal pronoun "I" in the elaboration of autobiographical memory.

Contrary to the commonsense assumption that there is a singular psychological self, subjectivity is in fact multifaceted; there are many different aspects of self. In place of a unified and reified concept of "self," psychoanalytic theory highlights several ideas about self. First, there is a multiplicity of selves, functionally organized. As we interact with others, we form concepts of ourselves, *self-representations*, and we identify with these; these concepts are who we take ourselves to be. But self needs to be understood as more than a set of concepts. It is better conceived (as it is in contemporary psychoanalysis) as a set of *functions*, independent of content and grounded in self-reflective awareness (Mitchell, 1993, 2000). These ideas will be elaborated in the discussion that follows. The major point here is that there are many different facets of subjectivity that must be functionally integrated in order to create the more or less cohesive experience that is referenced in common parlance by the word "self."

Different organizations of subjective experience contribute to the way we know ourselves. Different selves, configurations of self, are called forth by different circumstances, emotions, or relationships; yet, despite these differences, it is unusual for any of them to function totally outside of the sense of "me-ness."

Some of the confusions surrounding "self" come about as a result of the way language is constructed. Consider, for example, what you might be inclined to say to someone who says, "Tell me about yourself." You may refer to yourself as a person rather than to your subjective experience; you may refer to yourself as a particular individual, in distinction from others; or you may even refer to particular psychological traits you have, qualities you identify with, or social roles you play.

This confusion of meanings becomes even more confounded when attempting to juxtapose the Buddhist view of self (Schuman, 1991; Falkenstrom, 2003). To be able to discuss the topic of self with clarity, these various meanings need to be teased apart and explicated, and that is one of the overarching intentions of this chapter.

Self-Experience and Self-States

As subjective experiences are cognitively elaborated in the mind, they become aggregated into qualitative experiences that can be termed variously **self-states**, mental states, or states of mind. A self-state is a stable configuration of functional organization within the psychological self. Its core dimensions include a particular level of *arousal* (e.g. relaxed, excited, calm, or speedy), *affective tone* (e.g. elated, depressed, frightened, or angry), and *quality of attention* (e.g. alert, dull, scattered, or focused). Note that these are states of mind *and* body—or, as we may say, of "mind/body."

Despite the fact that self-experience can never be fully captured in words, its subjective texture can, however, be evoked and communicated through the expressive use of language, image, and metaphor. For example, states of low-arousal may be variously described as "groggy," "languid," "lazy," or "enervated." Self-states are most often described in ways that encompass more than one of these core dimensions. For example, we may describe our mental state in words such as "upset," "frozen," "trapped," "out of control," "uptight," or "high," representing some particular and familiar subjective constellation of arousal, affect, and attention. Some word-labels for mental states have a lot of psychological overlay embedded in their very verbal description, for example, "paranoid," "regressed," "fragmented," or "chaotic."

Mental states can also be described through the use of verbs: descriptions of the mind's activities described in action language. This is a process-oriented lens for viewing the mind. For example, we can observe cognitive activities such as paying attention, thinking, visualizing, or fantasizing; affective behavior such as loving, hating, defending, or blaming; or psychodynamic functions such as attacking, defending, projecting, or splitting. Mental activities associated with self-functions include initiating action, organizing perceptions, narrating experience, and interpreting the meaning of things.

In the above discussion, the psychological self is equated with subjective experience, which may be conveniently abbreviated as *self-experience*. However, this is actually a misnomer, because—as inquiry readily reveals—self is not a specific experience at all. The self cannot be seen, heard, tasted, smelled, or touched. It cannot be located anywhere. This was one of the Buddha's central teachings, and some of its basic implications will be explored later under the heading "The Problem of Self." An evocative simile used by dharma teacher Joseph Goldstein is that "self" is like a rainbow: something that emerges out of constituent elements of experience. Be that as it may, there is a fundamental similarity between the Buddhist and psychoanalytic views in the understanding that *self* is a *constructed* or *formulated* experience; it is always interpenetrated by symbols, concepts, and/ or narratives about our subjective experience.

The Structural Self

The term "self" is often used in theoretical literature to refer to a presumptive superordinate structure that is thought to be responsible for organizing and coordinating the activities of mind into a coherent whole. This concept of self as a "structure" has the unfortunate implication that it tends to reify the self as a *thing*, and for our purposes here structures may be better understood simply as processes that have a very slow rate of change. Self, in these terms, is a stable function that organizes the flow of energy and information in the mind.

Self-Awareness and Self-Reflection

One quintessential function of the human self is *self-awareness*: awareness of ongoing subjective experience (*self-reflective awareness* is a more inclusive and accurate term). This is the basic parameter of subjectivity by which the mind is able to become aware of itself. It is metacognitive awareness brought to bear on any aspect of the mind's functions: sensations and perceptions, thoughts and feelings, concepts and processes operating in the mind, even self-reflective function itself. Self-reflective awareness helps to create a sense of continuity between one subjective state and the next, and it is therefore instrumental in organizing the mind into a coherent sense of self. Qualitatively, it can also vary in its subjective depth and clarity, and it may be different in different self-states.

As the mind self-reflects, it elaborates its concepts or representations of itself (and of others). Such self-representations—of one's personality, history, and identity—are extremely significant because they constitute the scaffolding upon which new experience is built. Like all concepts, self-representations shape the way experience gets constructed. Although experience can never be entirely disentangled from its self-representational underpinnings, we can bring consciousness to how we think of ourselves and become more aware of how these representations shape our experience.

Self-representations are especially important in clinical work because they are so often dysfunctional, distorted by unconscious identifications with others, and stubbornly intractable to change. It is also important to call attention to the mind's tendency to defend its self-representations when there is a threat to the sense of self. In the framework of inquiring deeply, this aspect of self is described by the verb *selfing*, connoting implicit or explicit engagement with narratives which center around self. Self as a verb highlights the active psychological processes by which the psychological self is constructed, with special reference to the mind's tendency to defend its self-representations.[4]

The discussion in this chapter focuses on self-reflective awareness as an aspect of subjectivity. However, it is important to recognize that self-reflective function also has direct impact on the intersubjective dimension of our experience with others. For example, when too much attention is engaged by awareness of self, someone may suffer from self-consciousness or be preoccupied with how they are viewed by others. At the other extreme, someone may be preoccupied with another's experience to the exclusion of being aware of self.[5]

It should also be noted that conflict, deficit, and trauma may impair self-reflective functioning. When psychological defenses are engendered, some segment of experience gets excluded from awareness. One of the great benefits of a psychotherapeutic relationship is that it can be helpful in illuminating blind spots in self-awareness. (If we could see our own blind spots, they wouldn't be blind!)

To summarize the major points, capacity for self-reflective awareness is a basic mode of therapeutic action (Aron, 2000). Self-reflective function is what allows us to become aware of the self-representations we live by and to gain insight into the patterns of our mental states over time. As will be illustrated in the clinical case vignette below, self-reflective function carries the imprint of our relational history with others.

Additionally, it is important to emphasize that self-reflective awareness is not only cognitive but also affective and relational in nature. It can be cultivated through engagement in psychotherapy and/or by meditation practice. Taking advantage of both, inquiring deeply develops self-reflective capacity by incorporating mindful awareness, inquiry, and investigation into the framework of Buddhist-informed, relational psychotherapy. This blended approach enhances the effort to bring awareness to psychodynamic process so that new experiences can emerge.

"Self-awareness" is not a singular state or experience. It includes a wide range of experiences with varying degrees of depth associated with them, and is a function both of what we focus awareness on and the quality of attention that is engaged. As was emphasized in preceding sections, the intention in psychodynamic treatment is to enhance self-awareness by engaging the patient's self-reflective function. This requires a mental capacity called *mentalization* (Fonagy et al., 2002).[6]

Exploring Mentalization

Mentalization is the imaginative capacity that gives us the ability to understand what we are experiencing and/or to fathom what is going on in someone else's mind. It is through mentalization that we develop representations of ourselves within our own minds, an idea of how others are thinking about us, and the interconnection between the two. It is through mentalization that we come to realize that having a mind mediates our experience of the world.

Mentalization is the matrix of our understanding of psychological motivations, attitudes, beliefs, and feelings—which, in turn, determines how we relate to others. In short, mentalization is the way that we think about subjective experience. To the degree that we can mentalize, we have the capacity to reflect on ourselves; to the degree that we can reflect on ourselves, mentalization becomes further elaborated.

Self-reflective awareness and its accompanying mentalization is the central focus in psychodynamic and psychoanalytic treatment. A detailed theoretical account of this fascinating topic goes beyond the intended scope of this book, but it is illustrated clinically in the following sequence of statements made over the course of one session in which a patient reflects upon and elaborates the emotional meaning of a simple experience he has become aware of.

Clinical Illustration 8.1: Barry, Part I

The following statements are distilled from self-reflective comments extracted from a lengthy narrative given by a patient I will call Barry:

- *I am angry at her.*
- *I am angry at her because she doesn't care about me as much as I do about her.*
- *It's probably because she feels that I am a burden on her.*
- *That makes me feel unloved, and unlovable.*
- *I am angry because I am hurt, and because I feel unlovable.*

At the most basic level of this self-reflection, the patient notices his experience and recognizes anger. This recognition is a kind of "mindful awareness" in the sense that the mind knows anger, and—although somewhat clumsy to say—knows itself knowing anger. Next, however, this simple awareness is followed by a series of thoughts and mentalizations about the anger. This is self-reflection.

In this first segment, Barry was simply exploring out loud some painful feelings he was having. His comments unfolded in a narrative form that was analytic yet conversational. This was Barry's "natural style," although it probably bears the imprint of several years of psychotherapy. Such mentalization is a staple of therapeutic exploration. By talking through thoughts and feelings with the therapist, the patient's experience becomes progressively more formulated and articulated; s(he) organizes experience into new frameworks of narrative meaning. From a relational viewpoint, Barry's expectation of my empathic understanding was a key element in allowing him to feel safe enough to begin to develop his mentalizations about his experience.

As our therapeutic conversation progressed over several sessions, Barry's self-reflections began to deepen. How his point of view evolved is expressed in the next series of observations he made about his feelings:

Clinical Illustration 8.2: Barry, Part II

Those feelings [angry and unloved] make me very depressed. They make me not want to get out of bed in the morning.

When I feel like my wife doesn't love me, I am aware that this is a very old feeling. I often felt this way with my mother when I was little.

It is confusing that at some moments I can feel that she loves me and at other moments not. Does all of this originate in me?

I have a related set of thoughts that also confuse me. Is it really true that my mother didn't love me, or did I just feel that way because she didn't love me the way I wanted or needed to be loved?

How can you know if someone really loves you?

Here, Barry spontaneously began to "inquire more deeply" into his feelings. There was no specific prompt on my part nor any "prescription" of self-reflective practice. This is typical in the process of psychotherapy: deeper layers of experience begin to rise to the surface of awareness, and the interconnection between past and present begins to reveal itself. Even though there is nothing Buddhist about this example, it does illustrate this book's thematic focus: that problems provide a natural point of entry into self-reflective inquiry.

As this particular dialogue was transpiring, it occurred to me to focus Barry's awareness on how difficult it can be to hold positive and negative feelings side by side, or on how rapidly feelings can and do change. I might also have pursued his spontaneous inquiry about the nature of love. I did not intervene in any of these ways, however; it felt more appropriate just to listen. How the therapeutic inquiry did in fact deepen will be shown later in this chapter, where a further excerpt from the work with Barry will be presented. Regarding mentalization, the basic point is simply that psychotherapy invites deep feelings to the surface to be experienced and understood. It is worth repeating that how the patient is received by the therapist—the therapist's *listening*—is a vital part of the "relational surround" that deepens self-understanding in psychotherapy (Atwood and Stolorow, 1984; Stern, 2010).[7]

Mentalization has a rather complex internal structure, some of which is codified in psychoanalytic object relations theory. But putting theory aside, mentalization underlies how someone relates to others; it allows for understanding an interpersonal interaction as a two-way psychological street. In the example above, for instance, Barry's feeling angry or unlovable was cognitively elaborated into a self-representation ("I am angry or unlovable") and a coordinated representation of the other (burdened and uncaring). One problem that arises in relationships is that mentalization is influenced by self-representations constructed as a function of personal history, and so feelings in the present can be "contaminated" by the past without the person necessarily recognizing that this has occurred.

This has profound implications. First, the quality of relationships depends upon what mentalizations about self and other are constructed in the mind. Second, since we live within these constructed meanings, it is important to become aware of them. What we are blind to in ourselves is the limiting boundary of our freedom.

The Interpersonal Origins of Self-Identity

In order to understand the psychological self and the way it is organized, it is important to bear in mind its roots in emotional attachment and relationship (cf. Chapter 6). The psychodynamics of self-development and function were first described in the "self psychology" of Heinz Kohut. Kohut posited that essential self-functions were played by significant others in the process of psychological development and coined the term *selfobject*[8] to describe these functions. Selfobject functions, according to Kohut, are needed throughout the lifespan to organize self-experience and form the psychic "structures" of the self. He also recognized that selfobject needs both change and mature during psychological development (Kohut, 1971, 1977).

The most basic selfobject needs are for holding, care, mirroring, and validation, all held within the frame of loving connection. These enable homeostatic regulation of basic psychophysiological processes, such as sleep and waking, as well as the modulation of basic affects. As development proceeds, children require increasingly complex empathic responses to the events in their emotional lives in order to metabolize experience and master the challenges of separation and individuation.

In addition to the selfobject functions already mentioned, Stolorow et al. also highlighted the importance of *self-delineation*: the process by which the child's world of personal experience is articulated and validated (Atwood and Stolorow,

1984). Self-delineation is the formation of self-identity: it structures the possibility of what we can say, think, and know.

As Kohut put it, the self at birth is a *virtual self*, a self that develops in the process of being seen and responded to by the (m)other (Wolf, 1988). This is true in earliest psychological life and remains so throughout the life span. Self arises in the matrix of relationship as experience becomes progressively articulated through attuned validation. What is not validated by others will tend to be repressed or will simply fail to come into being. In other words, self is brought forth in relationship to others.

The psychodynamic aspects of the process of self-delineation can be restated this way: we identify with those aspects of self-identity that are responded to by significant others with mirroring, approval, and love. Self-delineating function and self-reflective function dovetail nicely. Just as conversation with another person can help us to define ourselves, so too can the "internal conversation" of self-reflection. We can "try on" new self-concepts in the way that we think about ourselves just as we can try on new behavior with other people. The deep and ongoing conversation we have with ourselves can expand as the development of subjectivity unfolds.

When selfobject needs are insufficiently met, self-function and self-experience become impaired, resulting in the likelihood of psychopathology and inhibited self-functioning (Stolorow and Lachmann, 1980). For this reason, the provision of needed selfobject functions is the cornerstone of therapeutic connection.

The Narrative Structure of Self and Self-Identity

Each person operates within a kind of personal idiom based on a complex concept of the *someone* they have become, including the stor(ies) of how they came to be that way. This is the (evolving) narrative history of self, the story that he or she lives "within." The major autobiographical themes are *who we think we are* (including who we are *afraid* we are); what we *are invested in having, doing, and being*; and *who we think we are supposed to be and/or are striving to become*. These reflect the total prior experience of how someone was related to during early development.

Because narrative shapes self-experience, it is a major focus in psychoanalytic psychotherapy: we explore the concepts someone has about themselves—i.e. their self-representations—and their related mentalizations about others. Self-narratives tend to determine the emotional texture of our subjective experience. Bottom line: when the Story of Me is validated, I feel good; when it is punctured or invalidated, I feel bad. Narrative meaning is a continually changing and developing construction within the mind, and psychotherapy works in part by bringing awareness to it.[9]

One of the most difficult aspects of narratives that define self-identity is that they tend to function as self-fulfilling prophesies, setting up the very circumstances in life that will tend to prove them true. We unconsciously engage others in seeing us in ways that validate our self-identity. Moreover, the whole narrative construction of self often revolves around emotional pain that has not been adequately recognized or processed (Welwood, 2000).[10]

For this reason, negative views of self are quite resistant to change and may often be found at the core of emotional problems. A particular narrative may be perpetuated even after it has been demonstrated how dysfunctional it is. Sometimes a narrative persists even when it has become quite clear that it is not accurate (i.e. it is either no longer true or never was true). Moreover, self-stories impose unconscious boundaries on what is possible for us to experience in life. Because self-narratives are the backbone of self-identity, penetrating our stories and seeing clearly who we think we are is an important key to psychological well-being.

The very concept of self can be understood as narrative: to paraphrase Roy Schafer's idea, *the self is a story; it is the story that there is a self to tell a story to* (Schafer, 1992). In practical terms, this means that the way we understand "self" is very important. When we illuminate the story that we tell ourselves (and others) about who we are, and when we come to understand it *as* a story, we can begin to shape and re-write the story of self in very helpful ways.[11]

The various facets of self and self-identity discussed in this chapter can be systematically investigated in psychotherapy and/or amplified by methods of investigation, inquiry, and self-reflection. We can inquire deeply about the stories of self, about our self-representations, our self-identity, and the way that *selfing* operates within our experience. We can mindfully investigate our ideas about ourselves, who we think we are. We can focus on seeing self-making in action. The structures of the self are also revealed in how one "part" of the self interacts with another part; for example, self-critical behavior may often be a vestige of an underlying dynamic between an angry parent and punished child.

Inquiring more deeply, we can engage in reflection about the power of narratives. Traits and qualities of "self" are concretized, made *real*, by thinking about ourselves in certain ways. We can reflect on the consequences of thinking of the self as having "parts," and we can reflect on the way the "committee of selves" divvies up the territory of our life experience.

In our culture, *self* is expressed in language,[12] and this language rests upon the pronoun "I." We are forever telling stories about ourselves; we are continually narrating ourselves to others. At the same time, however, we are also telling this Story of Me to ourselves—in effect, enclosing one story within another. In his book about the narrative process in psychoanalysis, Roy Schafer (1992) put it this way: "A person can only *tell* a self or encounter it as something *told*" (p. 27, emphasis added). In telling the Story of Me to ourselves, we are in effect imagining into existence an audience who is one's self or oneself (Loy, 2010). To paraphrase Schafer, the self is the story that there is a self to tell to.

Once we recognize that self is narratively *constructed*, we add a very important dimension to awareness practice. It is illuminating to see *selfing* in the stories we tell about ourselves, and, especially, how tenacious this tendency is.[13] Seeing deeply into the process nature of mind is a key dimension of dharma practice.

As has long been recognized in psychoanalysis, there are many narrative aspects of the self to notice. To single out one which is of particular importance (already implied in what is written above), self tends to view itself as singular, integral, and continuous, despite the fact that this is demonstrably untrue; even the briefest experiment with mindfulness meditation clearly shows that experience is discontinuous. Nonetheless, the mind is able to—and does—construct a sense of unique personal identity from the patterns in experience over time. Some psychoanalytic thinkers have recognized that, for this reason, self-identity must be considered to be a narcissistic illusion; it has even been termed "the very mother of illusions."[14]

Inquiring More Deeply about Subjectivity and Self

In Buddhist-informed psychodynamic psychotherapy, time and energy are focused on understanding self in multiple ways:

- By observing emotional reactions, one becomes aware of areas of self that are poorly integrated into the mainstream of the mind, and energy can be directed toward integrating them.
- By learning to see how relationships between self and other are involved at every level of subjective experience, relational entanglements can be recognized and relational problems can be resolved.
- By looking at self-representations and self-identity, as well as how the mind defends them, it becomes possible to diminish narcissistic defenses.
- By exploring subjective states and their vicissitudes, the psychodynamic structure of experience can be illuminated.
- By focusing on articulating the stories in the mind around which "I" gets organized, the story of self becomes more conscious, delineated, and coherent, and self-functions operate more smoothly.

In sum, inquiring deeply attempts to "peel away" the layers of self-identity through the deliberate application of mindful, self-reflective awareness. The fundamental purpose is to see how self-experience is put together in the mind. By observing how self presents itself in our experience, we see the stories that we are made of more clearly and gain a deeper experience of ourselves. This self-reflective awareness begins to transform the experience of self.

Inquiring deeply as described in this book begins with psychotherapeutic dialogue. As was illustrated in the work with Barry, above, self-reflective awareness is an embedded aspect of psychotherapeutic exploration. Where relevant, we can also deepen experience by using self-reflective "practice" adjunctively to amplify awareness of anything that is of particular psychological interest. This can be done in one or both of two ways: (1) as a framework for "living in the question" of something between psychotherapy sessions, and/or (2) as a guided meditative process within a therapy session, with the therapist functioning as a partner or guide to help the patient feel his or her way further into experience.

Simply through the intention to investigate what is going on in the mind—i.e. through the application of mindful attention and self-reflective awareness—experience tends to deepen and unfold. To reiterate the basic idea presented in Chapter 3, inquiry means simply to hold a particular question in mind with the intention to invite a deeper experience to unfold and emerge. Feeling one's way into the experience, one listens inwardly as well as outwardly for answers, alert to discovering one's subjective truth. Indeed, experience tends to deepen simply by setting this intention and mindfully noticing what arises. The key dimension of inquiry is **receptive presence** in the mind; this is an internal space of mindful awareness, relaxing, observing, and allowing experience to arise in whatever way it does. This meditative attitude is akin to lying back and watching the clouds come and go in the sky.

On the surface, this may sound somewhat similar to the classic "rule" of free association in Freudian psychoanalysis: watch thoughts and say whatever comes to mind.[15] However, it is important to note that inquiring deeply does not aim for a stance of detached observation—standing *apart from* experience—but rather mindful *immersion in* experience. Unless experience filters down to include the body and feelings, observation of mind can tend to be intellectualized and sterile. Inquiring deeply is a process of embodied awareness, similar to the "felt sense" in Focusing.

Just as inquiring deeply cannot be equated with free association, it also cannot be equated with mindfulness meditation. It does have a certain similarity to the "open awareness" practice of Buddhist meditation in that it welcomes every subjective experience into awareness. In contrast, however, inquiring deeply focuses on what is of psychological interest. I call it "self-reflective practice" rather than a meditation practice in order to highlight this essential difference in frame and purpose. Similar to mindfulness meditation, however, it does foster an ability to disidentify with the content of awareness.

The use of "prescribed" self-reflection is illustrated in the following clinical material, which unfolded out of Part I and II of the clinical illustration reported earlier.

Clinical Illustration 8.3: Barry, Part III: Inquiring More Deeply

> M.S.   You raised the question of how much of that experience [feeling unloved or unlovable with his wife] originates with you. You might find it useful to investigate that question experientially the next time this set of feelings comes up. Two specific suggestions: first, see if you can notice what story you are telling yourself that connects with those feelings. And second, make a point of feeling deeply into the feeling, as you do when you meditate; get a felt sense of it. Ask yourself: what is this feeling? What does it want/need for me to recognize? See if you can feel where the epicenter is. What is the thorn in your paw? And what specifically do you find so uncomfortable about it?

[Several weeks later.]

B.   *I have been doing the investigation you recommended. What I have noticed is a feeling in my chest, actually a sensation of my heart aching. Then the thought, "I am heartbroken!"*

I associate these feelings with when I was very young and my brother was born. I wanted so much to still be my mother's baby, and it seemed like all she wanted to do was hold my brother. If I needed anything, she acted like my needs were a burden. I think the worst part of it was that when I got really angry at her about it, then I didn't get any sweetness from her at all, and I felt like it was my fault ... I was bad ... who could love such a bad boy?

I can feel how this idea of myself as bad goes very deep. The funny thing is, when I tried to feel my way into the experience of "being bad," as you suggested, it actually didn't feel very true. I know that I am basically a good person. This must be one of those kind of "splits" we've talked about: a feeling that I am bad, side by side with a knowing that I am not bad ...

M.S.   *Yes! There is a lot in what you are saying here. At the core of your experience of being unlovable is the notion that you are bad. And that feeling grew out of the fact that really important needs for love and attention went unmet after your brother was born. You felt like you were bad and wrong for having those needs, and for being angry at your mother for not meeting them. You thought it meant there was something wrong with you, and that you were to blame for the whole situation.*

When you were angry with your mother and your younger brother, your mother conveyed to you that you were a bad boy, and you took that in as a definition of yourself.

Another way to frame what you discovered in your inquiry is that you are beginning to recognize that feeling you are bad is a feeling, not who you are. You are starting to see more clearly that having angry feelings isn't the same as being an angry person, much less being a bad person.

[Soon after this session, Barry described an insight that emerged spontaneously in his morning meditation:]

B.   *As I was meditating in the morning, I found myself thinking about our session on Monday, and it suddenly dawned on me: this same kind of thing must also be true of lots of other views I have about myself. I confuse my thoughts and feelings for who I really am!*

At this point in our work together, Barry was still very much "in the story" of his relationship with his wife and its origins in his early experience. As our work progressed, his experience deepened into ongoing awareness of the *felt sense* of open-hearted and loving connection with his wife (or its absence).

As we inquire deeply and probe self-representations with self-reflective aware-ness, we also begin to see what views of self we are attached to and how and why we perpetuate them. Insights of this nature emerged for Barry as his self-inquiry deepened. Following the work reported in Part III, he had an important insight that started to shift his sense of self:

> *I started to contemplate an important question: who is the real me, in my core, beneath all the things I find ugly and defective about myself? I didn't come up with any answers, but this was very deep. I felt like I was onto something really important for our work as well as for my meditation practice.*

A number of inquiries spontaneously unfolded as a result of this insight. A few of the topics and insights that presented themselves included the following:

> *When something good happens, my mind starts casting about for the familiar anxieties … it reminds me of when I was a child and my adult teeth were starting to come in … the first thing in the morning and all day long I would keep searching for the feel of the loose tooth in my mouth."*
>
> *"I think I locate myself in suffering … it's an important cornerstone of my identity. I have absolutely no idea who I would be without it: maybe I wouldn't even exist. Suffering is a proof of life for me."*
>
> *"I noticed that it is moments when I have open time and don't know what to do with myself that I start ruminating about my relationship with my wife … it's like worrying and ruminating is a default position in my mind.*

This is what I would describe as a wise relationship to narrative. Rather than feeding the fires of suffering with the automatic repetition of painful stories in the mind, the patient brings mindful attention to them. Such self-reflection can yield psychodynamic understanding and, at the same time, it begins to engender a progressive process of self-transformation as the structure of self becomes increasingly transparent.

In this work, as the patient and I engaged in a collaborative inquiry about his concepts about himself relating to current-day problems with anger, he began to be able to see into blind spots that once developed in response to unbearably painful feelings.

As was discussed in Chapter 5, the healing experience in psychotherapy depends upon empathically attuned resonance in the therapeutic relationship. The therapeutic connection and the deepening understanding that psychotherapy provides make it possible for the patient to *be with* what previously had to be defended against. This deepens self-awareness and also reveals defenses that support, justify, and protect dysfunctional views of oneself. The twin poles of this inquiry are the narrative matrix of self-identity, on the one hand, and the psychodynamic underpinnings of relational life, on the other. This psychoanalytic inquiry led Barry naturally and organically into the question, "Who am I?"—a contemplation on the nature of self.

Self-States and Subjective Positions in the Psyche

We may delineate three primary aspects of self-experience: *affective coloration*, sense of *agency*, and *continuity of experience* (Stolorow and Lachmann, 1980).

The first, *affective coloration*, is the embodied experience of emotion. Affect is the core of the psychological self. Much of experience unfolds from this emotional core "outward" into cognition and behavior. The second basic characteristic of self-experience, *agency*, is the ability to form intentions and implement plans of action. The exercise of agency is one of the principal ways that the psychological self organizes meaning. In fact, in self psychology, self is *defined* as this subjective center of initiative and creativity (Kohut, 1971). Concepts of who we are—self-identity—becomes a set of guiding fantasies which organizes what we do and how we do it. The third basic characteristic of self-experience is the experience of *continuity of experience* (*going-on-being*). The felt sense of going-on-being is the bedrock of a cohesive sense of self (Winnicott, 1965a).[16]

These three basic aspects of self-experience—affective coloration, agency, and continuity—are functionally organized into different configurations of experience, termed **self-states** in the preceding discussion: psychological organizations in the internal world with a distinctive quality of thinking and feeling. As self develops, there are predictable shifts in the way subjectivity is organized, referred to in psychoanalysis as **subjective positions** in the psyche.[17]

A subjective position may be defined as an organization of a set of self-states that represents a certain configuration of self and world. We can notice that the very experience of being the subject (to whom experience is happening) is constantly changing as we shift among different subjective positions, different organizations in the mind. In one position, subjective experience may be coherent, with a sense of agency; in another, we may be caught up in a world of thoughts and feelings in which we feel ourselves to be more object than subject. Important experiential characteristics of subjective positions include feeling expansive vs. contracted, cohesive vs. fragmented.

Another important dimension is that of *flow*: immersion in experience with a feeling of energized focus, alignment, and enjoyment (Csikszentmihályi, 1990).[18]

With these experiential qualities in mind, we can conceptualize two contrasting states of subjectivity, or perhaps states of Being. In the first of these, things are going along well and we feel subjectively cohesive. There are no major threats to our models of self and world; we feel alive and integrated. We feel safely expansive, and our psychic structure is able to contain and metabolize our experience. When our minds are optimally tuned and responsive in this way, there is energy available for being present with our experience, and we tend to have a clear sense of Being. There is an experience of going-on-being, which Winnicott called "true self" (called here *true subjectivity*) (Winnicott, 1965b).

In the second state, we encounter events, internal or external, that are so disturbing we can neither effectively process nor let go of them. Psychic defenses are engendered and true subjectivity is interrupted; the effort to avoid experience overwhelms the capacity to be present. In this state, we are reduced to a small segment of our ordinary capacity to respond and may become caught up in dysfunctional thoughts and action. The more intense the emotional reaction, the more constricted our subjectivity tends to become. At such moments, energy goes toward surviving rather than Being.

The idea of true subjectivity was understood by Winnicott in terms of the earliest psychic events in infancy. Attuned maternal attention, Winnicott explained, is necessary to the continuity of the baby's nascent sense of self; absent this maternal attention, reactions to external events impinge upon and disrupt the baby's experience of continuity. Therefore, the development of a cohesive sense of self-experience depends upon the provision of "holding" by the "good enough mother" in early life. When this is not adequately provided, dysregulations of various kinds occur, and subjective experience becomes unstable. Essentially, the mind gets disrupted by strong emotional reactions. Being and reacting are the two alternatives. In Winnicott's words, "reacting interrupts being, and annihilates it" (1965a, p. 47).

Subjective states are dynamic, changing from moment to moment as life events and our reaction to them unfold. In the framework of inquiring deeply, it is posited that it is possible to cultivate and develop a mode of subjectivity called **transcendent subjectivity**: subjective experiences in which awareness is heightened, clarity is sharpened, and things are deeply felt. Further, with sufficient practice and experience, such experiences can in turn become organized into a new subjective position, the **transcendent position**.[19] As defined here, the transcendent position includes but expands beyond Winnicott's idea of the *going-on-being* of true self. It is a subjective position in the psyche characterized by both a stable configuration of going-on-being and keen self-reflective awareness of that state. The transcendent position is a form of subjectivity epitomized by heightened awareness of Being. This subjective experience often emerges in the course of mindfulness meditation practice and deepens as a function of depth of meditation.

Transcendent subjectivity may come about in a myriad of ways: in meditation practice, in experiences of nature, or in music or art. It also frequently involves a deepening of one's interiority. Regardless of how it comes about, this heightened sense of being allows for wise knowing of what is so. And, it invites a deepening experience of compassion.

Summarizing the different threads of this discussion, inquiring deeply develops and sharpens self-reflective function and, in so doing, facilitates the emergence of transcendent subjectivity, a new "subjective position" in the psyche.[20] This enhancement of self-reflective function leads to greater cohesion of the psychological self.

At first blush, this view may seem confusing to Buddhist practitioners: isn't *developing* the self at odds with the Buddhist teaching of non-self (**anatta**)? Isn't Buddhism supposed to encourage *dissolution* of the self? This apparent contradiction is actually a misunderstanding based on confusion between different meanings of "self." Mindful self-reflection strengthens the psychological self. At the same time, however, it also allows us to see the truth of non-self, as will be further described in the next section.

The "Problem of Self": Understanding the Buddhist View

One of the cornerstones of Buddhist thought is the premise that we are mistaken in the belief, the assumption, that personal self *exists*—that there is a personal self (noun), the identity of which is singular, separate, and independent of the world that constitutes it. This misguided view of self, and the personality-based perspective on which it is built, entraps most people in a tangle of psychological suffering. This is the essential "problem of self" (Schuman, 1991) and the remedy for it, according to Buddhism, is a radical alteration of world view, called "non-self" (or "not-self"). In the words of one teacher, "no self, no problem" (Thubten, 2009).

This idea is quite challenging for many people to understand because it seems to fly in the face of ordinary subjective experience. What can "non-self" possibly mean when being a self seems to be a given? The mind feels boggled in attempting to comprehend it.

The ordinary (given) experience of self is based in the assumption that body, feelings, perceptions, thoughts, and even consciousness belong to *this* person (identity view). In contrast, the Buddhist truth of non-self is based in the understanding that there is no independently existing separate self, no "I," "me," or "mine" independent of the network of relationships in which I am embedded. In other words, "self" is embedded in a web of being, interdependent and co-arising with everything else; self has no existence independent of the other.[21] Note that this is an ontological, not a psychological proposition: it simply means that no one thing has existence independent of all others.[22] As one Buddhist teacher puts it, the psychological self is real, it's just not *really* real. It is phenomenologically real, but not ontologically real.

Apart from clarifying what Buddhism is pointing to when it says "non-self," it is important to emphasize that this understanding is not conceptual so much as intuitive and experiential. Apart from directly experiencing the truth of non-self, usually in a meditative context, non-self can be discovered in ordinary experience in several different ways:

- *By seeing that every aspect of what we call self intrinsically involves relationship: to other people, to other living beings, to the environment, and to human culture.*
- *By becoming self-reflectively aware that self is not a thing, but rather a set of activities of mind that varies continually from moment to moment.*
- *By recognizing how self lives in the mind as narrative.*

Inquiring deeply addresses the "problem of self" very differently than does Buddhist psychology. In place of advocating that we drop the story of the self,[23] it delves into the experience of self by probing the layers of self-identity. From a self-psychological, psychodynamic vantage point, the "problem" is not self *per se*, but the fact that *selfing* gets overinvested as a defensive response to narcissistic injury or threat. Selfing has the function of protecting the vulnerable psyche from psychological pain.

This understanding re-casts the "problem of self." From this view, it is clear that too much self is not the problem at all. Quite the contrary, selfing is a defense against an insufficiently cohesive sense of self. We need to *strengthen* the self, not in the sense of shoring up our self-representations, but rather by cultivating self-awareness and developing a more cohesive experience of going-on-being.

Buddhist psychologist Jack Engler expressed this same insight in his well-known statement, "You have to be somebody before you can be nobody" (Engler, 2003, p. 35).

The nature of self becomes more transparent as mindful exploration deepens and more subtle levels of awareness are engaged. It becomes quite apparent that all self-experience is constructed of simple experiential phenomena and narrative. Non-self in Buddhism is not an esoteric philosophy, but rather a method for bringing mindful attention to self-experience. The realization of non-self is intended as a remedy to free people from the trap of painful illusions of separateness and alienation. Only through the realization of non-self, the Buddha taught, is it possible to find liberation from the web of suffering in which every human self is entangled.

In conclusion, self is not a problem; it is an essential activity of mind which provides and maintains positive affective coloration, temporal continuity, and cohesive self-experience. This is not only not a problem; it is a necessity for well-being. The proposition that self is a problem can itself cause problems, if this is understood to mean that we should somehow defend against who we are. Although there is deep truth in what the Buddha taught, we need to balance the truth of non-self with wise understanding of the psychological functions of self. Inquiring deeply is informed by both points of view.

Mindful Awareness, Self-Reflection, and the Development of Subjectivity

The discussion presented in this chapter is intended to provide a conceptual framework for inquiring deeply into subjective experience. The process described begins with psychotherapeutic exploration, and sometimes includes self-reflective awareness practice as an adjunctive intervention. Although inquiry can focus on anything of psychological interest, its epicenter is typically psychological wounds, long-standing painful patterns of emotional reaction.

As explained in preceding chapters, narratives tend to congeal around painful emotion, encapsulating areas of unprocessed experience and trauma within the psyche. While narratives protect the psyche by providing a context of meaning for painful experience, ironically they often wind up repeating and perpetuating difficult feelings. Inquiring deeply begins from the assumption that psychotherapeutic narratives entail communication that is in search of understanding and recognition. It is important to emphasize that *narrative* here refers not only to what is communicated in spoken language, but also to what is expressed in the body, what is enacted in behavior, and what is revealed in the form of problems. Deep emotional understanding of narratives within the psychotherapeutic relationship is the foundation of psychological healing.

Psychotherapeutic exploration and inquiry in the framework of the above discussion highlights narratives of self, including mentalizations about self and other. It focuses therapeutic attention on how subjectivity is organized in the mind: psychodynamic awareness of self, other, and how relationship is held in mind. In and of itself, engaging in this process contributes to the development of further self-reflective capacity. Also, because narrative constructs create meaning, they lead to more constructive, compassionate, and self-empowering mentalizations.

Self-reflective awareness practices amplify subjective experience through the intention to pay attention to and observe what one is aware of from moment to moment. De facto, mindful awareness enhances the ability to de-center and take a step back from experience. It can yield insight into the fact that mind is essentially a continuously unfolding process rather than a set of fixed conditions—"*minding*" rather than simply "*mind*." And, articulating observations and insights within the relational therapeutic field further reinforces self-reflective awareness.

The starting point in inquiring deeply is not different from what might occur in mindfulness meditation when a difficult experience arises. Some nexus of reactivity within oneself has surfaced. In Buddhist practice, the aim would be to bring "bare attention" to the experience—that is to say, to *be with* reactivity, to notice the experience in the body and associated thoughts and images. In contrast, in a psychotherapeutic framework the aim is to explore the context of meaning in which reactivity is embedded, including its story line, and the experience of self and other connected to it.

As explained above, narratives are a primary matrix/structure that organize each person's subjective reality, sense of self, and relationships with others. It is vitally important for narrative structure to remain open and pliant, alive and responsive to changing circumstances. When instead, however, it becomes rigid and inflexible, it may become like an outgrown exoskeleton, confining us within meanings that have long outgrown their psychological usefulness. So the primary goal in inquiring deeply is to unpack narrative, see the stories in the mind as *story*, and feel the underlying feelings more fully. In this way, self-understanding deepens, wiser versions of our stories can be created, and self-experience can shift profoundly.

When a therapist and/or patient has their awareness and cognitive skills honed in mindfulness meditation, this entire process is aided and abetted. The combination of mindfulness and psychodynamic self-reflection furthers the development of self-reflective awareness.[24] Together, this promotes cognitive flexibility and emotional resilience by virtue of the repeated alternation between direct experience of subjectivity and the observation of one's experience.[25]

The focus on narrative in inquiring deeply is not at odds with the Buddhist understanding that stories in the mind are empty. It is true that narratives are fabricated, but it does not follow that they are simply conditioned associations devoid of value. At the same time, however, this does not imply that we should attempt to explore every narrative in the mind (which would in any case be impossible).[26]

What is needed is a wise relationship to narrative. It is easy to get lost in our stories, and it takes a particular kind of self-reflective awareness to recognize when we are in the grips of one. Narratives can be quite mindless and repetitive in a way which pulls the mind into dysphoric experience. To the extent that we do not hold narratives consciously, they tend to have *us* unconsciously.

Even when we know on a rational level a particular narrative is untrue and/or unhelpful, the narrative may often be quite resistant to change.[27] Narratives represent unprocessed emotional pain and often substitute for feeling things fully. For example, when we are angry with someone, all of our energy may be drawn into the narrative of what they have done wrong; and to that extent, we don't take the time to really feel the hurt that is underneath. For this reason, it is important that inquiring deeply be grounded in and integrate experience of both body and mind. Absent embodied feeling and compassion—i.e. without "heart experience"—inquiry becomes dry and flat, and, what's worse, useless.

To reiterate, narratives have subjective truth that can be recognized. They often represent unprocessed emotional pain and are driven by an inability to feel the underlying feelings more fully. Simply by engaging in a process of self-reflection with an attitude of inquiry, subjective truth is given the opportunity to reveal itself. For example, in Clinical Illustration 8.3, by investigating his experience with the simple inquiry, "What is this feeling?" Barry was able to notice a deep experience of "heartbroken" that might otherwise have been overlooked.

Meanwhile, the therapist's role is to listen empathically to what is said, what is not said, and often to what has never even been thought. Narratives are reworked in the form of the spontaneous dance of conversation, ideas, and feelings which emerge in the here-and-now of the therapy process. This deep understanding can untangle painful knots of story and reactivity.

Inquiring deeply in psychotherapy also has a didactic dimension, as the therapist intervenes to highlight the process of *listening for* and *being receptive to* what is emerging at the leading edge of the patient's experience. Patients expose aspects of themselves for review, and the therapist's role is to illuminate what might be usefully investigated in more depth. Sometimes, the role may be to devise practices for constructive self-reflection, such as the one "prescribed" for Barry in the clinical illustration. As patients articulate their experience and the therapist reflects aloud about what is being said, new possibilities for how to relate wisely to life often come into view. Moreover, the Buddhist-informed psychotherapist can help to bring Buddhist insights about self into the relational field of psychotherapy. In both of these ways, inquiring deeply can further the emergence of creative responses to old problems. This amounts to a newly delineated sense of self.

In sum, as the stories of a life are reexamined and retold in psychodynamic treatment, self-experience develops as a function of how the therapeutic connection is *felt*. This was described in Chapter 5 as both *present moments* and *moments of presence*. Inquiring deeply in psychotherapy is a *co-created process of self-reflection*, in which the therapist is partner and sometimes guide.

Inquiring Deeply and Self-Reflection: Conclusions

We come full circle now, back to the opening questions about self-reflective awareness and its role in mindfulness-informed psychotherapy. The fundamental point elaborated in this chapter is that the capacity for self-reflection is the bedrock on which self-function is built. (The truth that "you are not the self that you take yourself to be" is a wonderful topic for contemplation.)

Through the ongoing process of self-reflection, awareness gradually permeates the entire spectrum of experience, from the embodied level through the psychological and relational, and metapsychological layers of the mind. Metapsychological self-awareness, informed by Buddhist meditation, can be defined most simply as awareness of how one *relates to* self-function and to the mind itself (cf. Chapter 9). In this complex interplay between self-awareness and narrative dialogue, a transcendent position in self-function is gradually consolidated, and self becomes more transparent. There is power in making this an explicit goal in psychotherapy.

Through the practice of self-reflection, we see more and more deeply into the body/heart/mind and the nature of self. Upon this foundation, the transcendent position is built. It has been said that mindfulness is the state of mind in which you realize that you are not your state of mind. By this definition, and in this way, inquiring deeply progresses seamlessly into dharma practice.

Notes

1 This chapter is primarily based on two psychoanalytic theories: the *self psychology* of Heinz Kohut and the intersubjectivity theory in the work of Robert Stolorow and his colleagues. These theories provide a foundation for understanding the primary aspects of self-experience and self-structure. See Stolorow, R. et al. (1994); Atwood and Stolorow (1984); Stolorow and Atwood (1992).

2 Although the term "subjective experience" is used repeatedly in this chapter, this is actually a redundant phrase, because *all* experience is subjective. "Subjective" is one of a pair of dualistically defined opposites, subjective vs. objective. This polarity highlights a presumed difference between what we experience in the mind—internal reality—and that which is assumed to have a different order of being, the external "objective" world.

3 The word "self" as a noun confers the idea that self is a *thing* and reifies the experience of selfhood. This reification, in the Buddhist view, supports the view of separate self in a way which underlies psychological suffering. In contrast, in action language self becomes a verb, "selfing," which conveys the idea of self as an activity of mind. Particular meanings of "selfing" are described later in the chapter.

4 "Narcissistic defenses."

5 Self-awareness always entails some interpenetration of self as the subject and self as the object in experience. Though easy to distinguish at a conceptual level, these two poles of experience—subject and object—are not experientially separate, but rather comprise a seamless whole. How experience moves between these two poles of self-awareness has been termed "self-reflexivity" (Aron, 2000). The degree of self-reflexivity is an important indicator of the development of subjectivity and the maturity of self-function.

6 It was Fonagy who clearly conceptualized the essential interconnections between relationship and mentalization and highlighted the importance of attachment and affect in

this process. A wonderful and very accessible summary of this work can be found in Wallin (2007).

7 The concept of "relational surround" comes from intersubjectivity theory.

8 Note that a Kohutian "selfobject" (no hyphen) is a function rather than a person. "Self-object," written with a hyphen, can be used more generically to mean either function or person who serves that function.

9 In addition to explicit autobiographical narrative, which continues to unfold throughout the life span, it is important to recognize that many aspects of self-identity are implicit. These are expressed in the form of personality traits developed during the gradual assimilation of life experiences. They are also encompassed within social roles we take on or aspire to as we develop. From earliest life, this aspect of self-identity is engaged by the question adults routinely ask of children: *What do you want to be when you grow up?* In broadest form, self-identity is one of the major developmental tasks of every life. John Welwood calls it "The Identity Project" (Welwood, 2000).

10 See discussion of metabolizing experience in Chapter 6.

11 Buddhist teachings shift the paradigm of self altogether in a way that is intended to be radically psychotherapeutic. See heading, "The Problem of Self."

12 The interested reader will find many interesting points in Schafer's book, *Action Language in Psychoanalysis* (1987). Fast (1998) also discusses self as an active process, which she terms "selving."

13 Note, also, that the relationship between language and mind is an important inquiry in its own right. Language is itself an important *action*.

14 J. Engler (2003) citing Harry Stack Sullivan.

15 Free-association is not only the basic instruction for psychoanalysis but also its intended result. When the mind can free associate freely and without impediment, the psycho-analytic cure is said to be complete.

16 This topic is also explored in the work of Epstein (1995), a psychiatrist who has written extensively about the psychodynamics of experience from a Buddhist point of view.

17 This concept was first elaborated by the psychoanalyst Melanie Klein. In Kleinian thought, the two major subjective positions in psychological development are called the paranoid and depressive positions, respectively. These are defined in terms of the "internal objects" that predominate in experience (see Chapter 9). In the para-noid position of infancy, unresolved hate toward the loved object—prototypically the mother—exists in an unintegrated state, resulting in fragmented and primitive state of emotional life. As the hateful feelings and "phantasies" of the paranoid position are resolved, the urge to repair can mature along with the capacity to mourn what has been lost or damaged; hence, the depressive position is seen as a developmental achievement.

18 Csíkszentmihályi defined flow as a state of immersion or absorption in whatever one is doing. Flow is a state of highly focused motivation in which the emotions are not just contained and channeled, but also positive, energized, and aligned with the task at hand. He defined it as a mental state of intrinsic motivation in which we become so involved in what is happening that nothing else seems to matter; we are aligned with ourselves and with the moment—"in the zone" or "in the groove." This is a feeling everyone has at times, characterized by a feeling of great absorption, engagement, fulfillment, and skill—during which temporal concerns (time, food, ego needs, etc.) are typically ignored. Note the similarity to Winnicott's concept of going-on-being.

19 This is similar to yet different from the "transcendent position" defined by Grotstein and Franey (2008) based on the work of W. F. Bion: a formless form of subjectivity that is within us, around us, and beyond us. A "transcendent function" was also described in the work of C. G. Jung in reference to the tension between conscious and unconscious

contents of mind; the emergence of fantasy, dream, or vision bridges the gap between these two mental domains.

20 In an earlier paper, I described it as an "evolution of subjectivity" (Schuman, 1998).

21 Or, as D. W. Winnicott pointed out in a different context, there is no such thing as a baby without a mother (1965a).

22 Ultimately, this means that there are no things at all!

23 This idea can more appropriately be attributed to Buddhist teachers than to the Buddha.

24 Mindfulness meditation practice supports and enhances this process. As the mind becomes more settled and unified in meditation, one sees more clearly what is going on. So mindfulness practice not only engages self-reflective awareness, it also *deepens* it.

25 "Self-reflexivity" (see this chapter, Note 5).

26 I also do not intend to suggest here that every narrative has encoded meanings; as Freud famously said, "Sometimes a cigar is just a cigar." The emphasis in the present discussion is on the purpose and meaning of narrative in the overall function of the psyche.

27 One of the major reasons why narratives are intractable to change may have to do with the relational ties that are involved.

References

Aron, L. (2000). Self-reflexivity and the therapeutic action of psychoanalysis. *Psychoanalytic Psychology, 17*, 667–689.

Atwood, G. E. and Stolorow, R. D. (1984). *Structures of subjectivity: Explorations in psychoanalytic phenomenology*. Hillsdale, NJ: Analytic Press.

Csíkszentmihályi, M. (1990). *Flow: The psychology of optimal experience*. New York, NY: Harper & Row.

Engler, J. (2003). Being somebody and being nobody: A reexamination of the understanding of self in psychoanalysis and Buddhism. In Safran, J. D. (Ed.) *Psychoanalysis and Buddhism: An unfolding dialogue* (pp. 35–100). Somerville, MA: Wisdom Publications.

Epstein, M. (1995). *Thoughts without a thinker: Psychotherapy from a Buddhist perspective*. New York, NY: Basic Books.

Falkenstrom, F. (2003). A Buddhist contribution to the psychoanalytic psychology of self. *International Journal of Psychoanalysis, 84*, 1551–1568.

Fast, I. (1998). *Selving: A relational theory of self organization*. Hillsdale, NJ: Analytic Press.

Fonagy, P., Gergely, G., Jurist, E. and Target, M. (2002). *Affect regulation, mentalization, and the development of self*. New York, NY: Other Press.

Gendlin, E. (1978). *Focusing*. New York: Bantam Books/Random House.

Grotstein, J. S. and Franey, M. (2008). Conversations with clinicians: Who is the writer who writes the books. *Fort Da, 14*, 87–116.

Kohut, H. (1971). *The analysis of the self*. Madison, CT: International Universities Press.

Kohut, H. (1977). *The restoration of the self*. Madison, CT: International Universities Press.

Loy, D. (2010). *The world is made of stories*. Somerville, MA: Wisdom Publications.

Mitchell, S. A. (1993). *Hope and dread in psychoanalysis*. New York, NY: Basic Books.

Mitchell, S. A. (2000). *Relationality: From attachment to intersubjectivity*. Hillsdale, NJ: Analytic Press.

Schafer, R. (1976). *A new language for psychoanalysis*. New Haven, CT: Yale University Press.

Schafer, R. (1992). *Retelling a life: Narration and dialogue in psychoanalysis.* New York, NY: Basic Books.

Schuman, M. (1991). The problem of self in psychoanalysis: Lessons from Eastern philosophy. *Psychoanalysis and Contemporary Thought, 14*(4), 595–624.

Schuman, M. (1998). Suffering and the evolution of subjectivity. Paper presented at a conference on Psychotherapy, Spirituality, and the Evolution of Mind. Santa Monica, Calif. May 15–17, 1998.

Stern, D. (2010). *Partners in thought: Working with unformulated experience, dissociation, and enactment.* New York, NY: Routledge Press.

Stolorow, R. D. and Lachmann, F. M. (1980). *Psychoanalysis of developmental arrests: Theory and treatment.* Madison, CT: International Universities Press.

Stolorow, R. D. and Atwood, G. (1992). *Contexts of being: The inter-subjective foundations of psychological life.* Hillsdale, NJ: Analytic Press.

Stolorow, R. D., Atwood, G. and Brandschaft, B. (1994). *The intersubjective perspective.* Northvale, NJ: Jason Aronson Press.

Thubten, A. (2009). *No self, no problem.* Ithaca, NY: Snow Lion Publications.

Wallin, D. J. (2007). *Attachment in psychotherapy.* New York, NY: Guilford Press.

Welwood, J. (2000). *The psychology of awakening.* Boston, MA: Shambhala Publications.

Winnicott, D. W. (1965a). Ego distortion in terms of true and false self. In Winnicott, D. W. (1965), *The maturational processes and the facilitating environment: Studies in the theory of emotional development* (pp. 37–55). Madison, CT: International Universities Press.

Winnicott, D. W. (1965b). Ego distortion in terms of true and false self. In Winnicott, D. W. (1965), *The maturational processes and the facilitating environment: Studies in the theory of emotional development* (pp. 140–152). Madison, CT: International Universities Press.

Wolf, E. S. (1988). *Treating the self: Elements of clinical self-psychology.* New York, NY: Guilford Press.

Chapter 9

Mind as Object

In relational psychotherapy, the central premise is that the way self, other, and connection are implicitly represented or "held in mind" is at the core of personality and of relationship problems. The mind is organized for relationship; actively seeking connection is one of its major functions. To restate this idea in psychoanalytic language, human beings are "object seeking."

The psychoanalytic jargon is unfortunate because it dehumanizes the actual human *other* (literally objectifying him or her). Making matters worse, the term "object" is indiscriminately used to refer to the actual Other or to the mental image of the other.

The term "object" is replete with additional confusions. In philosophy and phenomenology, an "object of mind" is anything symbolically represented, known, or thought about in the mind; it is a mental image or idea of something not currently sensed or perceived.

The different meanings of "object" will be clarified in the present chapter, beginning with the philosophical object in Western philosophy, progressing to the Buddhist object, and from there delving into the nature of the psychoanalytic "internal object." After these preliminary reflections, the chapter will take up its principal topic: how the mind relates to *itself* as an internal object.

The Object in Western Philosophy

"Objects" in Western philosophy refer inclusively to anything that is apprehended by the mind: sensations, perceptions, feelings, thoughts, concepts, and ideas. They include beliefs, interpretations, assumptions, theories, images, fantasies, dreams, and anything else that is a product of the mind.

Implicit by definition as well as in the structure of language, the *object* is *what* is experienced and the *subject* is *who* does the experiencing. The subject of experience is thus separated from its mental object. This "subject–object dualism" creates problems for how to give a coherent account of the relation between the two. The question "Who is experiencing?" is one conundrum. ("Who?" also poses interesting issues about *subjectivity*, taken up in the previous chapter.) A complex set of questions about "What?" also comes into play. Is *inside* fundamentally different in substance from *outside* (external reality)? Is there such a thing as "objective reality"—reality that is independent of the perceiver or observer?

Attempts in Western philosophy to solve these philosophical dilemmas have given rise to a number of different theories/conceptualizations about these fundamental issues: materialism, idealism, etc.[1] A full discussion of the philosophical implications goes well beyond the scope of the present chapter (Wallace, 2003). For our purposes here, the philosophical object is understood to be any sensation, perception, concept, or idea that is noticed in experience. Such objects of mind, "mental objects," have no sensory properties, no mass, and no location.

The Buddhist Object

In essence, the Buddha's core teachings about the mind are stated in the opening verse of the Dhammapada, a classic Buddhist text: all experience is mind made, preceded by mind and led by mind (Fronsdal, 2005). The premises of Buddhist psychology are spelled out in the Abhidhamma, the part of the Pali Canon that descriptively catalogues the varieties of mental experience (Olendzki, 2010).[2]

The basic objects of mind recognized in Buddhism are identical to those described in Western philosophy: sensations, perceptions, feelings, thoughts, concepts or ideas in the mind, and so forth. Buddhist psychology spells out how basic elements of experience—"aggregates"—combine to form the stream of subjective experience. What is most fundamental in the Buddhist approach is its focus on the importance of becoming aware of how experience is constructed. For this reason, it teaches a method for seeing the construction of experience as it happens.

The fundamental nature of the mind, as taught in Buddhism, is to know different experiences in each moment. The mind is said to know itself only through moment-to-moment experiences as they arise—i.e. through mental objects; it is nothing other than these successive objects of mind (Gunaratana, 2012). The Buddhist view is that the subject and the object of experience cannot be separated. There is no "subject" at all apart from the object of experience, nor vice versa. In other words, the Buddhist mind is not predicated on subject–object duality.[3]

Buddhism recognizes many different mental states as well as altered states of consciousness brought about during periods of strong concentration. Awareness deepens as the mind becomes increasingly unified and balanced. One aspect of such deepening is increasing awareness of awareness: awareness of the background state of awareness, which underlies subjective experience. Background awareness—referred to here as Awareness with capital A—may be thought of as a space that "contains" mental objects. Awareness of Awareness is one of the intended consequences of mindfulness meditation practice. It is a state of deep stillness and awareness of now.[4]

Although Awareness is essentially ineffable, it can be conveyed to some extent through poetry and metaphor. For example, it has been described as "the sound of silence" (Sumedho, 2007). In another metaphor, this essence of mind is likened to an infinitely reflecting mirror, perfectly clear and luminous: it is not possible to distinguish between the surface of the mirror and what is reflected in it, and we cannot say whether the image seen is "in" the mirror or "in" the world. Along the same lines, in Zen it is said that essential mind is like the moon reflected on water: the moon does not get wet, the water isn't broken, and the reflection occurs equally in the vast expanse of a mountain lake or a drop of water. Even the whole moon, the whole sky, rests perfectly in a single dewdrop on the grass.

In this poetic language can be found inklings of deeper truth. As Hokusai says in the lines of poetry that open this book, there is no end to what can be seen. Though the deep nature of mind is essentially empty of anything, the emptiness contains infinite possibilities for the manifestation of experience. It is a space of potentiality that we cannot grasp intellectually, but whose qualities we can explore by deliberately focusing on experience as it arises from moment to moment. By learning to engage attention in certain specific ways—through meditation, contemplation, and self-reflection—we can deepen direct experience and *intuitive awareness* of the nature of mind.

The intention in meditative practice is to learn to relax and let go into experience, and also to develop a quality of consciousness which is clear and unified. Such a mind, it is said, is diamond-like in its capacity to reflect experience, and the more the mind can be stilled, the more clearly and deeply reality can be seen.

The Psychoanalytic Object

Distinct from the "object" in Western philosophy or Buddhism, the ***internal object*** of psychoanalysis is a cognitive representation of the relationship between self and other: memories, feelings, and fantasies stored in the mind as composite representations of experiences with significant others. According to psychoanalytic object relations theory, these cognitive representations are captured in the psyche as *schemas*—embodied patterns of memory. Schemas are acquired through learning, i.e. internalized in the psyche as mental structures. Personality thereafter bears their imprint.

Object relations theory is a fundamental structural hypothesis in psychoanalysis. It is a way of understanding the organization of relational experience in body/mind/brain. To reiterate its basic premise, memories of relationships become incorporated in the structure of the mind as internal objects. This process can be conveyed in architectural metaphor:

- The mind is constructed.
- Internal objects are an important set of building blocks in its construction.
- Internal objects are connected together into an organizational/relational matrix, a blueprint that gives shape to experience as it unfolds from moment to moment.

Hopefully it has been made sufficiently clear in the foregoing that mental "structures" are themselves concepts. Any implied reification of them is entirely unintended.

Adding to the theoretical complexity, we can also think of the psyche—either in toto or in part—as an internal object in its own right. The basic idea here is that the mind can and does relate to itself (or aspects of itself) in a manner analogous to the way it relates to others. In other words, subjective experience has an intrinsically relational, self–other dimension; our relationship to our own minds mirrors both how others have related to us and how we have related to them. To give some commonplace examples, we may dislike or even disavow some aspect of ourselves that reminds us of a parent or sibling. Or, enacting familiar ways of being treated by others, we may be impatient with ourselves, punish ourselves, etc. We may also speak of our reactions to things we have said, done, or thought as if they were perpetrated by another, e.g. "I was disappointed in myself." Psyche takes on characteristics of an Other.

Just as all relationships are complex and multidimensional, so too is the mind's relationship to itself. We may relate to the mind as a whole (generally considered to be "my mind" or "myself") or we may relate to particular aspects of mind.[5] Moreover, the quality of relatedness varies. For example, most commonly one feels a sense of **agency**, an experience of being the *doer*. At other times, however, one may feel acted upon *by* a mental state. For instance, someone may feel desperate for sleep but find their mind stuck in a series of thoughts that do not permit relaxation and sleep to occur; insomnia may even take on a persecutory quality.

With deep mindful awareness, the relationship to mind may sometimes take on a new quality: objects of mind may be experienced as simply happening, arising without a sense of agency (or with a sense of *non-agency*: "thoughts without a thinker" (Epstein, 1995)). In this regard, the mind seems to have a mind of its own. (This is one possible experience in the "transcendent subjective position" discussed in Chapter 8.)

To summarize and restate the basic idea in the language of psychoanalysis, the mind itself has the aspect of a complex internal object (Levin, 2010).[6] A dynamic dance occurs between different parts of ourselves, just as occurs in interpersonal relationships. We may project onto the mind as an internal object(s) and develop transferences toward these internal objects in much the same way as we enact our internal world in relationship to other people.[7] This mental architecture of internal objects governs the design and organization of the mind's relationship to itself.

Psychological Functions of Mind as Object

According to psychoanalytic theory, the mind's capacity to function as its own internal object goes through several preliminary stages of development during the earliest years. One archaic form is the phenomenon of "hallucinatory wish fulfillment." For example, sucking a pacifier presumably helps to soothe the infant by evoking a fantasy/memory of being at the breast. The experience of soothing—a mental state—is in this first stage engaged by the use of sensory reminders; later in development there will be more symbolic ways to evoke the memory of maternal holding.

Transitional objects are probably the most well-known example of the mental representation of maternal soothing. In the transitional stage of development, the baby learns to use an external object, generally something soothing such as a soft blanket, to deliberately evoke this experience for himself or herself. This is a primal act of self-soothing.

D. W. Winnicott (1971) characterized such *transitional phenomena* as involving both creation and discovery in the baby's mind. Later in development, the experience of comfort will come to be mediated by a broad repertoire of possible stimuli, including physical activity, interpersonal interactions, creative endeavors, music, or various symbolic enactments in the form of reading, writing, or listening to stories. Although the experience of comfort may occur within the domain of the "private self," it has relational underpinnings. It helps the mind metabolize experience (see Chapter 7).

The "Mind-Object"

As development progresses toward increasingly complex mental capacities, the cognitive mind becomes able to take over doing what originally was needed from the parent, providing support, comfort, and assistance to the psychologically vulnerable self. Executive functions of *planning*, *organizing*, and *doing* in particular are substituted for relational functions that are missing to at least some degree from the interpersonal milieu. In essence, the mind becomes a parentified internal object. This results in a reliance on the mind at the expense of bodily experience, a fracturing of what is presumed to have been, originally, a seamless connection between psyche and soma.

Corrigan and Gordon (1995), following upon the earlier ideas of D. W. Winnicott and others, termed this kind of mental structure the "mind-object": precocious development of the intellect that compensates for what was missing developmentally. A mind-object is likely to develop most strongly in children who are bright as well as highly anxious.

Corrigan and Gordon reported on a series of patients whom they described as "fiercely attached" to their mind as an object, and some of the self-reports of the people they described clinically are worth quoting to give the flavor of a mind-object:

- One patient, "Mr. A.," described the recognition of his effort to be in "fierce control. The very act of making something happen—no matter how insignificant—is what that is about for me."
- A second patient, "Mr. B.," tells his therapist, "My mind is like a factory; it has to produce work."
- "Miss C.," a profoundly depressed woman, speaks of "never being able to relax or trust her academic and career accomplishments." Despite exemplary achievement, fears of failure and exposure are ever present.
- "Mrs. D.," a young physician and mother, describes how "I do everything in a hurry ... I'm always ahead of time ... but I feel if I wait, it won't happen."

What can be seen in these brief clinical descriptions is a personality pattern in which the mind is used in the service of doing, thinking, and striving for achievement. Using the mind in these ways becomes overvalued and exploited; these functions are vigilantly protected, and their loss is constantly dreaded. The mind-object promises perfection and omnipotent control, but in place of satisfaction this ceaseless search may instead yield anxiety, depression, and threatened breakdown. This way of functioning denies the person the ability to relax into just being; instead, s(he) gets caught in the constant effort to stimulate and enliven themselves.

The concept of the mind-object sheds light on common personality traits such as obsessionality, perfectionism, and the need for control, as discussed further in the remainder of this chapter. This is not one personality style, however. As Corrigan and Gordon commented about their series of cases, patients varied in the nature and extent of their pathology as well as in personal style; some were narcissistic, some depressed, some boringly obsessive, while others were wonderfully quick and humorous.

In psychodynamic terms, the mind-object represents reliance and focus on intellectual function at the expense of bodily experience. None of this group of patients were on particularly good terms with their libido or with their bodies in general; many suffered from medical conditions with significant psychosomatic components. Investment of psychic energy in the mind-object fractures what is presumed to be, originally, a seamless integration of psyche and soma (Corrigan and Gordon, 1995).

Some Clinical Illustrations: Inquiring Deeply and the Mind-Object

Inquiring deeply provides an opportunity to gain insight into mind-object functions. I have found this perspective to be very useful in my work, and it has come to be one of the cornerstones of my clinical thinking. The following case examples will, I hope, show how valuable the mind-object concept is within the paradigm of relational–psychoanalytic psychotherapy.

These vignettes are fairly representative of how mind-object issues "show up" in inquiring deeply. They are also intended to show how self-reflective practice can be used within this therapeutic framework. With patients, I sometimes frame this as inquiry into *how mind is held in mind*. An analytically oriented clinician might regard it as exploration of the mind as internal object.

In any event, the following clinical illustrations summarize selected aspects of my work with two long-term psychotherapy patients who happened also to be practitioners of mindfulness meditation. The patients were very dissimilar in terms of their presenting problems, but each struggled with mind-object issues. Some general characteristics can be gleaned from the descriptions given earlier in the series of patients reported by Corrigan and Gordon. The emphasis in the clinical summaries reported here is on patients' self-reflective observations and insights.

Clinical Illustration 9.1: Daniel

*Daniel was referred to me by a dharma colleague for help with "person-
ality issues" that came up in his efforts to learn how to meditate. Despite
a lot of reassurance and the fact that he "knew better, intellectually,"
Daniel felt defeated by his difficulties with concentration and considered
himself a bad meditator. Mindfulness meditation was the latest in a long
series of situations in which Daniel fell short of his own standards of
performance.*

*Daniel was a 50-year-old man, a successful technical writer. He described
himself as a hard worker and a chronic worrier; he suffered—among other
problems—with a painful degree of shyness, social awkwardness, and a sense
of isolation from others. He tended to be very perfectionistic about everything
he did in life. It seemed quite clear to me from his presenting problems and
the psychological history associated with them that Daniel was chronically
depressed. His negative self-assessments in regard to meditation seemed to
reflect a deep vein of negativity toward himself. While we would need to
explore the dynamic origins of this, my first intervention was to focus clinical
attention on the harsh self-criticism.*

*At the time he first came to see me, Daniel viewed his self-assessments as
"true" and completely justified. (The pattern was quite egosyntonic.) Since
he was eager to apply his meditation practice, I suggested to him that mindful
noticing and self-reflective awareness of his "report card mentality" would
be a good place to start.*

*It was not difficult for us to discover that the bad marks that Daniel gave
himself for "monkey mind" in meditation (and many other things) were associated with a deep-seated belief he had developed during his school years
that he was stupid. This belief had roots, also, in comparisons frequently
made to his older brother, who was (according to Daniel) smarter, a better
student, a better athlete, and preferred by their father.*

*I made some suggestions in regard to Daniel's mindfulness practice:
When he found himself unable to concentrate, what actually was going
on? In addition to the frustration, tension, and "squirmy antsy feeling" he
reported, what else did he notice? What were the psychological themes that
pre-occupied him?*

*(In place of working so hard at concentration, I suggested, perhaps he
could try to simply observe "monkey mind is like this" (Sumedho, 2007).)*

*Daniel noticed that most often when he was highly distracted he found
himself ruminating about things he had said/done or not said/done in his connections with others. He worried continually about what kind of an impres-
sion he had made, or what he might have done wrong. The obvious clinical
question that emerged was whether he had those same concerns in his relationship with me. (He did.) This line of inquiry brought Daniel's anxiety and
insecurity alive in the here and now of our experience together. The work*

focused on the vicissitudes of the transference, as it would in any analytic treatment, but with the added element of meditative/experiential focus on the relational connection.

In working with Daniel's felt sense of all of this, a couple of things struck me. First, in response to the probing questions I asked, he would most often first close his eyes and take a long pause. Only then would he share his thoughts, which he tended to speak slowly and meditatively. Second, I found in working with him that my own state of mind quickly settled into one of still-ness and presence. Third, a ritual developed between us of sitting silently for the last three minutes or so of each session, and this shared meditative space felt very deep to me.

I shared these observations with Daniel and commented that I found all of this quite curious given what he had reported about his typical meditation experiences. He readily agreed that yes, the feel of this experience was differ-ent for him. There was a quality of spacious quiet he felt in our connection, which was exactly what he felt was missing when he meditated alone.

As we explored this further, Daniel shared something else he had noticed: his concentration always tended to be better when he was meditating with others.[8]

I wondered aloud about whether perhaps he felt alone or lonely when he was sitting by himself. He was intrigued by this idea and could hardly wait to "try it out" the next time he was meditating at home. He quickly discovered that, yes, he did *feel rather lonely. Soon after he had a powerful thought/ insight while doing his sitting practice: "I think maybe monkey mind is a way I keep myself company in my mind so I won't notice the void at the core of my being."*

Relational themes were central in Daniel's psychotherapy. As the work pro-gressed, we looked together at the dimension of intimacy and connection in his life. Here, I am emphasizing only what he discovered in his inquiry regarding anxiety and "monkey mind." In the context of our ongoing conversation about this, I made the comment to Daniel that I supposed it only made sense that we have monkey minds because, after all, we humans are primates at heart. The deep laughter which ensued felt like a deeply connected and mutual Now Moment, which I punctuated by saying, "Well you know, it takes one monkey mind to know another!"

Inquiring deeply in the therapeutic space brought into sharp focus Daniel's pervasive sense of aloneness. We looked at this in terms of the environment of harsh judgment he grew up in and the way this had colored his relationship with himself and significant others. As we talked about the importance of connection, Daniel began to focus mindful awareness on the experience of connection (and/or the lack thereof), and in our work together he discovered the embodied feeling of having an open heart. This led him to an interest in and focus on the practice of mindful self-compassion.

Ironically—given his conviction that he is cognitively defective—Daniel's mind is his strong suit. In place of feeling his way through his challenges, his approach to every situation has been to work harder to figure it out. Part of his attraction to meditation is a strong drive to find freedom from the prison of his own mind-object. The blend of psychotherapy and dharma practice in our work together, and our therapeutic connection in particular, has provided a structure which has allowed Daniel to develop a greater gentleness toward himself.

Clinical Illustration 9.2: Nancy

Nancy struggled with chronic anxiety. Aided and abetted by natural perceptiveness and keen intelligence, her defensive posture was one of hyper-vigilance. She was quick to notice any and every change in my office, my appearance, or my facial expression.

Exploring these patterns in psychotherapy, Nancy spoke of the pressure she had felt while growing up to try to know everything ahead of time. Her strategy to stay safe in life had been to collect information and suss out what was going on. This defense protected her from mental surprises: "When I don't sense something in advance," she reported, "I am apt to feel flooded by feelings which are too much to bear."

As we explored the relational dynamics in her family of origin, the psychodynamic underpinnings of Nancy's hypervigilance became very clear. I understood Nancy not only from her psychological narrative, but also by identification—from the inside out. Nancy's experience resonated with my own personality. In the beginning of our work together, I would often find myself pressuring myself to know and understand things and had to remind myself to slow down and let things unfold. This countertransference reaction relates to an embedded aspect of my character which is seldom present in my recent clinical work.

Among the various integrative insights that crystallized, one which stood out for me was that hypervigilance forecloses the opportunity to discover that things can settle out organically and find their own way to clarity. In mindfulness practice, learning to relax into experience begins to reopen that possibility.

Since childhood, Nancy's way of coping with overwhelm had been to retreat into a subjective fantasy space she called a "tunnel," which came into focus in the clinical dialogue between us. In current day, she observed, she was apt to retreat there whenever something was particularly upsetting emotionally. As we explored Nancy's reliance on this fantasy for self-sooth-ing, she began to understand the functions of this space; in her words, "I go into the tunnel to protect myself, to try to hold onto myself; or to hold onto you." Gradually she internalized our connection in a way that began to sup-plant this experience of being alone and underground. As her psychotherapy progressed, she seldom went to the tunnel anymore.

Concomitantly, Nancy's mindfulness practice deepened, and she saw that there were many layers to her familiar experiences of anxiety/agitation. She noticed an essential disquiet she experienced when she had free time at home by herself. "I don't know how to get comfortable in my own skin." In this self-state, it was hard for her to be with herself; instead, she typically chose to escape into being compulsively busy. I suggested that she make it a mindful practice to simply try to just be with—observe and allow—the felt sense of disquiet. Over time, it became clear to her that the disquiet had deep roots in her discomfort with being alone.

I learned a great deal about the function of mind-objects from the therapeutic inquiry we engaged in together and from Nancy's penetrating insights into herself. For example, we were speaking one day about the false self she presented to the world, how put together she thought she probably seemed to others. This was at odds with the "anxious mess" she sometimes felt herself to be on the inside. She said:

"I used to have only two choices: either I would go into the tunnel and hibernate with fear and mind-entanglement ... or else I would push through whatever it was and look fine on the outside while, all the while, feeling crappy. Neither place allowed me to be freely me."

The relationship to her mind-object, represented in her fantasy of the tunnel, stood in place of Nancy being able to tolerate the experience of overwhelming feelings. The tunnel was a way for her to batten down the emotional hatches, relating only to her own mind when being connected outside felt unbearably stormy or intense. The retreat into fantasy stood in place of experiencing what her feelings actually were (i.e. in place of being).

This shared understanding Nancy and I developed deepened my insight into the mind-object as a defense against intimacy: Nancy retreated exactly when—and to the degree that—there was a pull (and fear) of getting more involved. In her words, "These bombardments create a set of feelings/ stories/experiences in my system—it's hard to disentangle and trust that it's safe to be close." In the typical irony of psychological symptoms, the mind-object defense precludes any possibility of getting the very nurturing one most needs.

Nancy gradually integrated these experiences into a new sense of self which was calmer and more confident. She learned to be more deeply present with her experience and experimented with trusting that if she articulated her needs she would be able to get them met in a good-enough way.

Exploring how mind is held in mind is one of my principal points of focus in psychotherapy—which it is, too, in dharma practice, albeit from a different point of view. I typically introduce the concept of *exploring how mind is held in mind* as an explicit premise of psychotherapy, explaining why it is important to pay attention to how we relate to experience. I also frame this inquiry by analogy with interpersonal relationships, which may sometimes be harmonious and at other times fraught: the idea is to observe in an ongoing way what kind of relationship one is having with oneself (or with one's mind) at different moments. In those who are meditation practitioners, I may "prescribe" this as a self-reflective practice.

By exploring relational psychodynamics within the psyche, the patient develops a new understanding of their experience and a more compassionate self-awareness.

Psychoanalytic Factors: The Grandiose Ego-Ideal

Psychoanalytic theory is very instructive in understanding the development of the mind-object. Consider the following experience shared by a patient who was herself a clinical psychologist.

Clinical Illustration 9.3: Melanie

"My father was 'an absent-minded professor'. I mean that literally: he was a college professor who was seldom present in a psychological way for me or my sisters. Reading out loud to us was pretty much the only attention he paid to us. One day when I was three, I was sitting next to my dad on the couch as he was reading and something amazing happened. I was looking at the words in the book, mouthing the ones I recognized, saying them under my breath. And then we came to one pretty big word I recognized, I don't know what word it was, but my dad got very excited and made a major fuss over this, calling my mother into the room to show her how I could read out loud. 'Can you believe it?' my dad said. 'This girl is a genius! Reading at three!'

The mastery of reading would I'm sure have been sufficient reward unto itself, but I believe that what happened in that moment—and I'm sure in many others—was that my ego got sold into slavery to approval.[9]

My father conveyed that having a bright daughter was narcissistically gratifying to him. Thereafter, and lifelong, I endeavored to perform in ways that would win both approval and recognition of my having exceptional intelligence. School was a perfect breeding ground for the development and elaboration of this deep-seated personality trait. I became an outstanding student and endeavored to make my parents feel that they must be wonderful parents to have such a bright and talented child."

In her well-known work on the drama of the gifted child and the search for the true self, Alice Miller (1981) wrote very insightfully about the search for admiration and its confusion with love. She understood attachment to admiration as a substitute gratification for the meeting of primary needs for respect, understanding, and being taken seriously—i.e. love. Miller further explains that a self-esteem based on performance, or on the possession of any specific qualities or traits, occludes the development of a healthy self-esteem based on the authenticity of one's own being.

Benjamin (1999) echoes these ideas in her conceptualization of the need for recognition in the development of subjectivity. The search for admiration defends against the pain of non-recognition, low self-esteem, and the loss of contact with the true (or authentic) self. In addition, the search for admiration may hide conscious and unconscious fantasies of grandiosity, functioning as a defense against an underlying depression.

The Mind-Object and Obsessionality

This next section explores obsessionality—one of the primary psychological characteristics of the mind-object.

Obsessionality as a psychological symptom or disorder is usually defined as a compulsive preoccupation with a fixed idea, unwanted feeling, or emotion, often accompanied by symptoms of anxiety. The anxiety is thought to result from a "false alarm" in the mind—an erroneous appraisal of danger—which the mind then attempts to address by thinking, resulting in compulsive thought patterns. These may present as persistent, recurrent thoughts, ideas, images, cravings, temptations, prohibitions, or commands. Generally speaking, obsessionality may be understood as the mind's attempt to solve an emotional problem by thinking (Moore and Fine, 1990). It also serves to defend against awareness of feelings of weakness or deficiency (i.e. narcissistic injury), or against thoughts that tend to produce shame, loss of pride, or status (Salzman, 1980). In the most basic terms, obsessions substitute for feelings that are unsafe to experience.

Some degree of obsessionality is a normal characteristic of the mind's problem-solving function. Rumination or worry occurs as the mind "chews over" a situation, resulting in thoughts that continually preoccupy or intrude into a person's mind.[10] Obsessing is the mind's attempt to solve the "problem" of a disturbing feeling.

"Normal obsessionality" as defined here is one component of papanca in Buddhism: the proliferation of concepts in the mind as thoughts reverberate through the network of meanings with which they are associated. This is the continual and ongoing process of discursive thinking. As is said in Zen (and as discussed in Chapter 7), it is in the nature of mind to form thoughts much as it is in the nature of water to make waves. This language-based, often repetitive thinking, is the mind spinning stories to make sense of the world (Gazzaniga, 2011).[11]

Some individuals are more obsessional than others; there is an obsessional cognitive style and personality. In his classic description of obsessive-compulsive character, David Shapiro (1965) emphasized several interrelated features that bear repeating here. (The reader will notice similarities to definition of the mind-object by Corrigan and Gordon.)

- The obsessive's character style is marked by rigidity in regard to thinking and intellectual activity, and this rigidity extends to behavior generally, including body posture and social manner.

- The obsessive person's attention operates with intense, sharp focus, but in a way that is inflexibly narrow and lacks the ability to be regulated at will. The cognitive inflexibility of the obsessive person is revealed in the inability to shift attention from one thing to another, a lack of volitional mobility of attention.
- The obsessive person is also described as "driven"; genuine motivation is replaced by the sense of necessity or requirement to do something that, in actuality, is a pressure that the person applies to himself. For example, the obsessive gives him or herself deadlines for activities, which logically may be quite arbitrary.
- But if the obsessive is driven, he is equally the driver. The obsessive person's life space is structured around a sense of "should" that is quite ego-syntonic (although the person may complain about the experience of the pressure).
- The activity—one could just as well say the life—of the obsessional person is characterized by a more or less continuous experience of tense deliberateness, a sense of effort, and of trying. The obsessive is overcontrolled, operating from a state of tense effort that restricts affect, playfulness, and spontaneity in general. There is thus little room to experience satisfaction in doing anything without a continuous sense of purpose and effort.
- Any relaxation of deliberateness or purposeful activity is felt to be improper, uncomfortable, or worse.
- The overcontrol of the obsessive is linked with a specific anxiety and discomfort over loss of control.

It is important to bear in mind that obsessional style and the attempt to be in control cannot be viewed merely as a dimension of psychopathology. The capacity to focus and to organize the *doing* of life in an obsessional manner is quite normal in our culture, and is quite adaptive in the right context. It can be used in the service of achievement and success in school and in adult life. Too much obsessionality, however, results in a loss of cognitive flexibility.

The process of recurrent and autonomous thinking in the mind reflects patterns of activity in the prefrontal cortex (Siegel, 2007; Schwartz and Begley, 2002).[12] Of great interest in the present context, this is the same area of the brain which is most engaged by mindfulness meditation practice. As relaxation occurs during mindfulness practice, prefrontal activation is modulated; less energy is engaged in obsessional thinking. Whether this effect is mediated by concentration (i.e. the systematic regulation of attention) and/or by mindful awareness (the cultivation of present-centered awareness) is not entirely clear. However, from a Buddhist perspective, the most important conclusion may simply be this: mindfulness meditation counteracts obsessionality by fostering receptivity in place of active effort, *being* instead of *doing*. In this way, meditation practice has direct impact on the functioning of the mind-object (Schuman, 2007).

Hyperarousal and the Mind-Object

There is an important psychophysiological dimension to the way we embody ourselves: indwelling patterns of energy/arousal that are associated with character and personality. People whose minds are organized around a mind-object tend to be "high strung." Mindfulness practice can be helpful in bringing conscious awareness to patterns of arousal and how we are driven by them.

The drive for achievement and associated performance pressures engenders stress and psychophysiological arousal. This pattern of hyperarousal recalls the Type A behavior pattern first described in cardiac patients by Friedman and Rosenman (1974). Physiologically, psychophysiological arousal is mediated by a high level of activation in the sympathetic branch of the autonomic nervous system. Cardiovascular correlates include elevation of heart rate and vasoconstriction ("cold feet").

Indwelling levels of high arousal get organized and expressed psychologically in many different ways. Regardless of the associated personality structure, "high strung" can be described as an adrenaline-dominated way of being.[13] One strategy to cope with performance anxiety or performance pressure is to race the engine of the mind in order to power through and feel in control of a situation in which we are highly invested. I call this the "adrenaline junkie" syndrome because it has strong elements in common with substance abuse: there is psychological dependence on a state of arousal which seems necessary for the performance of certain psychological tasks, especially when there is anxiety associated with them. In Western culture, this pattern of behavior is fostered by the performance pressures connected with school.

The desired arousal state may be self-generated or may be facilitated by the ingestion of exogenous substances such as caffeine and nicotine. Such "autoaddiction" to adrenaline[14] seems quite parallel to substance abuse. If we think of the state of arousal (or hyperarousal) as a self-state, then we might further theorize that some people become "autoaddicted" to their own self-states, repeatedly inducing those states in themselves (albeit unconsciously). This is the mind-object in action.

When states of hyperarousal are sought as a way of *coping* with anxiety, these states both *manifest* and *sustain* anxiety. This complex relationship between performance anxiety and hyperarousal is one of the underpinnings of obsessional character. The chronic and repeated experience of states of anxious hyperarousal generates obsessional defenses as a way to defend against and contain them.

Buddhist Meditation, Obsessionality, and the Mind-Object

Mindfulness practice makes states of hyperarousal more noticeable, salient, and egodystonic. As awareness settles more into the body, the mind relaxes, arousal lessens, and one's subjective state shifts. While no particular experience can be reliably predicted, experience begins to take on a different coloration or resonant frequency; an alternate state of consciousness, a *meditative state(s)* begins to emerge. Meditative states represent a new organization of subjectivity which has its own coherence and flow; the mind becomes more relaxed, alert, present. Over time, the repeated experience of meditative states begins to change the habitual organization of energy patterns in the psyche.

One patient expressed it this way:

> *I am always a little bit hyper when I wake up in the morning ... typically I'm thinking about everything I need to do before I am even fully awake. My list-making self kind of takes over. Then, when I do my morning sitting practice, I always get to a point where I realize how revved up I've been without even noticing. For instance, when my mind comes back from wherever it goes when I'm distracted, I will find myself holding my breath, shoulders tensed.*
>
> *I guess that tension is my default mode. It generally takes quite a bit of steady and patient effort for me to settle down from this jangle into a calmer, more embodied state. That's why I have to go on retreat periodically. If I don't, I don't stand a chance of really calming down.*

Obsessional thinking rests on a foundation of anxiety. The most important focus clinically is bringing awareness to the embodied experience of anxiety that underlies recurrent thoughts. In obsessional mode, the mind/body tends to be in a state of high arousal. Unfortunately, this is a process that feeds on itself, because obsessing distracts attention from grounded awareness of the body. Obsessionality has the overall effect of displacing the feelings it is defending against.[15] It is only when the cycle *arousal > thinking > arousal* is interrupted that it becomes possible to establish a state of calm presence in which awareness can deepen.

Considering obsessional cognitive style in relation to mindfulness meditation poses intriguing questions. While the answers are not entirely straightforward, the important questions seem to converge on the faculty of paying attention. Attention may be focused/stable or distractible/labile and is a function of both *state* and *trait* attentional factors. Also, how we pay attention is heavily determined by the emotional energy connected both to the moment and to what we're trying to pay attention to.

The overview of obsessionality presented in this chapter is that it reflects the mind's efforts to metabolize affect and figure out solutions for emotional problems. However, what emotional problems most need is to be *felt*. They need to be received and understood by an empathic other. While thinking about problems can be very useful, it can also go around in circles in a way that heightens anxiety rather than dissipating it. Moreover, the very things that most need attention may also flood the mind with anxiety, causing thinking to veer away from important "targets." In short, paying attention is a complex psychodynamic process. This is precisely why the relational milieu of psychotherapy is so very useful: it supports focus on emotional matters that are in need of deep understanding and is conducive to psychological integration.

Mindfulness meditation is also extremely useful, engaging and strengthening the capacity to *be with* experience. Sitting quietly with the intention simply to notice *what is* creates a subjective state of calm focus in which affects can be more comfortably tolerated.

The ability to sustain mindful attention reflects cognitive processes which are embedded in personality. In addition to psychodynamic determinants mentioned above, there are several interrelated cognitive/neural capacities involved in selecting, sustaining, and switching attention. These have been designated as arousal, activation, and effort (Pribram and McGuinness, 1975).[16] Overall, two general functions may be distinguished: (1) executive functions that organize the process of paying attention and (2) the ability to flexibly "shift gears" between different objects of attention. These correspond, generally, to concentration and mindfulness, the two interrelated attentional components highlighted in Buddhist mindfulness meditation (Wallace, 2006).[17]

Because it is possible to control attention in meditation with mental "force," obsessionally inclined individuals may concentrate quite well.[18] Although their executive control of concentration may be very good, their characteristic tense effort is, however, actually antithetical to effective mindfulness. Skillful mindfulness practice requires, instead, relaxation and letting go. In short, mindfulness requires flexibility of attention and mental balance as well as attentional focus.

Fortunately, one of the benefits of mindfulness practice is that it also trains and improves needed attentional capacities. One important factor is the effect of repeated practice. Also, as the mind becomes more settled and unified in meditation, arousal in the body/mind decreases, which further facilitates calm focus. In both of these ways, over time meditation practice may help develop the attentional flexibility that the obsessional mind most lacks.

From the above discussion, the basic question which most goes to the heart of the matter seems to be: what factors determine the degree to which attentional *state* in mindfulness practice brings about changes in attentional *trait*?

It seems likely that amount and depth of mindfulness practice have cumulative effects. Perhaps the tenacity of mind-object structures is also key. If so, then the question becomes: what allows the mind to let go of "psychological imperatives" of obsessionality, perfectionism, and drive for achievement in favor of an experience of equanimity?

Summary and Conclusion: The Mindful Mind-Object

Mind-object is a psychoanalytic concept that describes psychological strategies that seek to manage and control experience. It is the set of executive functions that are engaged in order to try to hold life together in the mind. During development, the intellect—the fabric of thinking—takes over in order to try to provide the sense of security that optimally is provided by safe connection with others. Absent that attachment security, the mind clings to knowing, to being in control, and to its relationship with itself. In essence, *knowing* functions as a kind of second skin that contains experience and attempts to provide a feeling of security.

Ironically, what often escapes notice is that this strategy is in itself a major source of insecurity and suffering. With the intellect-dominated mind-object, authentic self gets replaced by compulsiveness, rigidity, and trying too hard; joyful experiences of flow get co-opted by obsessional efforts to keep track of everything, including oneself. Achievement, striving, and *doing* can never remedy the sense of emptiness and unworthiness that lies beneath. They do not provide a sense of connection with who we are, which ultimately is the only cure for a core experience of separateness and isolation. Moreover, immersion in compulsive productivity may tend to eclipse experiences of relational connection with others, thereby creating the very isolation that it seeks to remedy.

The effort to be in control is, in any event, futile, since so many aspects of life are beyond human control.

Elaborating this point further, it should be noted that when we are identified with ourselves as cognitive beings[19]—when we assume that who we *are* is this intellect—we become locked into a particularly limiting form of self-identity. As the Buddhist teacher Gregory Kramer puts it, "Thinking we know costs us all that we don't know, which is nearly everything" (Kramer, 2007, p. 144).

Transforming and healing of the mind's relationship to itself is the basic aim of both Buddhist practice and psychodynamic psychotherapy, each in its own way. (Perhaps we can call this the development of a mindful mind-object.) I will briefly reiterate here the important factors that bear upon the healing of the mind-object with mindfulness practice and/or relational psychotherapy:

- Mindful awareness of the experience of being driven allows recognition of feelings that are buried beneath obsessional thinking. (Observing ego is developed.)
- Mindfulness of embodied experience counters self-organizations that are based on intellectual function. (The split between mind and body is overcome.)
- Increased ability to *be with* feelings deepens emotional understanding of oneself. (Affect modulation is improved.)
- Feeling deeply understood fosters self-understanding and self-compassion. One develops compassion for what one has suffered and may still be suffering as a consequence of emotional wounds. One learns to be kinder and gentler toward oneself. (A more "loving and beloved superego" is developed (Schafer, 1960).)
- Directly and deeply encountering one's psychological pain allows one to recognize lifelong patterns of thwarted psychological needs, which underlie the development of a mind-object. (This opens a doorway to liberating insights.)
- Through becoming aware of the mind-object in its broader relational context, it becomes possible to appropriately redirect one's energies toward more nurturing connection with others. (More rewarding relationships with others can then be sought.)

- By decentering from and disidentifying with entrenched and previously unconscious states of mind, transcendent subjectivity is cultivated. (New self-states may be acquired and problematic self-states can be healed.)

As previously discussed, transcendent subjectivity is cultivated in mindfulness meditation practice; it can also be facilitated intersubjectively. In many instances, transcendent experience may be intersubjectively *communicated*—it exists in potential or virtual form in one person until it is brought into being by another.[20]

While it may be psychodynamically helpful to become familiar with the functioning of the mind as an internal object within psychic reality, from a Buddhist perspective this conceptualization is intrinsically misguided, in that it perpetuates the dualism between one part of the mind and another. Indeed, when the concept of mind-object was first delineated by Corrigan and Gordon (1995), they made that precise point: "When the mind takes on a life of its own, it becomes an object—separate, as it were, from the self." This may tend to generate a dissociative split within the sense of *agency*. To the extent that someone feels driven and does not own that pressuring behavior, s(he) may not fully take responsibility for the way that he or she is being.

Even within a dualistic frame, it is a mistake to conceive of a singular self in relation with a singular mind-object. We might do better to speak of multiple mind-objects. We also need to remember that the concept of mind-object tends to reify what is in reality a set of complex and dynamic *processes* in the mind. Do we attempt to live up to the performance standards of our mind-objects? Do our minds boss us around, drive us to distraction? Do we ignore the imperatives of our mind-objects in favor of sensory pleasure or impulsive acting out? Alternatively, can we become aware of and learn to *be with* the mind-object in a way that begins to heal the split between mind and body?

Mindfulness is practice with *being* which begins to inform and transform subjective life. As we inquire deeply into what we are striving for, and why, we can begin to see more clearly how anxiety within us gets expressed as a mind-object dynamic. Bringing consciousness to the experience of being driven opens the possibility for greater being and freedom from everyday compulsive *doing*. This allows us to be more aligned with our intentions and to create our lives in a way that has more coherent meaning.

As may be said of ego generally, the mind-object bears the stamp of defense. More than anything else, attachment to doing—to staying busy—defends against anxiety. "Dancing as fast as we can" provides the illusory sense that we are protected against existential fears: the freefall of groundlessness and the fear of non-being (death). It fortifies the illusion of self.

In conclusion, psychotherapy and Buddhist mindfulness meditation in tandem—inquiring deeply—provide a unique opportunity for subjectivity to evolve beyond blind domination by our mind-objects. As was discussed in Chapter 8, self-reflective awareness, whether in meditation or in everyday life, reveals many different states of mind and states of consciousness. Such states were described psychologically/clinically as different modes of subjectivity, each with its own organization, contents, and objects of awareness.[21]

Together, therapeutic inquiry and self-reflection heighten awareness of how we relate to our experience and to our minds—to the fluid, constantly shifting relationship between the experiencing self and the mind as object. At the heart of such inquiry lies the core issue of how people change. This question will be taken up at length in the next chapter.

Notes

1　According to the uncertainty principle posited by the German philosopher Heisenberg in 1927 (discussed in Chapter 7), what is observed is always and necessarily affected by the process of observation (cf. www.britannica.com/science/uncertainty-principle). Alan Wallace (2003) gives a good overview of the relevant philosophical issues.

2　The basic objects of mind are spelled out in the classic Buddhist text Abhidhamma (Pali language). An excellent description of the basic components is summarized in Olendzki (2010).

3　A further implication of the lack of subject–object duality is the idea that fully knowing something entails being that which is known.

4　In Buddhism, it is posited that Awareness is transparent and clear: without form, without boundary, and infinite.

5　This issue is unpacked in the discussion of subjectivity and Self in Chapter 8. In object relations language, we would say that there are multiple facets of the mind as an internal object, just as there are multiple selves.

6　This may be especially likely when some aspect of self is reminiscent of a particular Other who is a family member, and it is helpful in generating psychodynamic insight. Clinically, it is useful to explain this concept to patients in terms of the idea of an "internal family."

7　Also, the baby receives the mother's projections and enactments of *her* object world, and so the world of internal objects is shaped by this influence as well.

8　There is a virtual community of meditators that subscribe to a cellphone app called "Insight Timer." Daniel felt comfort in the company of this virtual sangha.

9　This example shows how authentic experience of "true self" in Winnicott's sense can be dominated or replaced by another mental function or psychological need.

10　Rumination is one of the prominent symptoms of depression, the so-called "automatic negative thoughts" that are addressed in cognitive behavior therapy.

11　Such thinking about experience is part of the "interpreter module" in the brain/mind, the part that spins stories to make sense of the world.

12　In cognitive science terms, prefrontal activity reflects baseline patterns of arousal and attention, as well as the energy of mental or "computational" activity in the brain.

　　An important related finding is that obsessive compulsive disorder involves hyperactivity of the orbitofrontal cortex, as reported by Jeffrey Schwartz (Schwartz and Begley, 2002). Schwartz pioneered the use of Buddhist mindfulness meditation in the treatment of patients with obsessive-compulsive disorder (OCD). His findings demonstrated that the habitual narrowing of attention which is pervasive and encumbering in OCD patients can be counteracted by mindfulness meditation in combination with cognitive behavioral interventions.

13　The Type A personality is intensely competitive, aggressive, and impatient. This clusters with persistent desire for recognition.

14　More accurately, the pattern of psychophysiological arousal under discussion is probably mediated by a combination of sympathomimetic amines: adrenaline and noradrenaline.

15 Sometimes the Vipassana technique of noting "thinking" can be used as a kind of obsessional defense, pushing experience *away* in place of fully feeling it.
16 Brain mechanisms in the control of selective attention are far more complex than can be adequately summarized here.
17 For a discussion of attentional factors in Buddhist meditation, refer to Wallace (2006).
18 One clinical topic that bears further investigation is the correlation between attention deficit disorder and obsessional behavior. Both have been linked to the same regions of the brain mechanisms: prefrontal cortex, responsible for executive control of attention and focus, and the cingulate cortex, which regulates shifts of attention. Obsessionality involves excessive focus coupled with insufficient flexibility of attention. Obsessive compulsive symptoms come about when the faculty of selective attention is not adequate to filter out emotional threat.
19 As expressed in the familiar Cartesian dictum, "I think, therefore I am."
20 It is not implied, however, that a psychotherapist necessarily needs to be a Buddhist or a meditator in order to facilitate development of transcendent subjectivity.
21 All of these ideas can probably be mapped onto the Buddhist Abhidhamma (compendium of mental states), although the task of doing so goes way beyond the intended scope of the present book.

References

Benjamin, J. (1999). Recognition and destruction: An outline of intersubjectivity. In Mitchell, S. A. and Aron, L. (Eds), *Relational psychoanalysis: The emergence of a tradition* (pp. 181–210). Hillsdale, NJ: Analytic Press.

Corrigan, E. G. and Gordon, P. E. (1995). *The mind object: Precocity and pathology of self sufficiency*. Northvale, NJ: Jason Aronson Press.

Epstein, M. (1995). *Thoughts without a thinker: Psychotherapy from a Buddhist perspective*. New York, NY: Basic Books.

Friedman, M. and Rosenman, R. H. (1974). *Type A behavior and your heart*. New York, NY: Alfred A. Knopf.

Fronsdal, G. (2005). *The dhammapada: A new translation of the Buddhist classic, with annotations*. Boston, MA: Shambhala Publications.

Gazzaniga, M. (2011). *Who's in charge: Free will and the science of the brain*. New York, NY: Harper Collins.

Gunaratana, B. H. (2012). *The four foundations of mindfulness in plain English*. Boston, MA: Wisdom Publications.

Heisenberg, W. (n.d.). In *Encyclopedia Britannica online*. Retrieved from www.britannica.com/science/uncertainty-principle.

Kramer, G. (2007). *Insight dialogue: The interpersonal path to freedom*. Boston, MA: Shambhala Press.

Levin, C. (2010). The mind as a complex internal object: Inner estrangement. *Psychoanalytic Quarterly, 79*, 95–127.

Miller, A. (1981). *Prisoners of childhood*. New York, NY: Basic Books.

Moore, B. E. and Fine, B. D. (1990). *Psychoanalytic terms and concepts*. New Haven, CT: American Psychoanalytic Association and Yale University Press.

Olendzki, A. (2010). *Unlimiting mind*. Boston, MA: Wisdom Publications.

Pribram, K. H. and McGuinness, D. (1975). Arousal, activation, and effort in the control of attention. *Psychological Review, 82*(2), 116–149.

Salzman, L. (1980). *Treatment of the obsessive personality*. New York, NY: Jason Aronson.

Schafer, R. (1960). The loving and beloved superego in Freud's structural theory. *The psychoanalytic study of the child, 15*, 163–188. New York, NY: International Universities Press.

Schuman, M. (2007). Driven to distraction: Observations on obsessionality. In Cooper, P. C. (Ed.), *Into the mountain stream: Psychotherapy and Buddhist experience* (pp. 77–97). Lanham, MD: Jason Aronson Rowman & Littlefield.

Schwartz, J. M. and Begley, S. (2002). *The mind and the brain: Neuroplasticity and the power of mental force*. New York, NY: Harper Collins Regan Books.

Shapiro, D. (1965). *Neurotic styles.* New York, NY: Basic Books.

Siegel, D. J. (2007). *The mindful brain: Reflection and attunement in the cultivation of well-being.* New York, NY: W.W. Norton.

Sumedho, A. (2007). *The sound of silence.* Somerville, MA: Wisdom Publications.

Wallace, B. A. (2003). *Choosing reality: A Buddhist view of physics and the mind.* Ithaca, NY: Snow Lion Publications.

Wallace, B. A. (2006). *The attention revolution: Unlocking the power of the focused mind.* Boston, MA: Wisdom Publications.

Winnicott, D. W. (1971). *Playing and reality.* London and New York: Routledge Press.

Chapter 10

How We Change
Inquiring Deeply and Psychological Growth

Inquiring deeply grew out of my abiding interest in the different theories of mind in Buddhism and psychoanalytic psychology. I wanted to understand how best to interweave these two narrative strands into an integrative view of emotional problems. This would then be a coherent basis for Buddhist-informed psychodynamic treatment.

This final chapter is intended to summarize and integrate the series of reflections that are presented throughout the book. It is also a meta-reflection on how mindful awareness helps bring psychodynamic efforts to fruition.

In the broadest sense, it considers the fundamental question: How do people change?

The Nature of Inquiry

I conceptualized several different factors that seemed to shape the process of my inquiry. First, the *questions* I asked were of paramount importance. Over time, I found, questions evolved, often going in directions I had not anticipated. (Some of the basic questions I inquired about were articulated in Chapter 1.)

As my inquiry deepened, it began to shape my clinical work, and those experiences in turn shaped my evolving inquiry. I increasingly recognized the pivotal importance of three basic things: (1) asking open-ended clinical questions, which tend to invite deepening inquiry (some of these were detailed in Chapter 4); (2) examining as deeply as possible the nature of the assumptions that seem to come into play in the construction of problems, including hidden existential attitudes; and (3) constructing self-reflective practices that deepen patients' awareness of the factors that hold problems in place. I also came to several conclusions:

- It isn't possible to be free of assumptions and beliefs. Be that as it may, an open mind and commitment to bringing awareness to our assumptions are essential.
- Inquiry encumbered with belief is less than optimal—not to mention self-fulfilling.
- The intention to be self-reflective about our assumptions seems to allow cognizance of many of our views and opinions.

My personal "assumptive paradigm" includes the idea that something useful invariably emerges from the process of reflection and inquiry whenever we bring deliberate focus and intention to that process. Life, I have found, tends to unfold in a way that answers people's sincerely held questions, especially when those questions are held in a frame of mindful, receptive inquiry. In similar manner, when we "go with the flow" instead of engaging struggle and effort to figure things out, solutions to problems seem to emerge of their own accord. It is as if life has a mind of its own.[1] So what we must endeavor to do is simply be receptive to the unfolding. This idea is evocatively expressed in the following lines of poetry:

> *not so much looking for the shape*
> *as being available*
> *to any shape that may be*
> *summoning itself through me.*
> *– A. R. Ammons*[2]

Inquiring Deeply: The Path of Problems

My experiences in the consulting room have been the fertile source of much of what I have come to understand about inquiry. Problems are a valuable opportunity for deepening our conversation with ourselves and with life. I do not regard this idea as simply cognitively "reframing" problems as opportunities, nor superficially looking for the "silver linings" problems may contain. Rather, it is a framework for using the contemplative method of inquiry for finding the opportunities within problems.

As described in Chapter 4, inquiry is a process of "living in the question of something." This has been likened to throwing a boomerang out into the universe and then waiting patiently for the answer to return. Using the method of inquiry to address problems entails the assumption that problems have innate wisdom embedded within them.

In the view presented here, problems are a basic organizing principle in psychological life. Consider, for example (as every reader can certainly notice), the fact that everyone has problems. The symbolic capacity of the human brain/mind gives us the ability to imagine different scenarios of what might have been, should have been, or could happen in the future, and we have a natural tendency to think and talk about problems in order to explore alternative possibilities for their solution. Taken together, these observations show us that problem-solving is a basic design function of the human mind. However, it is also often true that the effort to find cognitive answers may get in the way. Some problems need to be *lived through* rather than *figured out*.

In my view, problems have a role in our minds analogous to the role of pain in the body: they call our attention to what we most need to see. As such, the goal of inquiry in this psychotherapeutic approach is not to *disappear* problems (which of course is what most patients *hope* will happen) but rather to deepen

negative word sense

our awareness of them in a way that frees us from the cul-de-sac of overthinking them. The receptive state of mindful awareness is the fulcrum of this approach. Its premise is that solutions to problems emerge as a function of how clearly we can see where we are stuck. From this perspective, problems and solutions can be seen to be two sides of a single coin. I often refer to this assumptive framework as the "path of problems."

The path of problems as I define it in inquiring deeply is a path of mindful awareness which follows along in the slipstream of our concern about a problem, especially when that problem is painful. Using mindful and self-compassionate attention to explore our associative connections gradually untangles the knots of pain and trauma in the psyche and helps to reveal aspects of the wisdom innate within us.

As discussed throughout this book, this is an ever-deepening process. Part of the work in psychotherapy is to identify the hidden existential views that obscure our clear seeing of the nature of problems. In an important sense, the problem *is* the problem: no particular circumstance or situation is inherently problematic. Rather, it is the holding of a problem *as a problem* which constructs it as such. By gaining insight into how problems are mentally (and relationally) constructed, ultimately we may be led to our fundamental assumptions about identity itself.

In any event, my understanding of the path of problems—a framework of understanding of how people grow and change—has sorted itself into ten categories, each of which will be discussed in turn. Each heading is followed by a series of reflections that expresses my integration of psychological/psychodynamic ideas, on the one hand, and Buddhist ideas, on the other. The ten headings are as follows:

1 Identifying a problem/leading edge or horizon of change
2 Deconstructing the experience of the problem
3 Developing insight, clarity, and deep emotional understanding
4 The role of narrative and the importance of relationship
5 Relaxation and unwinding of experience
6 Intention, commitment, and action: blueprint for change
7 Coming into being: its intersubjective dimension
8 Wise relationship to the story of self
9 Reorganization and transformation of meaning
10 Transcendent subjectivity

1 Identifying a Problem/Leading Edge or Horizon of Change

The surface layer of a problem is generally not very subtle: it announces itself with an experience of suffering. So, the first step—both in Buddhist practice and in psychotherapy—is calling attention to suffering and then inquiring into it.

Recognition of suffering in its broadest sense is evoked by the phrase used by the Buddhist teacher Ajahn Sumedho: "Suffering is like this" (Sumedho, 2004).

One suffers and knows that one is suffering. This is mindful awareness of suffering, the heart of Buddhist practice.[4]

Suffering can be felt (recognized) at many different levels. In its most basic aspect, it highlights the *direct experience* of what we see, hear, touch, smell, and taste, as well as the perceptions, images, and thoughts associated with the unpleasant experience called suffering.

In addition to the sensory experience of the moment, there is an associative network in the mind that provides both the affective tone and "paradigm of meaning" that makes experiences of suffering feel psychologically distinct. For example, in a particular moment we may feel unhappy, burdened, dejected, or hopeless, as though things are falling apart.

In the most general sense, a problem/leading edge or horizon of change presents itself as an awareness of some difficulty accompanied by the upsurge of unpleasant emotion: "reactivity." Pema Chodron (1997) uses the Tibetan term "shenpa" to describe this phenomenon of getting hooked by something "sticky" in the mind. Reactivity may be triggered by an acute event or may be a long-standing reactive emotional pattern, and it is generally associated with upsetting or unhappy thoughts, images, fantasies, and/or narratives in the mind. Our reactivity shows us the surface of a problem that needs to be explored, grounded in the intimacy of our embodied experience, and met with compassionate understanding.

Investigation of "problems" can take many different forms. We can focus on a given moment through a meditative lens, amplifying our awareness of direct experience—each moment as distinct as the proverbial snowflake. We can focus on the emotional texture of the moment, amplifying our awareness of our "felt sense" of it. Or, we can expand upon its "meaning" by reflecting on it, or by speaking with someone about it.

In psychotherapy, problems are understood within a personal framework; their meaning is elaborated in relation to psychological history. In contrast, Buddhist practice aims toward extending presence beyond the conditioned aspects of experience, pointing awareness away from organization of experience around concepts of self and toward a broader awareness of the **background field** that pervades all existence. (From the perspective of this limitless, unbounded intelligence, there is no problem to fix (Amaro, 2007).[5]

Inquiring deeply honors both of these perspectives, meeting problems on their own terms. It is a way of working with problems by feeling our way into and through them. There are layers upon layers of experience—"no end to seeing," as Hokusai tells us.[6] We meet each of them as they arise within the psychological world of lived experience. In addition to the personal layers, themselves somewhat endless, we can discover many other layers which are existential/archetypal/universal. Over time and with open and receptive curiosity toward experience, intuitive awareness uncovers the intelligence within problems. Mindful awareness unfolds and deepens.

Inquiring deeply has some essential similarity to dharma practice.[7] However, because it does not privilege the spiritual dimension of experience, and, because

free assoc

of its focus on "personality view," it has a different "flavor" than does mindfulness meditation. It highlights what in psychodynamic language is called "working through" (Epstein, 1995).[8]

The major importance of the way that we identify problems—how we define the leading edge and horizon of change—lies in the fact that they are part of the narrative structure within which life unfolds. Inquiring deeply is based on the fundamental premise that there is innate wisdom in problems. If we use a problem as a guide to inquiring deeply into the structure of our experience, it will take us exactly where we need to go to discover important opportunities for change and healing.

With or without explicit goals for change, the way that we "construct" a problem is the way that we "incline the mind." In the teachings of the Buddha, "all experience is preceded by mind, led by mind, made by mind" (Fronsdal, 2005, p. 1).

2 Deconstructing the Experience of Problems

At its most basic level, both Buddhist and Western psychology highlight the idea that experience is constructed. Buddhism conceives of the mind as consisting of "aggregates"—heaps of mental "stuff." Psychoanalytic theory thinks of the mind or psyche in terms of structures which house experience.

The fundamental structure of problems can be understood in a way which is consistent with both of these views. Problems are configurations or patterns in the mind that are organized around a nucleus of something too painful to be fully experienced ("metabolized"). Such knots or tangles in the mind have been aptly termed areas of "non-experienced experience."[9]

Non-experienced experience may be thought of as a logjam in the free flow of mental energy in the mind. Such patterns (aggregates) comprise the traumatic core of problems[10]: when repeated over time, they calcify or rigidify into a kind of "scar tissue" on the psychic structure, including character.

These kinds of patterns and structures in our minds interfere with the experience of "optimal flow" and being.[11] As the psychoanalyst D. W. Winnicott expressed it, "reacting interrupts being, and annihilates it" (1965b, p. 47). And so, it is skillful to bring mindful awareness to moments of reactivity.

The task of deconstructing problems is complicated by the operation of psychological defenses that automatically screen some experiences out of conscious awareness. Since we cannot see our own blind spots, it can be helpful to have another person who can help us focus in on our patterns of reactivity. This is one of the key functions of psychotherapy.

Mindful awareness of the present moment of experience reveals that any experience—all experience—can be deconstructed into what we see, hear, touch, smell, taste, and think. Only six primary experiences. What we experience in the moment-to-moment flow of experience is not a problem unless we resist its unpleasantness. By paying mindful attention to the experience of resistance and the deconstructed experience of the associated reactivity, problems momentarily dissolve.

Despite the fact that this is quite easy to describe, it takes considerable practice to automatically and consistently do the first two tasks that have been described here: first, to identify reactivity as it arises in the present moment; and second, to bring mindful awareness to the direct experience that is occurring here and now. These basic skills of mindfulness need to be practiced if they are to be incorporated into the mind as a new attentional habit—a new structure of subjectivity or way of being.

"Deconstructing of experience" is one of the most frequently emphasized interfaces between meditation and psychotherapy. While it is an important element in working with problems, it is rather ineffective as a stand-alone strategy for meeting difficult moments of experience. "Deep emotional understanding," as it is termed in this book, extends "downward" toward the embodied present moment, but it also extends "upward" to levels of psychological meaning. And, surrounding all, it is essential for experience to be met by compassion (from the self and/or the other).

Thus, in inquiring deeply, deconstructing experience is only one of several important layers.[12] Once we have first understood that experience is actually constructed, the next—and more challenging—task is to begin to understand more clearly how subjective experience is put together, and what governs its organization.

3 Developing Insight, Clarity, and Deep Emotional Understanding of Problems

Once we have identified a problem, and as we continue to practice "being with" the basic elements in our experience of it, effective change requires that we develop clarity about and insight into the patterns in which we are stuck and their psychological roots. This is "deep emotional understanding." It includes our felt sense of what is going on, our psychological understanding, and our intuitive wisdom.

The first step, described in the first section, is mindful awareness of reactivity. Investigating "upsets" is itself a therapeutic intervention, since discerning and naming patterns of reactivity empowers change.[13] It is extremely helpful to realize that thoughts are merely thoughts and we don't need to believe everything we think. (This is the fundamental premise both in Buddhist practice and in mindfulness-based cognitive therapies such as mindfulness-based cognitive therapy (MBCT) and acceptance and commitment therapy (ACT).)

As we investigate reactivity with mindful awareness, we develop our capacity to recognize innate affects such as anger, fear, shame, etc. and begin to see the process by which our feelings are shaped and "biographized" in narrative. This awareness includes both mental *content* and mental *process*. Awareness and understanding of these psychological aspects of reactivity are important in "working through" feelings and learning to modulate affect.

There are a number of different elements that can be investigated with mindful awareness and self-reflection: (1) Distortions in cognition. Some of these are readily noticed and are familiar points of focus in cognitive therapy (such as taking things too personally, mind-reading, jumping to conclusions, catastrophizing, seeing things in black or white terms, etc.). Other distortions are egosyntonic and therefore relatively "invisible,"[14] for example, the psychological defense of projection. Nonetheless, we can be alert to these possibilities and inquire about them. (For example, "Is it possible that *I* am the one who is angry here, not him?") (2) Subjective differences in quality of thinking. For example, the mind may feel cluttered, chaotic, or paranoid. Thinking may feel confused and/or confusing ("I can't think clearly right now"). Or, we may feel driven by anxiety, urgency, or pressure, caught up in overthinking and unable to flexibly "shift gears." (3) We can notice the content as well as the tone of voice of our inner speech; and (4) we can explore the narrative themes and meanings in what the mind is thinking about.

One of the major themes in this book is that psychological clarity about problems depends in part on paying attention to (and, of course, being aware of) the stories that accompany being upset: noticing, reflecting on, and carefully considering what our narratives say about how our psychological experience is organized. By doing this, we gain insight and see into things more deeply.[15] It is important to emphasize here that attending to meaning in this way does not mean that it is good to get caught up in narratives, nor does it preclude mindful awareness. We can both engage in psychological self-reflection *and* practice mindfulness.

It may be useful here to compare *psychological* clarity and insight with the idea of "clear comprehension" in Buddhism. In Buddhism, the focus is on clear seeing and knowing of "what is so" as it was taught by the Buddha. It entails being fully alert and aware, applying attention and discriminating wisdom to awareness of the moment, *and* clearly seeing and having insight into the universal characteristics of existence—"dharmas."[16] For example, one focus is on clear awareness of the interdependent co-arising events which result in suffering.

In contrast, clear seeing in a psychological sense implies being fully alert and aware, applying attention and discriminating wisdom to awareness of the moment, etc., in regard to our personal psychological world. When we are clear in the psychological sense, we are aware of our "psychological world of lived experience," including our mentalizations and what we can discover about the dynamics of our minds and interactions with others. We have psychological understanding and insight.[17] So, for example, we can investigate what negative feeling(s) are hooking attention, what we are resisting in our experience, and what holds pain in place. By attending to the story line, we can gain insight into the "organizing principles" in our minds. However, this does not necessarily imply that we have insight about the dharma. We may be very aware psychologically yet remain quite "deluded" in the Buddhist sense.

Buddhism teaches that clear comprehension is best served by letting go of discursive thinking and anchoring the mind instead in direct experience. This teaching makes good sense in view of the fact that, other things being equal, the mind tends to get lost in narrative in a way that reifies it—assuming it to be objectively real. Therefore, narrative tends to impede clear comprehension. It does this to the extent that we fail to notice that there is a process of mind ("minding") that participates in creating realities and holding them together (i.e. "dependent origination"). Mindfulness practice trains the mind to sidestep the web of mental narrative and abide instead in embodied awareness of the present moment.

Though on the surface this may seem diametrically opposed to inquiring deeply into mental narrative, both views converge in the idea of "wise relationship" to storyteller mind. Stories in the mind have an important function: to hold, contain, and express feelings. To relate wisely to them, we need to be aware of their *content* (including their meaning), keep track of their *process*, and simultaneously register the *context of awareness* in which they are held in mind.

Reactivity of mind/body underlies the stories and interpretations that are endlessly proliferated in our minds. Unless we can work through reactivity to the point where the mind settles down, our clarity will be impeded: not only clarity about our personal situation, but also clarity about the fundamentally empty nature of things that we seek to "clearly comprehend" in Buddhist practice.

In sum, clarity and insight are important cornerstones of change. The "middle way" in regard to storyteller mind is to notice and reflect on the content of our thoughts with discernment. By noticing the stories and narratives that frame experience, we can develop psychological wisdom and learn to create narrative which supports us in the change we aspire to.

Psychological understanding works in concert with intention and action to facilitate the unfolding of this multilayered process. (See Section 6.)

4 The Role of Narrative and the Importance of Relationship

Particular narrative themes hold important clues as to the unresolved emotion that has been stimulated in the mind. Paradoxically, narratives *arouse* emotion as well. Either way, mental narratives reveal what needs to be "worked through" psychologically. Sometimes we may need to "let go" of a particular story, hold it more lightly, or make it not so significant. But at other times, we may need to delve into the story: reflect on it more deeply, think about why we are so invested in believing it, and understand why we may have told it. This is wise when relating to narrative.

When we dig down into human problems and experience, underneath we find relational underpinnings. Relational patterns underlie narratives and hold them in place. As discussed at length in Chapter 6, the mind is organized for relationships, and this includes patterns acquired implicitly (i.e. nonverbally) with significant others in early childhood. This is the "relational software" that runs the human "biocomputer" (Lilly, 1967).

To summarize the major points presented in previous chapters, psychological wounding and trauma occur when painful events befall us, not only actual (objectively real) events, but also those we construe in painful ways. We may, for example, feel rejected, betrayed, or abandoned, and we may also judge or blame ourselves in relation to what happens.[18] How adequately we are able to negotiate the travails of human life depends in large measure on how well our significant others were able to help us make sense of (and therefore "metabolize") what happened to us as we were growing up.

When significant others have been insufficient to our developmental emotional needs, we are left with feeling unsafe and emotionally overwhelmed, and we develop psychological defenses which in turn cause their own difficulties. In order to heal these wounds, we need what Robert Stolorow (2007) has called a "relational home" for our pain, a place where we can bring our metaphorically bruised knees to be examined, soothed, and bandaged. We need time and a compassionate space that can hold pain as we learn to accept it and be with it. This is one way that emotional healing occurs.

Alongside deconstructing experience and developing deeper emotional understanding of problems, a key step in psychological healing is the provision of empathic understanding by another. Being deeply understood in this way is primary and its value cannot be overstated. The other side of this same coin is the healing value of *articulating* our experience. When we speak deeply and from the heart *out loud*, subjective truths emerge which might otherwise remain in the shadows of our minds.

The intimacy of deep conversation, both speaking and being heard, is the heart of emotional growth and integration. It is the third leg of the "stool" in inquiring deeply: mindful awareness, self-reflection, and deep connection. Beneath and interwoven in narrative is the lived experience of the relational field. Depth of connection is what gives the words spoken in therapeutic conversation—symbols of connection—the power to contain the patient's experience.

Our essential human nature is relational; every new relationship calls forth new versions of ourselves. The evolving process of change needs to be biographized and understood within new narratives of meaning. In inquiring deeply, therapist and patient become partners in the construction of this new narrative.

Various ways that the psychotherapeutic conversation/relationship can help in resolving problems are explored in this chapter and throughout this book. The bottom line is this: once we have truly understood how something has been brought about, and how and why it came to be in that particular form, those insights may themselves constitute the beginning of change.

When we inquire deeply (in psychotherapy or otherwise), we create the possibility of discovering the organizing principles which have been unconsciously shaping our experience, thereby facilitating change. A few examples from my psychotherapy practice that occur to me right now are the impact on one man, when he realized that he was magnetically drawn to the experience of being a victim; or the liberating effect on one woman, when she recognized that she had made happiness into a personal project against which she measured herself. In both examples, these insights enabled the person to make different choices and grow in significant ways.

Sometimes therapeutic change comes about of its own accord, through the quality of the interpersonal exchange without any explicit intervention. The patient takes in the therapist's way of thinking about problems, the reflective frame for exploring suffering, and the capacity to hold conflicting ideas in suspension while examining connections, meanings, and significance of events. Under these circumstances, one may begin to feel a profound change in oneself without quite knowing how or why. As the saying goes, when we change the way we look at things, the things we are looking at change. This is the intersubjective alchemy of deep psychotherapy.

As discussed in Chapter 5, the calm and spacious state of mind contributed by the mindful presence of the therapist provides a platform of awareness from which things not previously recognized can be seen.[19] I sometimes describe this process to patients as a metaphorical hike we will take together up a mountain, talking together on the way about the terrain we encounter. It is a hike that reveals whatever is in our way.

Problems can be understood in an unlimited variety of ways, and there are as many points of view as there are individual differences. This is where the clinical acumen and creativity of the mindful therapist becomes most relevant. In my view, what arises in the process of psychotherapy is a function of the breadth of understanding of the therapist, as well as the depth of his or her presence. We can only "take people" into the psychological territory we ourselves are able to go. This is the art of psychotherapy: it develops nuanced awareness of our experience and points the way toward strategies for change.

5 Relaxation and Unwinding of Experience

One of the primary phenomena that need to be recognized and understood, both in psychotherapy and dharma practice, is resistance—which, in turn, is based in unconsciousness. When we can bring the light of consciousness to what we are resisting, unconsciousness dissolves and pain begins to be released. In other words, what has been unconscious becomes conscious.

Mindful awareness is undefended consciousness (Kurtz and Prestera, 1977). One of the impressive aspects of mindfulness practice, especially retreat practice, is the slow but steady "unwinding" of experience that occurs as relaxation deepens.[20] As previously described, problems live in both body and mind—i.e. in body/mind. Knots of energy in the body/mind are held as patterns of somatically encoded sensation, muscle contraction, emotion, and memory, all intertwined ("non-experienced experience"). As mindful awareness is brought to each pattern, and as we meet each experience as it presents itself, without resistance, these knots begin to dissolve into the space of open awareness.

As the mind becomes increasingly settled and unified in mindfulness meditation, and as awareness deepens, knots of "non-experienced experience" begin to loosen and unwind as a function of the inherent intelligence of the mind/body. This is one of the major functions of bringing conscious attention to something: mindfulness engages self-regulation, renewal, and reorganization (Varela et al., 1993; Kaparo, 2012).[21, 22]

We can elaborate this idea as regards the basic mechanism of psychotherapeutic change. When we focus awareness on problems, they begin to untangle and resolve by virtue of the consciousness we bring to them. Mindfulness in some ways functions as a clutch for the engine of ourselves, heightening our ability to shift gears and providing for greater flexibility in experience. The back and forth movement of attention lights up the unfolding process of experience in a way that confers choice (see Section 6) and, by virtue of this deeper awareness, we become more able to inhabit ourselves from deep within ourselves.

This potential for "unwinding" in the nervous system was first identified by Wolfgang Luthe (1965). During states of deep relaxation, Luthe found, paroxysmic motor and sensory discharges would occur, seemingly correlated with a person's trauma history. These "autogenic discharges" were accompanied by emotion and autonomic nervous system reactions (changes in heart rate, blood pressure, and the like) connected to fight-or-flight responses.

It is now well understood that such phenomena represent traumatic memory stored in the body, as explored in the work of Peter Levine, Bessel van der Kolk, and many others. Later, methods were devised for integrating autogenic release into psychodynamic work, a new method for uncovering the unconscious called "autogenic abreaction."

Autogenic discharges occur during mindfulness meditation as a function of attention to the present moment experience in a passive and receptive frame of mind, and as a function of the psychophysiological relaxation engendered by this practice.[23] Under these conditions, the conscious mind gains access to "non-experienced experience." Previously repressed memories, thoughts, and impulses (the psychodynamic unconscious)—as well as other previously unrecognized material, such as the physical aspect of trauma—become conscious.

The nervous system relaxation and attentional focus that occur during meditation practice are optimally conducive to autogenic "unwinding" and release. Energy previously bound up in the brain and body as engrams of "non-experienced experience" is thereby released. Memories are "metabolized" through the very act of becoming aware of them, and their energy becomes available for more integrated and coherent states of mind—states of alert flow (Csikszentmihalyi, 1990). Mindfulness practice thereby engenders highly coherent mental states marked by intense yet effortless focus, engagement, and deep presence (Siegel, 2007, 2010).[24]

6 Intention, Commitment, and Action: Blueprint for Change

By and large, psychodynamic psychotherapies emphasize the causal role of the past in the present, with little emphasis on the shaping impact of awareness going forward. It was left to New Age spiritual psychologies to fill in that vacuum with various forms of "thinking from the end," the fundamental idea that consciousness manifests that which it focuses on. Visualization, affirmation, positive thinking, *push pull NB*

and prayer, for example, are said to "create" whatever outcome is desired. In metaphysical terms, *energy follows thought*.

We can use the metaphor of pushing and pulling to explore these ideas of cause and effect. If we think of the past as a push and visualization as a pull, push and pull come together in the present moment by influencing how we interpret and respond to events in an ongoing fashion. In the act of bringing new awareness to the present moment, the next moment is already changed because of the alteration in view. In this way, awareness (or insight about) how something was brought about may become the beginning of what comes next.   *OK*

Without resorting to metaphysics, the concept of *intention* in Buddhist psychology elegantly illuminates the complexity of this process. Everything that happens, the Buddha taught, begins with our thoughts; for good or ill, our thoughts are the foundation of what arises. Intentions are an important dimension of thought because what we intend directs our energy and attention. The back-and-forth movement of attention lights up the process of "minding" that is the unseen background of experience as it arises. Intentions frame our interpretations and determine how we hold things in mind. When we form a conscious intention, this then becomes an integral part of what unfolds next. Attention and intention light up experience and support living from the inside out.

Simple examples abound. If you are looking for someone to marry, everyone will be evaluated as a prospective mate. If you are angry and have the energy of ill will, you will find someone to have a fight with. If you expect good things to happen, the quality of your attention will itself amplify possibilities of something good. At an existential level, bumper sticker wisdom says it all: "If you look hard enough for something, eventually it will appear" (Brilliant, 1980).

Because intentions are what "incline the mind" in one direction or another, it behooves us to be conscious of what these intentions are. Having clear intentions is a soft form of "thinking from the end." When our purpose is clear and coherent, we are on course toward a particular outcome. Moreover, intentions keep us centered in the moment by keeping our attention focused on what is important, and that helps us stay optimally responsive to what is unfolding.

To reiterate the major point from previous sections, understanding how something has been brought about in our lives often holds the key to finding a constructive response. By providing a space uniquely dedicated to *looking* in a way that infuses psychological insight with mindful awareness—and also by acknowledging the importance of intention—inquiring deeply invites change. As the psychoanalyst Allen Wheelis put it, "Something lies behind us, something goes before us, consciousness lies between" (Wheelis, 1973, p. 86).

Clear seeing and clear intention segue into strategies for action. Once we are clear about what the problem *is*, we are poised to take whatever action is appropriate and indicated. (And conversely, our failure to see or understand important aspects of the current situation keeps us blind to important possibilities.) Intention leads to constructive action in the spontaneous unfolding of the journey forward. It remains only to commit to what we most deeply value[25] and stay on the path defined by putting one foot in front of the other.

Spontaneous?

The structure of this blueprint for change is expressed in the following aphorism[26]

First comes understanding, without which action is blind
Then comes action, without which understanding is ineffective
Finally, understanding and action become one.

7 Coming into Being: Its Intersubjective Dimension

Sometimes problems resolve without explicit intent or action. Something may simply "happen" in a way which settles things. Whether intentions are consciously formulated or not, an intermediate step which may be expedient is to explore the problem or dilemma in conversation with another. As discussed earlier, the intersubjective moment that ensues contributes important new elements to the way we are thinking about something and, hence, what happens. It also helps to shape who we become.

The importance of the intersubjective dimension of change cannot be overstated. In early life, our personalities and characteristics are first brought into being through the ways that intimate others interact with us. Our parents see us in certain ways, determined by their own psychology, and those perceptions, in turn, shape who we become. Psychotherapy is very much like this: the way that we as therapists see the person and his or her predicament—and the way that we consequently relate to him or her—is what allows new qualities of self to emerge into being. Then, as change begins to appear, our role is to recognize and validate it.

In a very real sense, deep connection is how human beings come into being. It is the process by which, as described in Chapter 8, the psychological self first forms during psychological development, and this process continues throughout the self-delineating experiences of adulthood. Psychotherapy contributes to transforming the patient's self by fostering new experiences of self-delineation: the therapist sees what is valuable in the patient and this seeing is instrumental in bringing forth that potential. The patient comes to see him or herself in the eyes of the therapist. New structures of self are birthed in these blood-moments of meeting.

From the point of view of inquiring deeply as a relational psychotherapeutic approach, deep connection in the *transference/countertransference* is an essential aspect of how people change. This *corrective relational experience* (or *corrective emotional experience*) is essential in helping the patient learn to contain experience, modulate feelings, and rest in a place of going-on-being. While mindfulness practice also facilitates this change, it may often be difficult for patients to access deep layers of psychological wounding and metabolize the associated trauma without the balm of a healing connection.

In psychoanalytic language, we can say that psychotherapy provides new (corrective) relational and attachment experiences: needed selfobject functions of empathy, mirroring, and validation. Taken together, these provide "earned attachment security." Pragmatically, this means that the therapist looks for and supports the core of what is sane in a person—their strengths as well as their constructive intentions—to help them discover strategies that support change and growth. We see who the person has the potential to become and, in that seeing, those qualities are invited into being.

Another way to say this is that as people grow and develop, change occurs not only as a function of what they choose *to do*, but also as a function of who/what they come *to be*. This process of healing in relational psychotherapy is one of co-creation, always reciprocal albeit asymmetric.

8 Wise Relationship to the Story of Self

The meta-narrative that organizes all other narratives is the story of self. To reiterate one of the major themes in Chapter 8, the self is itself a story; it is the story that there is a self to tell a story to. As we "biographize" and construct new narratives of meaning in psychotherapy and/or in dharma practice, narratives about self slowly evolve, gradually allowing us to be divested of "mistaken identities," limiting images of the self we have believed ourselves to be (Moffitt, 2012).

The concept of non-self (***anatta***) is one of the foundational teachings of Buddhism. The basic idea is that holding on to our sense of separate self, of "I," is one of the root causes of human suffering. Once the illusion of a reified "I" can be dispelled through meditation and practice, it is taught, patterns of fear and reaction based on that sense of self will also dissolve. The Buddhist path to the end of suffering is predicated on this idea. It is one of the defining characteristics of liberation.

This aspect of Buddhist practice can be summarized as non-identification with any or all concepts of self—non-identification with the mind. In order to clearly comprehend this in our own experience, the basic guideline for practice is to notice and then let go of any and all of the stories in the mind about who or what we are. This concept of non-identification is often codified in the idea of "dropping the story of self." It can be illustrated in the following teaching parable, "Drop the Rock" (Gould, 2014):[27]

> This is the story of a girl who got a rock for Christmas from her parents instead of the Barbie doll she wanted. The girl was hurt, disappointed, angry, but decided to keep it, as a reminder of all the things she never got as a child, and how dysfunctional her family had been.
>
> But then, as the girl grew up, she discovered that it was actually a magic rock; it grew larger every time she had a disappointment, got hurt, or felt rejected. She became fascinated by the rock, which carried with it the story of her life. It was cumbersome to carry around, and sometimes she was ashamed or embarrassed about how big it was, but she was also secretly proud of it, because it represented all that she'd been through. She felt it defined her so accurately that when she went on a date or met with a therapist, she felt all

she really needed to do was show them the rock, and they'd know all there was to know about her.

As the story goes, the girl was invited by friends to go by boat to a picnic on a beautiful island. The girl was late for the boat (it was difficult to haul that big rock), and it sailed away without her (the rock got a bit bigger). Eager to catch up with the boat, the girl jumped into the water to swim to meet the boat. But the rock was weighing her down, and as hard as she tried to swim, she was drowning instead. Her friends on the boat called to her, "Drop the rock!" But she couldn't. She loved that rock so.

But she was drowning.

"Drop the rock!" they kept calling.

"But it's my rock," she thought.

"Drop the rock!" they shouted.

Finally, something caught her attention, and without meaning to, she dropped the rock. The rock quickly sank, and she herself (became) wonderfully buoyant. She swam easily to the boat, climbed in, joined her friends, and had a wonderful time at the picnic.[28]

The Buddhist moral of this teaching story is clear: Clinging to the things that are making us unhappy is the source of all of our troubles. We need only "let go" in order to become liberated.

But when we reflect more deeply on this teaching story, it is evident that it is not so simple to "drop the rock." People cling to things that make them unhappy for many different reasons. Being exhorted to let go is seldom of lasting help.

In the parable quoted, the girl had constructed an identity as a victim. She had located a sense of self in the pain of not having gotten what she had wanted (and needed in a psychological sense). This psychological mechanism can be understood psychodynamically as a defensive wall of judgment which has formed to protect the vulnerable parts of the self. It is a very tenacious, albeit dysfunctional, psychological defense. Although it is possible to disentangle constructions of identity which are based in pain, to do so involves working through, not just letting go.

Based on the understanding that the sense of self is constructed through the proliferation of stories (and vice versa), it is often implied in Buddhist teachings—as in the parable—that we should just "drop the story" of separate self. (A good example can be found in the Buddhist book *No Self, No Problem* (Thubten, 2009).) Because the Buddhist view is that suffering arises from deluded identifications with the separate self, this may seem at first blush to be a sensible inference. Unfortunately, like "dropping the rock," dropping the story of self is easy to say but difficult or well-nigh impossible to do. Understanding *why* it is so hard to do goes to the heart of the psychotherapeutic endeavor.

The story of self is held in place by relational structures and attachments deeply based in psychological needs and developmental history. Some of these factors are discussed in Chapters 6 and 8; of paramount importance, shame causes us to cling to defensive representations of ourselves[29] and impedes our ability to disidentify with experience.

It may be important to recognize that dropping the story of the self is actually not something which can be *done* at all, except moment by moment through mindful recognition of here-and-now and the act of letting go. However, it *is* something which may *happen* for longer or shorter periods of time as a function of deep meditation practice, for example.[30] In such transcendent moments, we clearly see the stories of self as story and become much less likely to get caught in identifying with them. In psychotherapeutic terms, this may be seen as a reorganization of the sense of self. In Buddhist terms, it is conceived as liberation.

In whichever frame of reference, "waking up" from the story of self occurs in layers and stages as we come to understand the forces that hold "self" together. In inquiring deeply, this is done by exploring the mistaken identities that form the carapace of the psyche. We inquire into our psychological needs, see clearly what we are holding onto, and invite deeper emotional understanding of our experience.[31] This is not so much "dropping the story" as it is *dropping into* the story: not getting lost in the story, but rather allowing the story to reveal itself.

Once we have identified a particular story of self that has been operating unconsciously within us, have consciously reflected on it, and have experienced the suffering of it more fully, our relationship to the story has already begun to change. Letting go begins to happen of its own accord, as a kind of spontaneous unwinding of mental tangles accompanied by insight.[32]

In inquiring deeply, wise understanding of the stories of self means to become more present to the stories that define us. It is not so much that we drop the story of self as that we cease to feel defined by obsolete stories of ourselves. As the relationship to both self and other become freer of the constraining influences of old stories, and as new aspects of self (and new "self-states") come into being, old ideas of self can become simply stories we no longer believe in.

9 Reorganization and Transformation of Meaning

The search for meaning is a primary motivational force in human life. As the renowned psychiatrist Viktor Frankl articulated in his writings on logotherapy, there is always a freedom which can be found in what we experience; at the very least, the freedom to take a stand for something, even in the face of unthinkable suffering. (Frankl proved this to himself while interred in a Nazi concentration camp.) Suffering becomes bearable when it is given meaning (Frankl, 1959).

Although the narratives about the meaning of suffering are different in Buddhism than they tend to be in inquiring deeply, there is a common denominator in the effort to change the matrix of meaning in which we live and construct our personal experience. In order to come to terms with our experiences in life, we have to have some place to "put them" and some sense that there is a path going forward. When we give meaning to an experience, we can accept and assimilate it. I believe that the creation of meaning is a quintessential part of healing.

One of the most distinctive aspects of inquiring deeply as a psychotherapeutic strategy is its perspective on the meaning of problems. Problems entail any number of dysfunctional, ego-centered assumptions, but the assumptive paradigm in inquiring deeply is that they also contain innate intelligence, directing attention to what we most need to see in order to discover how we are unnecessarily limiting ourselves. When we approach problems from the perspective that they have value and contain opportunities within their very structure, that new mindset can itself represent an important existential shift. This point of view invites us to relate to problems with curiosity and awareness rather than from the limiting perspective of (only) trying to fix them or make them go away. Once the felt sense that something is a problem dissolves, we may come to appreciate the value or even the perfection in the situation. In this light, we can better accept problems and embrace the possibility that they may resolve.

As has been said many times in this book, reorganizing the meaning of problems is not only a cognitive process but also one of deep *emotional* understanding. To be transformative, it necessarily includes the felt sense of connection with an empathic other. Being understood is a relational process which reorients awareness away from defensive identifications with limiting narratives of self and toward a sense of being-with others based in appropriate boundaries and a mature sense of autonomy.

Over time, such experiences can evolve into an increasingly non-dual frame of reference; we can become more cognizant of the intrinsic relatedness between self and other (and of the connection between how we feel "inside" and what is happening "outside"). This is an important development on the path of insight. It may be experienced as a process of "waking up" from the story of self. This reorganizes and transforms the experience of meaning in life.

10 Transcendent Subjectivity

Although liberation in the spiritual sense is not an explicit goal of inquiring deeply in psychotherapy, there is a fundamental change in subjectivity that can develop adventitiously in the midst of this therapeutic process.

The spiritual dimension of healing is this meta-level understanding that the experience of a problem is a necessary part of its solution, that problem and solution are two sides of a single coin. Each time we live into the unknown and consciously experience how we are complicit in creating and sustaining a problem, that awareness constitutes a new threshold, a portal of opening into a new realm of possibilities. To glimpse the interpenetration of problem and solution constitutes a transformational or existential shift. This new awareness begins to reorganize the sense of self as it was previously known. It is *transcendent subjectivity*.

Such transcendent or transformational moments involve the insight that one's problems actually represent an appropriate unfolding of one's self in one's life space. This is what Paul Tillich (1952) called existential knowledge: non-conceptual insight born of an encounter in which new meaning is created and recognized. And, as in all existential knowledge, both subject and object are transformed by the very act of knowing.

Transcendent subjectivity is not limited to shifts in the subjective experience of *problems*. It can be any experience of opening in which a new dimension of being can suddenly be seen.

Ever since I first experienced spontaneous, transcendent states of subjectivity early in my childhood, it has been a major interest and narrative theme in my own life. My first language for it was "altered state of consciousness"; later I thought of it as a new "persona" or an "emergent self-state." Although it can be described roughly as a kind of "waking up," I think the idea is better conveyed by analogy with a perceptual shift between figure and ground. Attention to the *background field* in mindfulness practice facilitates the emergence of transcendent subjectivity.

As previously discussed, transcendent subjectivity is marked by an expansion in the depth, fluidity, and locus of awareness, as well as a shift in the relationship between subjective sense of self and the contents of experience, so that we seem to flow *with* and *through* experience. The word "transcendent" is misleading to the extent that it implies an experience apart from ordinary, embodied human existence. What we transcend in "transcendent subjectivity" is only the frame of our accustomed ego-centeredness; the content of experience is, if anything, *more* ordinary, *more fully* embodied.

As I conceptualize it, transcendent subjectivity is a meta-level of subjective organization which includes ordinary subjective awareness at the same time as it expands beyond it. (It can come to constitute what was termed in Chapter 8 "the transcendent position.") I should add, however, that while transcendent subjectivity is an aspect of ordinary psychological awareness, there are many degrees and forms of transcendent subjectivity, including mystical states, which *are* extraordinary.[33]

Over time, experiences of transcendent subjectivity are consolidated as they become increasingly more integrated into our psychic structure. We can also cultivate our relationship to this experience, first by recognizing it, and then through the practice of mindful awareness, directing our attention and intention toward it.

States of transcendent subjectivity lead to a sense of freedom that comes from being able to function more coherently and integrate experience more effectively. These are the essential building blocks of self-actualization. Transcendent subjectivity is the foundation of growth and change.

Conclusions: Are Mindfulness and Psychotherapy Different?

Following the recap provided in the ten headings of this final chapter, I want to return again to the general questions with which *Inquiring Deeply* began and make some concluding comments.

Are mindfulness and psychotherapy different? Zen-like, I conclude *both* yes and no; *neither* yes nor no.

The practice I have called inquiring deeply in this book can, I believe, be construed as a form of dharma practice. Basically it is a psychodynamic/psycho-analytic elaboration of the strategy of R.A.I.N. widely taught today within the American Vipassana tradition of Buddhist mindfulness practice.[34] The funda-mentals of the R.A.I.N. practice are recognition, acceptance, investigation, and non-identification. Inquiring deeply incorporates and expands upon each of these elements.

At the same time, the R.A.I.N. model of Buddhist practice moves dharma prac-tice into the realm of psychotherapy. Using similar reasoning, we might also say that the Buddha was advocating a form of "psychotherapy" in the idea of *mindful-ness of mind*. We bring attention to whatever is arising in the present moment of experience, suspend judgment, and reflect on it.

"Investigation" and "non-identification" are interwoven. Before we can let go of identifications, we first have to see them clearly. We need to look into *what* we are attaching to and how or why we got hooked. This looking deeply at one's thoughts and feelings is an example of what I have called the self-reflective func-tion. Once we have engaged the process of reflecting on something with mindful awareness (noticing it and cognizing that noticing), our subjective process has already started moving in the direction of letting go of identifications.

The idea of non-identification is a key concept in both Buddhist mindfulness practice and inquiring deeply. It is based on the fundamental teaching of the Buddha that nothing whatsoever has the nature of being *I*, *me*, or *mine*. What I wish to emphasize here is that non-identification is not something that someone *does*, but rather something that *happens* as a result of insight into identification. And since identification most often entails ideas of *self*—who we take ourselves to be—psychodynamic exploration is a natural outgrowth of this element of dharma practice.

In *Inquiring Deeply*, I have tried wherever possible to emphasize the process nature of all mental states. In place of *having* a mind, think *minding*. In place of *having a self*, think *selfing*. Mind is a body of processes, or, if you will, a "process body."

Because minding is organized around relationship, inquiring about our rela-tionships with others is primary if we want to understand and let go of identifica-tions. Therefore, inquiring deeply, as elaborated in this book, expands on the idea of R.A.I.N. by focusing on the relational dimension of human life.

When it comes to understanding experience in terms of its relational "causes and conditions," in my view contemporary psychoanalytic theories—including self psychology, intersubjectivity theory, object relations theory, and relational psychoanalysis—are state of the art. They comprise a wonderful explanatory par-adigm for deep understanding of the relationship between self and other.

Contemporary psychoanalysis goes beyond R.A.I.N. in its explicit acknowl-edgment that the mind is by nature relational and intersubjective. There is no self without other. (D. W. Winnicott (1965c) made this clear in his famous saying that there is no such thing as a baby without a mother.) If we look deeply enough into our intersubjective life, we realize that "me" and "you" are arbitrary points of reference in the dance of you and me. There is no answer to the question "Whose unconscious is it, anyway?" (Bass, 2001). This is congruent with the Buddhist understanding of mind (Kramer, 2007).[35]

To summarize, inquiring deeply can be understood as mindfulness of mind in a psychodynamic (relational/psychoanalytic) framework. It is a form of "practicing with problems" in a way that blends psychodynamic exploration and mindfulness. Inquiring deeply is mindfulness-informed psychotherapy; whether we consider this mindful "practice" to be Buddhist or psychotherapeutic is in my view largely a function of the narrative of meaning we choose. These are simply two different methods and narratives for working with difficult emotional states.

In my (relational) view, healing is ultimately about connection. We can experience person-to-person connection as one *particular* instantiation of belonging—intimacy with another—as happens in psychotherapy. And/or, we can experience "intimacy with all things" (as the Zen master Dogen (1995) famously said) in Buddhist practice. Either way, there is "true refuge" in the awakening of the heart (Brach, 2012).

Moreover, I have found both in my own experience and that of others that reading and hearing the dharma is itself comforting; as one of my patients often said, it is a "good feed." In psychoanalytic parlance, dharma practice serves self object functions for the mindfulness practitioner.

I believe that the most fundamental difference between Buddhism and psychotherapy lies in their goals. While there is a shared goal to alleviate suffering, Buddhist practice is about "liberation." It is about learning to abide in awareness rather than in identification with the mind. In contrast, psychotherapy focuses on untangling the knots in the mind. In this regard, it is I think wise to bear in mind a point eloquently made by Ajahn Sumedho (2004): personality doesn't get enlightened.

Be that as it may, personality and spiritual path are closely interwoven. As John Welwood (2000) has said, personality is not just an arbitrary "error," but serves instead as an essential stepping stone on the path of spiritual unfolding. When we bring psychotherapeutic intention to the practice of mindfulness, mindfulness and psychotherapy converge. Inquiring deeply is Buddhist-informed psychotherapy; it is a method for applying mindful awareness and self-reflection (investigation and inquiry) as strategies in achieving psychotherapeutic goals of growth and change.

One of the most profound messages to be found both in Buddhism and psychotherapeutic traditions is the idea that we can become aware of many of the disowned aspects of our thoughts and feelings. We can come to understand that the unconscious is bigger than we are, and bigger than our ego-centered sense of our subjectivity. Spiritual practice reveals the possibility that we can transcend our identification with self (ego). In this sense, the spiritual is the completion of the psychological.

The practical goal in both Buddhist practice and psychotherapy is the alleviation of psychological pain. Both are aimed at reorganizing meaning in a way that makes hope real; both transform hope from a conceptual belief in the future possibility of something into a genuine acceptance of what is unfolding in the present. This broadens the scope of what we take to be the healing process, suggesting the possibility that, in Stephen Levine's words, "Healing occurs not in the tiny thoughts of who we think we are and what we know, but in the vast undefinable spaciousness of being" (Levine, 1987, p. 4).

Notes

1 These ideas are in accord with the Taoist principle of *wu wei*: life doing *itself* (non-action).
2 "Poetics." Copyright 1969 by A. R. Ammons, from *Collected Poems 1951–1971* by A.R. Ammons. Used with permission of W. W. Norton & Company, Inc.
3 Risa Kaparo (2012) has a similar way of understanding the awakening of somatic intelligence in regard to pain, stress, trauma, and aging in the body.
4 For example, recognition, acceptance, investigation, and non-identification in the process of R.A.I.N., which was presented in Chapter 3.
5 Suffering does not, from this perspective, constitute a "problem." Problems always entail intrinsic resistance to what is being experienced.
6 Opening poem, Chapter 1.
7 To whatever extent we consider it to be and engage with as such.
8 Epstein's seminal volume, *Thoughts Without a Thinker* (1995), is a wonderful rendering of the basic goals of psychodynamic treatment incorporating Buddhist perspectives.
9 This language was used in the EST training of Werner Erhard (Rhinehart, 1976).
10 And encode memories of actual trauma.
11 See Chapter 8, Note 18, for a more complete definition of flow.
12 In Buddhist teachings about mindfulness practice, it is often implied that deconstructing experience is all that is necessary to achieve the end of suffering; bare attention to direct experience is viewed as the totality of practice, itself liberating. Through the systematic practice of deconstructing experience, it is taught, we school ourselves in the perception that suffering is "empty," lacking in any real substance, and we are thereby liberated. In contrast, the discussion of deconstructing experience in this chapter is about *psychological change*, an issue that is somewhat separate from questions of liberation from suffering.
13 This is the "r" of the R.A.I.N. approach: recognition.
14 This does not imply that everything that is egosyntonic is necessarily unconscious.
15 As I frequently say to patients, insight often begins with bad news.
16 Dharmas are phenomena conceived in the non-personal, abstracted terms that the Buddha taught: perception, pleasant and unpleasant experience, grasping and clinging, and so forth.
17 As has been repeatedly emphasized in this book, psychological clarity includes but is not limited to cognitive understanding: it is insight that involves deeply felt intuitive recognition.
18 We have the tendency to add to the wounds inflicted by others by what we tell ourselves about ourselves. This is called the "second arrow" in the teachings of the Buddha.
19 This need not necessarily be a state of non-dual awareness in order to contribute to and enhance the unfolding of the patient's experience.
20 Indeed, psychophysiological relaxation is an essential precondition of meditative consciousness.
21 This is "autopoiesis," a characteristic of living systems in which self-generated dynamic feedback mechanisms maintain the state of balance within the system in a way which supports its function.

22 Awareness is also healing for the body.

23 These are hallmarks of the alpha/theta brain wave state that characterizes meditation (see for example Schuman 1980).

24 As neuroscientist Daniel J. Siegel has described (2007), such patterns of flow of energy and information define mental states, including meditative states.

25 For an excellent discussion of intentions, values, goals, and aspirations, the interested reader is referred to Phillip Moffitt's book *Emotional Chaos to Clarity* (2012).

26 Source unknown.

27 "Dropping the Rock" is 12-step language for "letting go."

28 "Drop the Rock" by Diana Gould (2014). Guest blog published in Insight LA newsletter, http://inside.insightla.org/blogs/2014/08. Reprinted with permission from Insight LA and Diana Gould.

29 Narcissistic defenses.

30 A fascinating autobiographical account of the experience of no-self as a spontaneous psychological occurrence can be found in Roberts (1985).

31 This is essentially the goal Freud was advocating in his famous dictum about psychoanalysis: "Where id was, there ego will be."

32 This is congruent with the Taoist idea of *wu wei*, a very useful construct in inquiring deeply.

33 Spiritual experience in general—personal experiences of the unity of all being—demonstrates the possibility of a way of being that transcends suffering. In this sense, the spiritual is the completion of the psychological.

34 Spirit Rock Meditation Center (Woodacre, northern California), Insight Meditation Center (Barre, MA), and insight centers all over the United States.

35 The inherently relational basis of Buddhist "awakening" has been articulated by Gregory Kramer in the *Insight Dialogue* method of Vipassana practice.

References

Amaro, B. (2007). The golden state. In *Rugged interdependency: A monk's dependency on the American Buddhist landscape 1990–2007* (pp. 7–11). Redwood Valley, CA: Forest Sangha Publications, Abhayagiri Monastic Foundation.

Ammons, A. (1980). Poetics. *Collected poems 1951–1971*. New York, NY: W.W. Norton & Co.

Bass, A. (2001). It takes one to know one; or, whose unconscious is it anyway? *Psychoanalytic Dialogues, 11,* 83–702.

Brach, T. (2012). *True refuge*. New York, NY: Random House.

Brilliant, A. (1980). *I have abandoned my search for the truth and am now looking for a good fantasy*. Santa Barbara, CA: Woodbridge Press.

Chodron, P. (1997). *When things fall apart: Heart advice for difficult times*. Boston, MA: Shambhala Press.

Csikszentmihalyi, M. (1990). *Flow: The psychology of optimal experience*. New York, NY: Harper & Row.

Davis, M. and Wallbridge, D. (1981). *Boundary and space: Introduction to the work of D. W. Winnicott*. New York, NY: Brunner-Routledge.

Dogen, E. and Tanahashi, K. (Ed) (1995). *Moon in a dewdrop: Writings of Zen master Dogen*. New York, NY: North Point Press/Farrar, Straus, & Giroux.

Epstein, M. (1995). *Thoughts without a thinker: Psychotherapy from a Buddhist perspective*. New York, NY: Basic Books.

Frankl, V. (1959). *Man's search for meaning*. Boston, MA: Beacon Press.

Fronsdal, G. (2005). *The dhammapada: A new translation of the Buddhist classic, with annotations*. Boston, MA: Shambhala Publications.

Gould, D. (2014). Drop the rock. Guest blog published in Insight LA newsletter, http://inside.insightla.org/blogs/2014/08.

Kaparo, R. (2012). *Awakening somatic intelligence: The art and practice of embodied mindfulness*. Berkeley, CA: North Atlantic Books.

Kramer, G. (2007). *Insight dialogue: The interpersonal path to freedom*. Boston, MA: Shambhala Press.

Kurtz, R. and Prestera, H. (1977). *The body reveals: Illustrated guide to the psychology of the body*. New York, NY: Joanna Cotler Books.

Levine, S. (1987). *Healing into life and death*. New York, NY: Anchor Doubleday.

Lilly, J. (1967). *Programming and metaprogramming in the human biocomputer*. New York, NY: Julian Press.

Luthe, W. (1965). *Autogenic training*. New York, NY: Grune & Stratton.

Moffitt, P. (2012). *Emotional chaos to clarity*. New York, NY: Hudson Street Press Penguin Group.

Rhinehart, L. (1976). *The book of est*. New York, NY: Holt, Rinehart & Winston.

Roberts, B. (1985). *The experience of no-self*. Boston, MA: Shambhala Press.

Schuman, M. (1980). The psychophysiological model of meditation and altered states of consciousness: A critical review. In J. M. Davidson and R. J. Davidson (Eds), *The psychobiology of consciousness* (pp. 333–378). New York, NY: Plenum Press.

Siegel, D. J. (2007). *The mindful brain: Reflection and attunement in the cultivation of well-being*. New York, NY: W.W. Norton.

Siegel, D. J. (2010). *The mindful therapist: A clinician's guide to mindsight and neural integration*. New York, NY: W.W. Norton.

Stolorow, R. D. (2007). *Trauma and human existence: Autobiographical psychoanalytic and philosophical reflections*. New York, NY: Analytic Press, Taylor & Francis Group.

Sumedho, A. (2004). *Intuitive awareness*. Hertfordshire, UK: Amaravati Buddhist Monastery.

Thubten, A. (2009). *No self, no problem*. Ithaca, NY: Snow Lion Publications.

Tillich, P. (1952). *The courage to be*. New Haven, CT and London, England: Yale University Press.

Varela, F. J., Thompson, E., and Rosch, E. (1993). *The embodied mind: Cognitive science and human experience*. Cambridge, MA: MIT Press.

Welwood, J. (2000). *The psychology of awakening*. Boston, MA: Shambhala Press.

Wheelis, A. (1973). *How people change*. New York, NY: Harper Colophon Books/Harper & Row.

Winnicott, D. W. (1965a). The capacity to be alone. In Winnicott, D. W., *The maturational processes and the facilitating environment: Studies in the theory of emotional development* (pp. 29–36). Madison, CT: International Universities Press.

Winnicott, D. W. (1965b). The theory of the parent–infant relationship. In Winnicott, D. W., *The maturational processes and the facilitating environment: Studies in the theory of emotional development* (pp. 37–55). Madison, CT: International Universities Press.

Winnicott, D. W. (1965c). Ego distortion in terms of true and false self. In Winnicott, D. W. (1965), *The maturational processes and the facilitating environment: Studies in the theory of emotional development* (pp. 140–152). Madison, CT: International Universities Press.

Glossary

affective coloration   Overall tone of mood or emotion (affect); one of primary determinants of self-experience. Experience unfolds from this emotional core "outward" into cognition and behavior.

affect regulation (dysregulation)   The ability to maintain or increase positive feelings and well-being states and to minimize negative feelings and defensive states.

agency   The subjective center of initiative and creativity, including the ability to initiate, execute, and control volitional actions in the world. The prereflective awareness or implicit sense of being the one who is doing things or thinking thoughts.

anatta   In Buddhism, one of the three marks of existence: non-self. There is no singular, independently existing self apart from its network of causes and conditions.

anicca   In Buddhism, one of the three marks of existence: impermanence. Everything is continually and constantly changing in response to underlying causes and conditions.

background field   The field of sentience or interconnected Being from which experience continually arises and disappears.

corrective emotional experience (corrective relational experience)   A new experience which takes the place of older, more dysfunctional patterns of behavior and feeling and is thought to heal or reverse the effects of childhood trauma or neglect. In psychotherapy, relational event in which the therapist recognizes misattunements, misinterpretations, or mistakes on their part and apologizes or otherwise attempts to repair the intimacy in the therapeutic connection.

countertransference   In psychoanalysis, the transferences the analyst unconsciously experiences and displaces onto the patient.

co-creation   In psychoanalysis, a model of interpersonal and intersubjective interaction which posits that all relational events between people are essentially dyadic and involve the participation and conscious or unconscious influence of both parties.

dharma   The teachings of the Buddha (Buddhadharma) and all of the understanding and wisdom those truths imply.

disidentification (non-identification)   To separate oneself from identifying with or defining oneself in terms of particular aspects of one's self-image or identity.

dissociation   In psychoanalysis, a defense mechanism which results in the disconnection between aspects of experience—thoughts, memories, or identity—which ordinarily are integrated and closely associated.

dukkha   In Buddhism, one of the three marks of existence: suffering; the essential unsatisfactoriness of all conditions and circumstances of life.

emergent (emergence)   New experiences, relational events, or psychological developments which arise unbidden and in a way that can be neither predicted nor controlled.

enactment   In relationship, the acting out or re-creation of implicit memories or unconscious schemas without awareness of the source of action or with distortion of its meaning—especially when it involves the attribution of dissociated parts of oneself to the other.

experience-near   Interpretation or explanation of a situation or problem in terms which match subjective experience rather than diagnostic concepts, theories, or labels.

felt sense   The holistic and implicit bodily sense of the emotional meaning of a complex situation.

going-on-being   D. W. Winnicott's term for the experience of continuity of being which defines the subjective sense of self.

implicit memory   The aspect of memory which lives in the mind without being consciously recognized as such; in psychoanalysis, the distillation in the patient's mind of how they were treated and how they felt with significant others in their lives.

internal object   In psychoanalytic theory, structures in the mind which represent the composite experience one has had with significant others.

intersubjectivity   In psychoanalytic theory, the field of reciprocal mutual influence between two (or more) minds as they meet in a space of shared thought and feeling, the subjectivity of each both determining and determined by the other. (Also refers to the theoretical perspective of Robert Stolorow and his colleagues, an explanatory psychoanalytic paradigm based on an intersubjective perspective.)

mentalization   The imaginative capacity that gives us the ability to understand what we are experiencing and/or to fathom what is going on in someone else's mind. It is through mentalization that we develop representations of ourselves within our own minds, an idea of how others are thinking about us, and the interconnection between the two.

narcissistic defense   Active psychological processes which implicitly or explicitly protect and maintain self-representations.

object relations   In psychoanalysis, theories based on the premise that the mind is comprised of elements internalized in the process of relating to significant others, forming psychic structures called internal objects.

organizing principles   Deep beliefs, mental schemas, and psychic structures—largely unconscious—which influence what becomes conscious and orchestrate our customary ways of seeing ourselves, others, and the world.

papanca   The discursive mind; the experience of the subjective world elaborating itself in language and concept.

presence   To be aware in the here and now in a way which is open, attentive, balanced, and flexible.

psychodynamic/psychoanalytic psychotherapies   A variety of depth psychotherapies have in common that they are derived from psychoanalytic theory. All focus on the influence of the past on the present and highlight the impact of unconscious processes in the mind on conscious thoughts and behavior. Psychoanalytic psychotherapy, a subset of psychodynamic psychotherapy, focuses on the development, interpretation, and working through of therapeutic transference and countertransference.

psychological world of lived experience   The subjective, experience-near world as it lives in our minds.

psychological self see **self**

receptive presence   Internal space of mindful awareness which invites relaxing, observing, and allowing experience to arise in whatever way it does.

relational field   The fabric of interpersonal interconnection; the conjoined surface of interplay between therapist and patient; the mingling of minds at the intersubjective intersection.

relational matrix   Framework of personal meanings which derive from the psychological history of self and other and which are encoded in the structure of the mind as representations of self, other, and the relationship between self and other.

relational mindfulness   Mindful awareness of the felt sense of connection and relatedness as it shifts and changes from moment to moment.

relational psychotherapy   Psychoanalytically based psychotherapy which is based on exploration of what is enacted and what is dissociated in the psychotherapeutic relationship.

samadhi   In Buddhism, the state of concentrated focus that can be developed through the practice of meditation.

second arrow   In Buddhism, judgment, interpretation, or attribution that adds to the suffering of an already painful situation.

self (psychological self)   The sense of continuity in the ongoing stream of subjective experience which gets narrated in language. It is what is referenced by the personal pronoun "I" in the elaboration of autobiographical memory. (Self can also be defined with reference to a set of *functions* which are independent of content and grounded in self-reflective awareness.)

self-awareness see **self-reflective awareness**

self-delineation   The process by which the child's world of personal experience is articulated and validated. Self-delineation is the formation of self-identity: it structures the possibility of what we can say, think, and know.

selfing   Implicit or explicit engagement with narratives which center around self. Self as a verb highlights the active psychological processes by which the psychological self is constructed, with special reference to the mind's tendency to defend its self-representations.

selfobject   In Kohut's self psychology, essential self-functions played by significant others in the process of development of the psychological self.

self psychology   A psychoanalytic theory developed by Heinz Kohut and his colleagues which elaborated upon concepts of narcissism and the self. Self psychology is characterized by its emphasis on the formation of the self as a superordinate psychic structure and the nature of selfobject functions.

self-reflective awareness (self-reflection)   The basic capacity of subjectivity by which mind is able to become aware of itself. This is meta-cognitive awareness brought to bear on any aspect of the mind's functions: sensations and perceptions, thoughts and feelings, concepts and processes which are operating in the mind, even self-reflective function itself.

self-reflective practice   Various introspective methods of exploring experience based on Buddhist meditation, including mindfulness (mindful awareness), noticing, investigation, and inquiry.

self-representation   Concepts or representations of the psychological self which the mind constructs both through interaction with others and through self-reflection.

self-state   A stable configuration of functional organization within the psychological self. Its core dimensions include a particular level of *arousal* (e.g. relaxed, excited, calm, or speedy), *affective tone* (e.g. elated, depressed, frightened, or angry), and *quality of attention* (e.g. alert, dull, scattered, or focused). Note that these are states of mind *and* body—or, as we may say, of "mind/body."

self-structure(s)   In psychoanalytic theory, aspects of the presumptive superordinate structure which is thought to organize and coordinate the activities of mind into a coherent whole.

separateness   The developmental psychological achievement of individuation and differentiation as an autonomous psychological being.

separation   The state of being apart from someone or something that we are attached to. (As a verb, *to separate from* someone or something.)

splitting   In psychoanalysis, a defense mechanism which separates the positive and negative qualities of self and other into *all* good or *all* bad, with no middle ground and no integrated whole.

subject   In psychology or philosophy, the presumptive psychological being who has a unique consciousness and/or unique personal experiences.

subject-object duality   In psychology or philosophy, the presumptive distinction between the subject who experiences and that which he or she is experiencing.

subjectivity   One-of-a-kind constellation of subjective sensations, thoughts, and feelings in the experiencing subject. Through the repetition of many such moments, the psychological self comes to be known to itself in a way which is unique to each person.

subjective position   Organization of a set of self-states which represents a certain configuration of self and world.

transference   The displacement of patterns of feelings, thoughts, attitudes, and behavior, originally experienced in relation to significant figures in childhood, onto a person involved in a current interpersonal relationship.

transcendent attunement   A state of deep therapeutic presence and interpersonal resonance which the therapist experiences in the countertransference, characterized by a transient suspension of duality between self and other.

transcendent position   Subjective position organized around transcendent subjectivity.

transcendent relational field/transcendent subjectivity   State of subjectivity in which awareness is heightened, clarity is sharpened, and things are deeply felt. It can be further characterized in terms of the experience of acceptance, harmony, and flow and the felt sense that everything is okay just as it is.

unconscious   Memories, images, and beliefs about ourselves, others, and the world that we are not aware of. Some of these, the "pre-reflective unconscious," are readily accessible to consciousness. Others are dynamically unconscious, disavowed, or repressed, and less readily accessible. Some processes are intrinsically unconscious while others can become conscious under appropriate conditions. In addition, some psychological systems posit a collective or transpersonal unconscious.

virtual self   The potential self which can go on to develop in the process of being seen and responded to by (m)other. This is true in earliest psychological life and remains so throughout the life span.

Index